GLOBAL GANGS
Street Violence across the World

Jennifer M. Hazen and
Dennis Rodgers, Editors

University of Minnesota Press
Minneapolis
London

Published by the University of Minnesota Press
111 Third Avenue South, Suite 290
Minneapolis, MN 55401-2520
http://www.upress.umn.edu

Library of Congress Cataloging-in-Publication Data

Global gangs : street violence across the world / Jennifer M. Hazen and Dennis Rodgers, editors.
  Includes bibliographical references and index.
  ISBN 978-0-8166-9147-0 (hc : alk. paper)
  ISBN 978-0-8166-9149-4 (pb : alk. paper)
1. Gangs. 2. Violence. I. Hazen, Jennifer M., 1973– II. Rodgers, Dennis.
  HV6437.G56 2014
  364.106'6—dc23
                    2013048784

Printed in the United States of America on acid-free paper

The University of Minnesota is an equal-opportunity educator and employer.

20 19 18 17 16 15 14   10 9 8 7 6 5 4 3 2 1

Contents

Acknowledgments

We thank the Centre for Conflict, Development, and Peacebuilding (CCDP); the Jacobs Foundation (Switzerland); and the Small Arms Survey for providing the funding for the workshop convened in May 2009 at the Graduate Institute of International and Development Studies, Geneva, that was at the origins of this volume. We are grateful to Thomas Biersteker, Oliver Jütersonke, Keith Krause, and Sandra Reimann for their organizational support for this event. We also thank Pieter Martin at the University of Minnesota Press and the contributors to this volume for their exceptional patience as we endeavored to finalize it.

Gangs in a Global Comparative Perspective

DENNIS RODGERS AND JENNIFER M. HAZEN

Frequently depicted as an almost pathological form of brutality, gangs are ubiquitously associated with senselessly destructive violence and have become popular bugbears and scapegoats. This is currently perhaps most obvious in the case of contemporary Central America, where gangs—known as *pandillas* and *maras*—are widely perceived as the most important security threat within a post–Cold War panorama of criminality often characterized by levels of violence that surpass those of the revolutionary conflicts that affected the region during the 1970s and 1980s (Rodgers 2009). This concern, heightened in the post-9/11 context, has Central American gangs commonly portrayed as a "new urban insurgency" aiming "to depose or control the governments of targeted countries" through "*coups d'street,*" thereby embodying a danger that has the potential to extend beyond the isthmus, in particular, to the United States and Canada (Manwaring 2005, 3). The corresponding policy response has been particularly repressive, to the extent that it is no exaggeration to talk of Central American governments having declared a veritable "war on gangs" in recent years (Jütersonke, Muggah, and Rodgers 2009).

Gangs are a global phenomenon, found in most societies around the world. On the one hand, this is likely due to a process of convergent evolution, whereby similar social contexts around the world give rise to similar social phenomena. On the other hand, however, processes of globalization have also increased the connections between societies around the world and enabled the spread of practices and culture between places separated by vast distances. "Gangs" and "gang culture" have been such exports, in particular from the United States and Latin America. There is worldwide enthusiasm for U.S. gangster rap music (see Hagedorn 2008), and we are now seeing Latin American gangs migrating to Spain, the United States, and Canada; U.S. gangs to Europe; Senegalese gangs to Italy and France; and Jamaican gangs to the United Kingdom. In some instances, this is more mimicry than migration, with local youth adopting gang names and culture that they experience online, in music, or through television and movies rather than having any real tie to the gangs. In other cases, there does appear to be some transplantation of gang members, leading to the actual geographical spread of gangs. However, considering the nature of worldwide migration flows, it would be surprising if gang members never migrated. Irrespective of whether there exists a gap between the real and perceived international movement of gangs, there is no doubt that concern with the phenomenon has become increasingly commonplace all over the world during the past decade, whether in policy-making circles, among law enforcement officials, or among the general public, as communities grapple with understanding and managing the phenomenon.

Gangs have not always been viewed as inherently oppositional. The first of a very long line of studies of gangs by the famous Chicago School of Sociology, for example, saw them as "interstitial" social organizations that emerged as alternative sources of order in areas—such as urban slums—where the state's authority was deficient (see Thrasher 1927). Much of the subsequent literature about gangs has highlighted how they are complex and multifarious social institutions that can take a variety of forms and be associated with a whole range of different practices and behavior patterns, from the cultural (e.g., Cohen 1955) to the economic (e.g., Sanchez-Jankowski 1991). At the same time, though there is much to be learned from the existing corpus of work on gangs, most studies tend to be national in scope or focus on a single group and therefore offer little in the way of an international comparative perspective, making it difficult to know to what extent particular gang practices are context specific, determined by global social processes, or simply more universal in nature.[1] In the ever-more globalized and interconnected world of today, this is arguably a major limitation, all the more so considering more generally that comparative assessments, whether across time, space, or discipline, have long been recognized as a primary strategy "for revealing the assumptions, limits and distinctiveness of particular theoretical or empirical claims, and . . . for formulating new lines of inquiry and more situated accounts" (McFarlane 2010, 726).

GLOBAL VERSUS TRANSNATIONAL GANGS

The perceived connection between gangs in different countries—whether real and strategic or simply mimical—has led to a growing discourse about the rise of "transnational gangs" (see Sullivan and Elkus 2009). Most recently, this discussion has focused principally on the notorious Central American *maras,* which are often depicted as transnational supergangs. The most commonly referenced groups—the Mara Dieciocho and the Mara Salvatrucha (also known as M-18 and MS-13)—supposedly operate territorially throughout the isthmus and in large swathes of the United States and Canada. Law enforcement studies have repeatedly alleged the existence of links between *maras* in the United States and El Salvador. The Federal Bureau of Investigation created a special task force focusing on *maras* in December 2004 and established an office in San Salvador in February 2005 specifically to monitor the phenomenon as a transnational security threat. By contrast, most academic studies of the *mara* phenomenon have generally emphasized that these are local-level social forms, and although local *maras* do explicitly identify with either the Mara Dieciocho or the Mara Salvatrucha, neither über-*mara* is a federal structure, much less a transnational one, with a federated nature more imagined and symbolic of a particular historical origin than demonstrative of any real unity, be it of leadership or action (see Jütersonke, Muggah, and Rodgers 2009).

Part of the reason for the transnationalism associated with the *mara* phenomenon is that *maras* have their origins in a particular transnational migratory pattern between El Salvador and the United States, more specifically Los Angeles. During the 1980s, large numbers of people moved from El Salvador, Guatemala, and Honduras to Los Angeles, mainly to escape the violence and civil strife affecting these countries. Many immigrant and refugee youths formed gangs to combat the poverty, exclusion, and racism they faced in the United States and exported this gang culture upon their return to their countries of origin following peace accords in the early and mid-1990s. Most of those who returned to their home countries did so through deportation, including—significantly—felons automatically sent back to their countries of origin after serving their prison sentences.[2] Deportee gang members rapidly reproduced the structures and behavior patterns that had earlier provided them with support and security in the United States, founding local chapters of their U.S. gangs in their communities of origin (see Jütersonke, Muggah, and Rodgers 2009). At the same time, *maras* are more than just transplanted U.S. gangs and are better understood as an amalgamation of U.S. gang culture and local Central American gang culture *(pandillerismo)*. The *maras* of Central America are culturally quite different from their U.S. counterparts, and the number of deportee gang members has also been declining steadily, to the extent that they now constitute a minority of contemporary Central American gang members (Demoscopía 2007, 49).

In other words, *maras* represent a particular kind of hybrid gang culture that combines certain U.S. gang practices with local dynamics. To this extent, the transnational nature of the *maras* is more imagined than real, at least in the present, and is based on a particular migratory origin and a number of common international reference points. Just because it is not accurate does not mean that it does not have very real consequences, however. The implementation of repressive antigang policies in Central American states has to a large extent been funded by international donor money, clearly with an eye to containing what is perceived as a threat that might potentially spread beyond the isthmus (Rodgers 2012). More generally, new emerging imaginaries about gangs are also a factor in some of the more recent discussions about the phenomenon, for example, in relation to other types of armed groups. In particular, gangs are being increasingly compared—and, at times, implicitly linked—to insurgents, organized crime, drug cartels, or international terrorist groups (see Hazen 2010c; World Bank 2011). Although there may be similarities on the surface that suggest comparisons could be valid and instructive—for example, parallels can be made between terrorist tactics of spectacular, targeted violence and the highly visible practices of certain gangs in Brazil (see Holston 2008, 300–309)—the application of such labels without serious consideration is potentially problematic. Certain labels carry with them not only expectations about how the group should function but also expectations about how the state should respond to such groups (see Bhatia 2005; Jones and Rodgers 2011).

Partly for this reason, we need a better understanding of the different types of gangs—and other violent groups—that manifest globally to truly understand the role that gangs, versus other armed actors, play in contemporary patterns of violence (see Hazen 2010a, 2010b). More generally, this is why we need a global rather than a transnational comparative dimension. At the same time, we need to be cautious with international comparisons. The conditions and assumptions that hold in one locale may not hold in another. Groups that appear similar at first glance may be quite different on closer inspection. In fact, variability is one of the major challenges to developing shared definitions, understandings, and assessments of gangs. We also need to be very careful with sensationalism and deriving unwarranted assumptions from comparisons. But it is through comparison, both explicit and implicit, and a constant willingness to rethink our assumptions that we will best be able to achieve these aims, and we hope that this volume will mark the beginning of a new phase of debate, discussion, and research within the broader context of gang studies.

DEFINITIONAL, TAXONOMICAL, AND DISCIPLINARY ISSUES

If there is one issue about gangs that is universally accepted, it is—as Frederick Thrasher (1927, 3) claimed in his pioneering study of gangs in 1920s Chicago—that they can be seen as "life, often rough and untamed, yet rich in elemental social processes significant to the student of society and human nature," and as such, they need to be studied. Beyond this, however, there arguably exists very little in the way of any consensus regarding gangs. A review of the literature suggests that gangs are a common and persistent facet of most societies, past or present, and that they are principally an urban phenomenon (see, e.g., Covey 2003), but otherwise, even the very term *gang* is used in a highly variable manner, and there is little agreement concerning what a gang is and does. Certainly the label is attributed to a whole gamut of phenomena ranging from organized crime syndicates to prison-based associations to more or less ephemeral groups of youths who gather spontaneously on street corners and engage in behavior that is frequently labeled "antisocial" but is more often than not simply linked to adolescent rebellion. Partly because of this, the term *gang* is highly contentious, and there is little agreement within national contexts—let alone internationally—concerning the kind of phenomenon that should be classified as such.

The most reproduced definition remains the one Thrasher originally proposed: "A gang is an interstitial group, originally formed spontaneously, and then integrated through conflict. It is characterized by the following types of behavior: meeting face to face, milling, movement through space as a unit, conflict, and planning. The result of this collective behavior is the development of tradition, unreflective internal structure, *esprit de corps,* solidarity, morale, group awareness, and attachment to a local territory" (57). Part of the continuing appeal of Thrasher's definition is the fact that it is sufficiently broad to apply to a whole range of social forms. This is a benefit, insofar as gangs are slippery social phenomena. As John Hagedorn (2008, xxv) argues, gangs exist as part of a continuum of armed groups, to the extent that "today's youth gang might become a drug posse tomorrow, even transform into an ethnic militia or a vigilante group the next day." Indeed, the most famous potential transformation that a gang can undergo is the one Charles Tilly (1985) posited in his classic essay "War Making and State Making as Organized Crime," where he contends that modern European states are effectively the descendants of medieval warlord gangs.

Much of the academic research that has been carried out on gangs over the past one hundred years has focused on refining the taxonomy of the phenomenon, proposing definitions and classifications based on factors such as the number of individuals involved, their origins, and the degree of violence exercised. As Hagedorn (2008, 145) has pointed out, this kind of "nit-picking" categorization ultimately provides little in the way of real insight into the underlying logic and dynamics of gangs. In particular, these efforts have provided little in the way of deeper insights into one critical aspect of gangs: their evolutionary nature. Certainly, Julie Ayling (2011, 2) contends that "gang research has so far failed to develop causal issues fully" and that to truly understand gang dynamics, it is necessary first and foremost to consider "the question of what accounts for the emergence, decline, spread and evolution . . . of gangs." Thus a primary focus of any study of gangs should be to understand how, as highly volatile social forms, they can emerge in a variety of ways, under a range of circumstances, and can potentially change from one type of social organization into another.

Gang studies are also plagued by a simultaneous compartmentalization and fragmentation that, according to Hagedorn (2007), have led to an "intellectual impasse." On one hand, gang studies exists almost as an autonomous subdiscipline and rarely relates with other fields of study, including, for example, those considering the nature of potentially analogous phenomena, such as other armed groups, and those exploring the broader structural contexts within which gangs emerge, both of which would arguably have much to offer when considering the evolutionary nature of gangs (see Hazen 2010d). On the other hand, although mainstream gang studies—particularly in the United States—tends to be dominated by criminology, the field more generally includes a veritable plethora of disciplinary approaches, ranging from anthropology to geography to economics, and it is striking how little communication and exchange there is between studies emanating from different disciplines. The fact that all of these have generated a whole range of theories of social change makes this all the more frustrating in view of the failure of gang studies to engage with the fundamentally evolutionary nature of gangs. There is also a general tendency for specific studies of gangs to remain focused on a particular approach or theme to the exclusion of related phenomena and variables; for example, studies of the relationship between gangs and politics rarely consider studies of gangs and economic activity, despite the intimate link between politics and economics.

This volume seeks to encourage a more relational and interdisciplinary approach to studying gangs by focusing on comparisons across gangs, their practices, and their contexts. It brings together contributions on gangs from different disciplines in a range of countries, including Brazil, China, El Salvador, France, India, Indonesia, Kenya, Mexico, Russia, Sierra Leone, South Africa, and the United States. The origins of the volume lie in a workshop that the volume editors co-organized at the Centre on Conflict, Development, and Peacebuilding at the Graduate Institute of International and Development Studies in Geneva, Switzerland. This brought together a unique group of individuals with experience of primary research on gangs across different global contexts, who engaged in intensive exchanges and debates about the similarities and differences between their respective investigations. Owing to the highly

variable and frequently contested nature of gangs, workshop partici-
pants were asked to adopt a broad approach to the gang phenomenon
and to base their contributions on a common definition of gangs that
drew on three primary criteria, namely, that a gang will (1) display a
measure of institutional continuity independent of its membership; (2)
routinely engage in violent behavior patterns that are considered illegal
by the dominant authorities and mainstream society; and (3) consist of
members who are principally, though not necessarily only, under the
age of twenty-five.

We offered this definition not as a definite global classification but
rather as a fuzzy common ground for the authors. As Kelly (2007, 1006)
has pointed out, "fuzzy definitions capture . . . diversity and heteroge-
neity," while at the same time providing a clear-cut starting point for
comparison. Our contributors therefore either worked with this definition or countered it with their own as they situated the gangs they
studied within a broader understanding of armed violence. This enabled
them to engage in a more contextualized approach and to relate different manifestations of the gang phenomenon to other types of armed
groups around the world—including some that are often referred to by
the "gang" label but that do not correspond to the preceding definition.
Taken together, the different contributions to this volume consequently
engage in a debate about the similarities and differences between gangs
across different contexts, revealing a number of comparative insights
that go beyond those typically associated with the simple juxtaposition
of individual case studies. A range of common trends and practices
across gangs consequently emerges from the volume contributions,
demonstrating the utility of such comparisons. While this volume does
not offer a definitive global gang definition or taxonomy—nor do we
believe such singular and narrow thinking is desirable—it does begin a
process of cross-cultural comparison that is greatly needed and should
be expanded in future gang research.

CHALLENGES FOR COMPARATIVE STUDIES

The polysemicity of the term *gang,* the broad gamut of social forms
with which it is associated, and the mutable nature of gangs as social
organizations clearly make it essential to think about the phenomenon

in relative terms. On one hand, this means approaching the study of gangs in a manner that avoids rigid typologies, disciplinary ghettos, and static assessments, all of which impair the ability to study the fundamentally dynamic nature of gangs. On the other hand, it also suggests that properly exploring gang dynamics demands a comparative perspective across both time and space. There is a lack of longitudinal studies within the field, with most investigations presenting gangs in a snapshot manner, as they exist at a specific moment in time. Similarly, most studies focus on a single gang or a group of gangs that operate in a single community and rarely consider the gang or the context relationally, particularly cross-culturally. The lack of longitudinal studies can be attributed to the intrinsic methodological difficulties involved in carrying out detailed primary research on gangs (see Rodgers 2007a), which means that many studies of gangs are often rather serendipitous in nature or the indirect result of other investigations, neither of which are necessarily conducive to repeated study over time.

The dearth of comparative research is more difficult to explain, especially considering the worldwide presence of gangs. At a national level, this perhaps has to do once again with the difficulties of conducting primary research on gangs and with turf issues among gang researchers. At a cross-cultural level, Hazelhurst and Hazelhurst (1998b, 3) suggest that this state of affairs is due to the existence of a particular bias within global gang studies, and more specifically of a widespread notion of "American exceptionalism" (see also Hagedorn 2005). They summarize the situation by citing the veteran U.S. criminologist Malcolm Klein, who once emphatically declared that "the street gang is basically an American product," and contend that this attitude has led to U.S. gang studies being very parochial in nature, largely ignoring research on gangs outside the United States, because these are not considered "real" gangs.

To a certain extent, however, this parochialism also exists because U.S. gang studies unquestionably occupy a hegemonic position within the field, as they constitute both the longest and densest tradition of scholarship on gangs in the world. Certainly since Frederick Thrasher published his seminal study of 1,313 gangs in Chicago in 1927, there has been a continuous stream of investigations on the issue in cities all over the United States.[3] Although some consensus has emerged concerning the logic and dynamics of gangs, including the fact that they are fundamentally urban phenomena, associated with low-income or socially excluded contexts, the scholarly output of U.S. gang studies is characterized by a veritable proliferation of theoretical approaches and explanations (Coughlin and Venkatesh 2003). The first generation of studies on gangs in the 1930s and 1940s were all more or less associated with the Chicago School of Sociology's social ecology approach and conceived gangs as epiphenomena of the "social disorganization" of poor urban areas (see Shaw and MacKay 1942; Whyte 1943), but this changed radically from the 1950s onward. The social ecology approach saw gangs as partial replacement structures for crucial social and socializing institutions such as the family, school, or the labor market, which the poverty and administrative breakdown characterizing slums and inner-city areas had weakened or rendered dysfunctional. New approaches, however, portrayed gangs as reflections or examples of lower-class (sub)culture (Cohen 1955), forms of resistance to limited or "blocked" opportunities (Cloward and Ohlin 1960), male maturation processes and identity creation (Bloch and Niederhoffer 1958), and economic enterprise (Sanchez-Jankowski 1991; Padilla 1992) or else in terms of gang members' supposedly deviant or sociopathic personality traits (Yablonsky 1963), to list the main tendencies.[4]

Jack Katz and Curtis Jackson-Jacobs (2004, 115) contend that the multiplication of theoretical approaches has effectively constituted the equivalent of an academic "smorgasbord" that has led to a "mystification of the field" of U.S. gang studies. Certainly, as Ruth Horowitz (1990, 53) has sensibly pointed out, in practice, different approaches correspond to "distinct aspects of the gang experience" that cannot be easily separated, and they should really be considered together because it is unlikely that the causes and processes of gang formation and practice derive from a single factor. Yet Katz and Jackson-Jacobs argue that there has in fact been a drift away from research based on "situationally specific data" toward more abstract intellectual tussles aiming "to tell a story about . . . gang life . . . on the grandest scale" (114). Although this is also partly due to the more general rigidification of disciplinary divisions within academia, as Hagedorn (2007) points out, there is no doubt that much of U.S. gang studies has over the past few decades become more concerned with conceptual rivalries than with empirical data collection and analysis. This has arguably reinforced the parochialism that exists within much of U.S. gang studies, and few studies ever look outside the

United States as a result, whether for conceptual or empirical inspiration, even as there is increasing discussion outside academic circles of the growing transnationalization of gangs operating in North America.[5]

ENGAGING WITH NON–U.S. GANG STUDIES

The parochial and segmented nature of U.S. gang studies contrasts sharply with other gang research traditions around the world. Although not as extensive or developed as the U.S. scholarship, where these exist, they have generally developed with individual researchers in explicit and continuous conversation with each other, both empirically and theoretically, in a way that has not usually been the case of U.S. gang studies, at least since the 1950s onward. The Central American gang literature, which is probably the second largest after the U.S. literature, is a case in point in this respect. The first in-depth investigation of gangs in the region was Deborah Levenson's (1988) pioneering research on Guatemalan gangs, on which Juan-Carlos Núñez (1996) drew to conduct his comparative study of gangs in Guatemala, El Salvador, and Nicaragua, and which also informed José Miguel Cruz and Nelson Portillo Peña's (1998) study of gangs in El Salvador as well as Leticia Salomón, Julieta Castellanos, and Mirna Flores's (1999) study of gangs in Honduras. Similarly, the first ethnographic study of a Central American gang, carried out in Nicaragua in 1996–97 by Dennis Rodgers (1997, 2000, 2007a), was built on by José Luis Rocha (2000a, 2000b, 2003, 2005) during his research on a different Managua gang in 1999–2000, with his results then taken up by Rodgers (2006, 2007b) to calibrate new field research in 2002–3, and further exchanges occurring for Rocha's continuing research in 2005–6 (Rocha 2007a, 2007b, 2008) and Rodgers's in 2007 and 2009 (Rodgers 2010, forthcoming), culminating in joint research carried out in 2012 (Rodgers and Rocha 2013).[6] This cross-fertilization resulted in a consistency of both empirical information and theoretical approaches that is quite rare within gang studies, and which has persisted since this first wave of scholarly investigation, with the ever-increasing amount of new gang research in Central America almost always drawing on this initial body of work to inform its investigations.[7]

Similar processes of sustained exchange and communication are also evident in the less developed—but no less significant—Brazilian, South

African, or French gang studies traditions. In the first, Alba Zaluar's (1983, 1994) foundational research on gangs in Rio de Janeiro was a major reference point for almost all subsequent studies there (e.g., Soares et al. 1996; Leeds 1996; Goldstein 2003; Gay 2005; Arias 2006) but also in other Brazilian cities such as Brasilia (Abramovay et al. 2002) and Sao Paulo (Adorno et al. 1998). In South Africa, Don Pinnock's (1984) early work on gangs in the Cape Flats is actively engaged with and used as both an empirical and theoretical anchor in the studies later carried out in the same area by André Standing (2006) and Steffen Jensen (2008), both of whom are in active conversation with each other, and it is also a major reference point for Clive Glaser's (2000) work on gangs in Johannesburg. Analogously active and continuous interactions can also be observed in the French gang literature, as Marwan Mohammed describes in his contribution to this volume, although it is interesting to note that, in contrast to the Brazilian or South African traditions, both of which actively seek to situate themselves within broader regional as well as the traditional U.S. gang literature, this French corpus of work tends not to engage with external comparison.[8]

There is clearly much to be learned from non-U.S. gang studies traditions, both theoretically and empirically, as a result of its dense interactive nature, and it is very much this observation that has motivated the current volume. But a case can also be made for the need to conduct primary comparative research on gangs across different contexts. In this regard, however, there exists almost no scholarship. The two major exceptions are John Hagedorn's (2008) groundbreaking global investigation, which ranges worldwide but includes a detailed comparison of gang dynamics in Chicago, Cape Town, and Rio de Janeiro, and the edited volume by Kayleen Hazelhurst and Cameron Hazelhurst (1998a), which offers a unique range of case studies from across Europe, North America, Australia, Oceania, and South Africa, which are all framed by a coherent and federating introduction.[9] The revealing insights from such works about the similarities and differences between gangs in different contexts and epochs highlight the critical need for more global comparative efforts. In particular, both works end up focusing on two key dimensions of gangs, first, what we might call their "trans/formation," including their genesis, development, and institutionalization over time, and second, the hugely problematic nature of both the label and the theory surrounding gangs. It is on these two key issues that the contributions to this volume focus from an explicitly comparative vantage point.

OVERVIEW OF THE VOLUME

This volume is organized into two halves: the first on "Gang Formation and Transformation," the second on "Problematizing Gangs." The former addresses questions about the emergence and evolution of gangs over time, whereas the latter addresses definitional and relational questions as these challenge common wisdoms about gangs, including, in particular, the labeling of certain groups as gangs. Even within the context of national-level gang research, these are arguably two of the most vexing issues to have been overlooked, as they have both critical theoretical and policy-related implications. This is arguably even more so the case at a global level, in view of the huge diversity of gang experiences across the world. Although the different contributions offer much in the way of both empirical and theoretical insights into gangs, this volume does not aim to generate a grand theory about the phenomenon, nor is it prescriptive in intent. Rather, it aims more modestly to stimulate a broader discussion about the need for comparative analysis within the world of gang studies and to challenge the field to explicitly address the two key themes identified as important issues often overlooked in the literature, namely, the dynamism and the variability of gangs. Our hope is that this comparative approach will provoke additional reflections by readers about gangs as well as encourage future endeavors in comparative gang studies. To this extent, this volume should be seen as a starting point rather than an end point.

The contributions in the first section can nevertheless be said to raise new questions and provide new perspectives on a range of factors that have been important to gang formation. These include the apartheid regime in South Africa (Jensen), immigration and migration in the United States (Vigil), economic crisis in France (Mohammed) and the Soviet Union (Salagaev and Safin), and the waning of mechanisms of social control in China (Zhang). These chapters explore how these factors contribute to gang formation and to gang membership, thereby contextualizing these processes within broader structural circumstances that often spill beyond national boundaries. There are clear parallels, for example, in the way that changing forms of state authority in the Soviet Union and China, albeit quite different in nature, can be linked to particular gang evolutions. The same can be said of the different forms of racial politics in South Africa, the United States, and France, although all three of the contributions dealing with this issue also highlight the intimate link between racialized gang transformations and broader economic processes—a link that is rarely found in significant swathes of the U.S. literature on race and gangs. Indeed, all of the contributions in this section explore how and why gangs can transform as a result of broader social, economic, and political factors. In particular, they highlight how economic restructuring in France (Mohammed), political change such as the end of socialism in Russia (Salagaev and Safin), and the implementation of *Mano Dura*—"Hard Hand," that is, repressive—policies vis-à-vis gangs in El Salvador (Cruz) have led to evolutions and transitions of gangs. As such, these contributions also highlight how such transformations are not always unidirectional or toward a certain end state but rather show that gangs can transform several times over the lifetime of the group.

This points to a potentially important element for the development of a truly global perspective on gangs, which is the role played by context in the evolutionary transformation of gangs. National-level studies, by their very nature, cannot consider the ways different types of socioeconomic contexts impact gangs, unless they are longitudinal in nature, something which, as observed previously, is very rare. Similarly, although there are more studies exploring the ways different types of policy environments affect gangs, these tend to be quite specific in scope, and because such policy changes are often incremental, they can be quite limited in their observation of difference—hence the importance of juxtaposing cross-national studies, moreover across radically different contexts, and even in terms of different structural processes. It is interesting to note the similarities between some of the consequences of economic restructuring in 1970s and 1980s France, on one hand, and political transformation in post-Soviet Russia, on the other, while there are uncanny points of comparison between Jensen's dissection of Apartheid-era oppression and social control in contemporary China.

It is also important to take into account processes of stability within any consideration of transformation. Although all gangs that last for any length of time involve some form of institutionalization that provides the basis for cross-generational longevity, they do not exist in stasis. Some gangs institutionalize more than others—meaning they have a higher level of organization; more formalized structures; and greater embedment in the social, economic, and political activities of a community. Some gangs become supergangs, whereas others turn into outfits more akin to organized crime, and yet still others become political organizations. Gangs go through a number of transformations. But not all transformations bring gangs to a higher level of organization. Much that is written about gangs seems to suggest an underlying presumption of a trajectory that gangs follow as they age—from unorganized street gang to hierarchical supergang (see, e.g., Sullivan 2006)—but there is little evidence to support such a hypothesis. What the case studies presented in this volume suggest is that gangs can follow a number of paths, reaching a number of end points; which path is chosen depends on a set of factors both internal (e.g., leadership, organization) and external (e.g., state response, politics, drugs), and what end state is reached may depend on an entirely different set of factors. The numerous similarities in the processes of institutionalization across different contexts is striking. However, it is important to stress the need for cautious comparison. As Cohen (1969, 219) famously pointed out, although there is obviously a relationship between form and function, neither form nor function is inherent to any given institution, and neither continuity nor change in either necessarily entails continuity or change in the other, because different forms can achieve a particular function, while conversely, a particular form can fulfill different functions.

The second section of this volume implicitly highlights the need for a broad-based global comparative approach by turning common wisdom about gangs on its head. More specifically, it questions the ways in which we think about the phenomenon and opens up areas of existing debate in current studies. The contributions address questions such as whether there is a difference between gangs and militias in postwar Sierra Leone (Utas); how child vigilante squads resist the notion of being "gangs" in India (Sen); the relationship between gangs and social movements in Kenya (Rasmussen); the strategic—and variable—political discourse about gangs in Brazil (Arias); the political instrumentalization of gangs in Indonesia (Ryter); and the social stigmatization of youth through the arbitrary use of the "gang" label in Mexico (Jones). By tackling these ambiguous situations, these chapters explore the very nature of what kind of group might be called a gang and how we should think about different types of groups that act in ganglike ways but either reject the "gang" label or else are not seen by wider society as such. The relationship with other armed and/or powerful groups is often a key issue in this respect, both directly, in terms of concrete links that might exist, and more indirectly, with regard to the general dynamics of the broader environment within which armed groups—whether gangs or otherwise—operate.

This section therefore offers examples of a number of ganglike groups around the world that may not meet the criteria of "gang" according to our fuzzy categorization but nevertheless oftentimes behave in a very ganglike fashion. These groups can occupy a space at the nexus of politics, economics, and security in the cities in which they operate that is often analogous to the space occupied by gangs. Indeed, these groups are sometimes directly linked to gangs, as the continuities in membership between peacetime gangs and wartime militias in Sierra Leone highlight well. The Sierra Leone case also has an added dimension of interest insofar as U.S. gang culture explicitly constitutes a point of reference for both peacetime gangs and wartime militias.

At the same time, there can also be major differences between ganglike groups and gangs. Although groups such as the Mungiki in Kenya or the Pemuda Pancasila in Indonesia are not trying to capture the national poles of power—something that makes them analogous to gangs—they are certainly trying to achieve some form of local political power, and they are definitely directly linked into national power play. Similarly, whereas child vigilante squads in Indian slums may not appear on the surface to be gangs, they provide similar benefits to members as gangs—family, prestige, power, security—and mimic many of the functions of gangs, such as territorial control, defense of space, and defense of community, that have been identified in numerous classic gang studies. There also exist analogous ambiguities surrounding the application of the "gang" label in Brazil and Mexico, which often occurs in an instrumental manner for political gain. To this extent, this section seeks to highlight the inherent slipperiness of the gang notion, thereby reinforcing our contention that the best gang definition is a fuzzy one— only in this way can we properly get to grips with a phenomenon that, despite enjoying a clear imaginary, is in the final analysis extremely polysemic, ambiguous, and fluid.

Overall, then, what this volume aims to highlight is the socially embedded nature of all gangs, regardless of their location, and how different environments can affect their origins and their transformation in different ways. The chapters underscore the great variation in gangs across space and time but also the recurring themes that suggest that further comparative work will generate important insights into the similarities and differences among gangs and ganglike groups across different sociocultural contexts. Such comparisons not only deepen our understanding of gangs, in all their forms, but also aid in suggesting better means through which to manage these groups, which are often deeply rooted in the social, political, economic, and security activities of their communities and as such may not be easily separated from their environments and the conditions that drive their development, regardless of whether they are labeled a gang, a national security threat, or a rational response to their situation. Achieving such insight, however, requires an approach that enables engagement with as wide a variety of experiences across the globe as possible, rather than sticking to traditional approaches founded on rigid taxonomies and limiting the scope of comparison.

NOTES

1. Venkatesh and Kassimir's (2007) edited volume is a partial exception to this, as it explores the impact of globalization on young people, including, in several chapters, gang members, but it does so focusing specifically on the role played by legal institutions and discourses and the way these shape the experience of young people.

2. Almost a quarter of the two hundred thousand deported from the United States to Central America between 1998 and 2005 were convicts, although not all were gang members (Jütersonke, Muggah, and Rodgers 2009, 380).

3. It is important also to mention Herbert Asbury's (1928) popular journalism on the gangs of New York, which was published to great acclaim just a year after Thrasher's foundational study. Asbury significantly popularized interest in gangs by subsequently writing a series of books on the gangs of Chicago, San Francisco, and New Orleans, all of which were commercially very successful. *The Gangs of New York* was, of course, also adapted as an acclaimed film in 2002 by director Martin Scorsese.

4. Other landmark studies that offer variations on these different themes include Spergel (1964), Short and Strodtbeck (1965), Suttles (1968), Keiser (1969),

Moore (1978), Hagedorn (1988), Harris (1988), Vigil (1988), Bourgois (1995), Klein (1995), Decker and Van Winkle (1996), Schneider (1999), Brotherton and Barrios (2004), and Venkatesh (2008; see also Venkatesh 2000, 2006).

    5. The volume by Zilberg (2011) is an important exception in this respect.

    6. Nicaragua is probably the country that has been studied in greatest empirical depth as a result of this rather unique process of longitudinal ethnographic conversation between Rocha and Rodgers (see Rocha and Rodgers 2008).

    7. This includes Hume (2007a, 2007b), Savenije and Andrade-Eekhoff (2003), Savenije (2009), and Wolf (2012a, 2012b) in El Salvador; Castro and Carranza (2001), Gutiérrez Rivera (2010), Wolseth (2011), and Brenneman (2012) in Honduras; Vermeij (2006) in Nicaragua; Winton (2004) and Merino (2001) in Guatemala; and Zilberg (2011), who conducted a transnational study of gangs "between Los Angeles and San Salvador," and Rubio (2007), who used self-reporting surveys among university students to conduct comparative research on gangs in Honduras, Nicaragua, and Panama. A multivolume study juxtaposing—although not explicitly comparing—research on gangs in each Central American country was also published in the early and mid-2000s by a conglomerate of regional research institutes (ERIC et al. 2001, 2004a, 2004b), and there have also been four overview studies based on primary research: USAID (2006); Demoscopía (2007); the work of the Transnational Youth Gangs in Central America, Mexico, and the Unites States (Pandillas juveniles transnacionales en Centroamérica, México y Estados Unidos) project coordinated by the Instituto Tecnológico Autónomo de México's (ITAM's) Center for Inter-American Programmes and Studies (Centro de Estudios y Programas Interamericanos, or CEPI), whose output is available online at http://interamericanos.itam.mx/maras/index.html; and the volume edited by Thomas Bruneau, Lucía Dammert, and Elizabeth Skinner (2011). We do not consider here the multitude of superficial overviews that have been written on the basis of secondary literature as well as works that touch on gangs within the context of a broader issue, such as Latin American youth violence (e.g., Jones and Rodgers 2009).

    8. The ethnographic study by David Lepoutre (1997) is a major exception, as is the collection edited by Marwan Mohammed and Laurent Mucchielli (2007), although it should be noted that while the latter's section on international comparisons does engage with a non-French literature, most of the volume's other contributions on French gangs only refer to French gang studies.

    9. Although a number of other collections also offer studies of gangs in more than one context, most of these tend to focus principally on U.S. gangs and simply add one or two non-U.S. case studies at the end of the collection, in contrast to Hazelhurst and Hazelhurst (1998a), who make cross-cultural comparison the organizing principle of their volume. Two further contributions to the literature that do provide very rich empirical material on a range of gangs around the world are Herbert Covey (2003) and Louis Kontos and David Brotherton (2008), but they are largely limited in their comparative insights because they are more encyclopedia-type reference works. Another initiative worthy of note is the

Eurogang project, which has developed a number of comparative methodological instruments aimed at facilitating the comparative study of U.S. and European gangs (see http://www.umsl.edu/ccj/eurogang/euroganghome.html). The project's publications are so far mostly country-specific studies but do include several overview volumes and articles (see, e.g., Klein et al. 2001; Decker and Weerman 2005; Esbensen and Weerman 2005; Klein, Weerman, and Thornberry 2006; Van Gemert, Peterson, and Lien 2008). These are, however, mainly ex post facto comparisons of studies conducted independently from each other, and it can also be argued that the Eurogang project implicitly defines and categorizes gangs in a restrictive manner against a U.S. benchmark, which goes against the grain of real comparative research and also privileges a deductive blueprint approach that is not necessarily the most suited to the study of gangs. Steffen Jensen and Dennis Rodgers (2008) have also written a short comparative history of the recent evolution of Nicaraguan and South African gangs, whereas Steffen Zdun (2008) has carried out comparative research on youth gangs in Germany and the Russian Federation.

REFERENCES

Abramovay, M., J. J. Waiselfisz, C. C. Andrade, and M. das Graças Rua. 2002. *Guangues, galeras, chegados e rappers: Juventude, violência e cidadania nas cidades da periferia de Brasília.* Rio de Janeiro: Garamond.

Adorno, S., R. S. de Lima, D. Feiguin, F. Biderman, and E. Bordini. 1998. "O adolescente e a criminalidade urbana em Sao Paulo." *Revista Brasileira de Ciencias Criminais* 6:189–204.

Arias, E. D. 2006. *Drugs and Democracy in Rio de Janeiro: Trafficking, Social Networks, and Public Security.* Chapel Hill: University of North Carolina Press.

Asbury, H. 1928. *The Gangs of New York: An Informal History of the Underworld.* New York: Alfred A. Knopf.

Ayling, J. 2011. "Gang Change and Evolutionary Theory." *Crime, Law, and Social Change* 56, no. 1: 1–26.

Bhatia, M. V. 2005. "Fighting Words: Naming Terrorists, Bandits, Rebels and other Violence Actors." *Third World Quarterly* 26, no. 1: 5–22.

Bloch, H. A., and A. Niederhoffer. 1958. *The Gang: A Study in Adolescent Behavior.* New York: Philosophical Library.

Bourgois, P. 1995. *In Search of Respect: Selling Crack in El Barrio.* Cambridge: Cambridge University Press.

Brenneman, R. 2012. *Homies and Hermanos: God and Gangs in Central America.* Oxford: Oxford University Press.

Brotherton, D. C., and L. Barrios. 2004. *The Almighty Latin King and Queen Nation: Street Politics and the Transformation of a New York Gang.* New York: Columbia University Press.

Bruneau, T., L. Dammert, and E. Skinner, eds. 2011. *Maras: Gang Violence and Security in Central America.* Austin: University of Texas Press.

Castro, M., and M. Carranza. 2001. "Las Maras en Honduras." In *Maras y Pandillas en Centroamérica,* vol. 1, 221–332. Managua: UCA.

Cloward, R. A., and L. E. Ohlin. 1960. *Delinquency and Opportunity: A Theory of Delinquent Gangs.* New York: Free Press.

Cohen, A. K. 1955. *Delinquent Boys: The Culture of the Gang.* Glencoe, Ill.: Free Press.

Cohen, A. 1969. "Political Anthropology: The Analysis of the Symbolism of Power Relations." *Man* 4, no. 2: 215–35.

Coughlin, B. C., and S. Venkatesh. 2003. "The Urban Street Gang after 1970." *Annual Review of Sociology* 29:41–64.

Covey, H. C. 2003. *Street Gangs throughout the World.* Springfield, Ill.: Charles C. Thomas.

Cruz, J. M., and N. Portillo Peña. 1998. *Solidaridad y violencia en las pandillas del gran San Salvador: Más allá de la vida loca.* San Salvador: UCA.

Decker, S. H., and B. Van Winkle. 1996. *Life in the Gang: Family, Friends, and Violence.* New York: Cambridge University Press.

Decker, S. H., and F. M. Weerman, eds. 2005. *European Street Gangs and Troublesome Youth Groups.* Lanham, Md.: Alta Mira Press.

Demoscopía. 2007. *Maras y pandillas, comunidad y policía en Centroamérica.* San José: Demoscopía.

ERIC, IDESO, IDIES, and IUDOP. 2001. *Maras y Pandillas en Centroamérica.* Vol. 1. Managua: UCA.

ERIC, IDESO, IDIES, and IUDOP. 2004a. *Maras y Pandillas en Centroamérica: Pandillas y Capital Social.* Vol. 2. San Salvador: UCA.

ERIC, IDESO, IUDOP, NITLAPAN, and DIRINPRO. 2004b. *Maras y Pandillas en Centroamérica: Políticas juveniles y rehabilitación.* Vol. 3. Managua: UCA.

Esbensen, F.-A., and F. M. Weerman. 2005. "Youth Gangs and Troublesome Youth Groups in the United States and the Netherlands: A Cross-National Comparison." *European Journal of Criminology* 2, no. 1: 5–37.

Gay, R. 2005. *Lucia: Testimonies of a Brazilian Drug Dealer's Woman.* Philadelphia: Temple University Press.

Glaser, C. 2000. *Bo-Tsotsi: The Youth Gangs of Soweto, 1935–1976.* Cape Town: David Philip.

Goldstein, D. 2003. *Laughter Out of Place: Race, Class, Violence, and Sexuality in a Rio Shantytown.* Berkeley: University of California Press.

Gutiérrez Rivera, L. 2010. "Discipline and Punish? Youth Gangs' Response to 'Zero-Tolerance' Policies in Honduras." *Bulletin of Latin American Research* 29, no. 4: 492–504.

Hagedorn, J. M. 1988. *People and Folks: Gangs, Crime, and the Underclass in a Rustbelt City.* Chicago: Lakeview Press.

———. 2005. "The Global Impact of Gangs." *Journal of Contemporary Criminal Justice* 21, no. 2: 153–69.

———. 2007. "Introduction: Globalization, Gangs, and Traditional Criminology." In *Gangs in the Global City: Alternatives to Traditional Criminology,* edited by J. M. Hagedorn, 1–10. Urbana: University of Illinois Press.

———. 2008. *A World of Gangs: Armed Young Men and Gangsta Culture.* Minneapolis: University of Minnesota Press.

Harris, M. G. 1988. *Cholas: Latino Girls and Gangs.* New York: AMS Press.

Hazelhurst, K., and C. Hazelhurst, eds. 1998a. *Gangs and Youth Subcultures: International Explorations.* London: Transaction.

Hazelhurst, C., and K. Hazelhurst. 1998b. "Gangs in Cross-Cultural Perspective." In *Gangs and Youth Subcultures: International Explorations,* edited by K. Hazelhurst and C. Hazelhurst, 1–34. London: Transaction.

Hazen, J. M. 2010a. "Force Multiplier: Pro-Government Armed Groups." In *Small Arms Survey 2010,* 254–75. Cambridge: Cambridge University Press.

———. 2010b. "Gangs, Armed Groups, and Guns: An Overview." In *Small Arms Survey 2010,* 84–99. Cambridge: Cambridge University Press.

———. 2010c. "Understanding Gangs as Armed Groups." *International Review of the Red Cross* 92, no. 878: 369–86.

———. 2010d. "War Transitions and Armed Groups." In *Ending Wars, Consolidating Peace: Economic Perspectives,* edited by Mats Berdal and Achim Wennmann, 157–70. London: IISS/Routledge.

Holston, J. 2008. *Insurgent Citizenship: Disjunctions of Democracy and Modernity in Brazil.* Princeton, N.J.: Princeton University Press.

Horowitz, R. 1990. "Sociological Perspectives on Gangs: Conflicting Definitions and Concepts." In *Gangs in America,* edited by C. R. Huff, 37–54. Newbury Park, Calif.: Sage.

Hume, M. 2007a. "Mano Dura: El Salvador Responds to Gangs." *Development in Practice* 17, no. 6: 739–51.

———. 2007b. "(Young) Men with Big Guns: Reflexive Encounters with Violence and Youth in El Salvador." *Bulletin of Latin American Research* 26, no. 4: 480–96.

Jensen, S. 2008. *Gangs, Politics, and Dignity in Cape Town.* Chicago: University of Chicago Press.

Jensen, S., and D. Rodgers. 2008. "Revolutionaries, Barbarians, or War Machines? Gangs in Nicaragua and South Africa." In *Socialist Register 2009: Violence Today—Actually Existing Barbarism,* edited by C. Leys and L. Panitch, 220–38. London: Merlin.

Jones, G. A., and D. Rodgers, eds. 2009. *Youth Violence in Latin America: Gangs and Juvenile Justice in Perspective.* New York: Palgrave Macmillan.

———. 2011. "The World Bank's *World Development Report 2011* on Conflict, Security, and Development: A Critique through Five Vignettes." *Journal of International Development* 23, no. 7: 980–95.

Jütersonke, O., R. Muggah, and D. Rodgers. 2009. "Gangs, Urban Violence, and Security Interventions in Central America." *Security Dialogue* 40, nos. 4–5: 373–97.

Katz, J., and C. Jackson-Jacobs. 2004. "The Criminologists' Gang." In *The Blackwell Companion to Criminology*, edited by C. Sumner, 91–124. Oxford: Blackwell.

Keiser, R. L. 1969. *The Vice Lords: Warriors of the Street.* New York: Holt, Rinehart, and Winston.

Kelly, J. 2007. "Reforming Public Services in the UK: Bringing in the Third Sector." *Public Administration* 85, no. 4: 1003–22.

Klein, M. W. 1995. *The American Street Gang: Its Nature, Prevalence, and Control.* New York: Oxford University Press.

Klein, M. W., H.-J. Kerner, C. L. Maxson, and E. G. M. Weitekamp, eds. 2001. *The Eurogang Paradox: Street Gangs and Youth Groups in the U.S. and Europe.* Amsterdam: Kluwer.

Klein, M. W., F. M. Weerman, and T. P. Thornberry. 2006. "Street Gang Violence in Europe." *European Journal of Criminology* 3, no. 4: 413–37.

Kontos, L., and David C. Brotherton, eds. 2008. *Encyclopedia of Gangs.* Westport, Conn.: Greenwood Press.

Leeds, E. 1996. "Cocaine and the Parallel Polities in the Brazilian Urban Periphery: Constraints on Local-Level Democratization." *Latin American Research Review* 31, no. 3: 47–83.

Lepoutre, D. 1997. *Cœur de Banlieue: Codes, Rites et Langages.* Paris: Odile Jacob.

Levenson, D. 1988. *Por sí mismos: Un estudio preliminar des las "maras" en la ciudad de Guatemala.* Cuaderno de Investigación 4. Guatemala City: Asociación para el Avance de las Ciencias Sociales en Guatemala.

Manwaring, M. G. 2005. *Street Gangs: The New Urban Insurgency.* Carlisle, Pa.: U.S. Army War College.

McFarlane, C. 2010. "The Comparative City: Knowledge, Learning, Urbanism." *International Journal of Urban and Regional Research* 34, no. 4: 725–42.

Merino, J. 2001. "Las maras en Guatemala." In *Maras y Pandillas en Centroamérica*, vol. 1, 111–218. Managua: UCA.

Mohammed, M., and L. Mucchielli, eds. 2007. *Les bandes de jeunes: Des "blousons noirs" à nos jours.* Paris: La Découverte.

Moore, J. W. 1978. *Homeboys: Gangs, Drugs, and Prison in the Barrios of Los Angeles.* Philadelphia: Temple University Press.

Núñez, J. C. 1996. *De la Ciudad al Barrio: Redes y Tejidos Urbanos en Guatemala, El Salvador y Nicaragua.* Ciudad de Guatemala: Universidad Rafael Landívar/ PROFASR.

Padilla, F. 1992. *The Gang as an American Enterprise.* New Brunswick, N.J.: Rutgers University Press.

Pinnock, D. 1984. *The Brotherhoods: Street Gangs and State Control in Cape Town.* Cape Town: David Philip.

Rocha, J.-L. 2000a. "Pandilleros: la mano que empuña el mortero." *Envío* 216:17–25.

———. 2000b. "Pandillas: una cárcel cultural." *Envío* 219:13–22.

———. 2003. "Tatuajes de pandilleros: estigma, identidad y arte." *Envío* 258: 42–50.

———. 2005. "El traido: clave de la continuidad de las pandillas." *Envío* 280: 35–41.

———. 2007a. "Del telescopio al microscopio: hablan tres pandilleros." *Envío* 303:23–30.

———. 2007b. *Lanzando piedras, fumando "piedras": Evolución de las pandillas en Nicaragua 1997–2006.* Cuaderno de Investigación 23. Managua: UCA.

———. 2008. "La Mara 19 tras las huellas de las pandillas políticas." *Envío* 321:26–31.

Rocha, J.-L., and D. Rodgers. 2008. *Bróderes Descobijados y Vagos Alucinados: Una Década con las Pandillas Nicaragüenses, 1997–2007.* Managua: Envío.

Rodgers, D. 1997. "Un antropólogo-pandillero en un barrio de Managua." *Envío* 184:10–16.

———. 2000. "Living in the Shadow of Death: Violence, Pandillas, and Social Disintegration in Contemporary Urban Nicaragua." PhD diss., University of Cambridge.

———. 2006. "Living in the Shadow of Death: Gangs, Violence, and Social Order in Urban Nicaragua, 1996–2002." *Journal of Latin American Studies* 38, no. 2: 267–92.

———. 2007a. "Joining the Gang and Becoming a *Broder*: The Violence of Ethnography in Contemporary Nicaragua." *Bulletin of Latin American Research* 26, no. 4: 444–61.

———. 2007b. "When Vigilantes Turn Bad: Gangs, Violence, and Social Change in Urban Nicaragua." In *Global Vigilantes,* edited by D. Pratten and A. Sen, 349–70. London: Hurst.

———. 2009. "Slum Wars of the 21st Century: Gangs, Mano Dura, and the New Urban Geography of Conflict in Central America." *Development and Change* 40, no. 5: 949–76.

———. 2010. "Génèse d'un gangster? De la *pandilla* au *cartelito* au Nicaragua post-Sandiniste." *Problèmes d'Amérique Latine* 76:61–76.

———. 2012. "Gangs of Central America." In *South America, Central America, and the Caribbean Regional Survey 2013,* 30–35. London: Europa.

———. Forthcoming. *Gangland Nicaragua: The Ethnography of Violence and Social Order in Central America.* Philadelphia: University of Pennsylvania Press.

Rodgers, D., and J.-L. Rocha. 2013. "Turning Points: Gang Evolution in Nicaragua." In *Small Arms Survey 2013,* 47–73. Cambridge: Cambridge University Press.

Rubio, M. 2007. *De la Pandilla a la Mara: Pobreza, Educación, Mujeres y Violencia Juvenil.* Bogota: Universidad Externado de Colombia.

Salomón, L., J. Castellanos, and M. Flores. 1999. *La Delincuencia Juvenil: Los Menores Infractores en Honduras.* Tegucigalpa: CEDOH.

Sanchez-Jankowski, M. 1991. *Islands in the Street: Gangs and American Urban Society.* Berkeley: University of California Press.

Savenije, W. 2009. *Maras y Barras: Pandillas y Violencia Juvenil en los Barrios Marginales de Centroamérica.* San Salvador: FLACSO.

Savenije, W., and K. Andrade-Eekhoff, eds. 2003. *Conviviendo en la Orilla: Violencia y Exclusión Social en el Area Metropolitana de San Salvador.* San Salvador: FLACSO.

Schneider, E. C. 1999. *Vampires, Dragons, and Egyptian Kings: Youth Gangs in Postwar New York.* Princeton, N.J.: Princeton University Press.

Shaw, C. R., and H. D. McKay. 1942. *Juvenile Delinquency and Urban Areas.* Chicago: University of Chicago Press.

Short, J. F., Jr., and F. Strodtbeck. 1965. *Group Process and Gang Delinquency.* Chicago: University of Chicago Press.

Soares, L. E., J. T. S. Sé, J. Rodrigues, and L. Piquet Cerneiro. 1996. *Violencia e Politica no Rio de Janeiro.* Rio de Janeiro: Relume.

Spergel, I. A. 1964. *Racketville, Slumtown, and Haulberg: An Exploratory Study of Delinquent Subcultures.* Chicago: University of Chicago Press.

Standing, A. 2006. *Organised Crime: A Study from the Cape Flats.* Cape Town: Institute for Security Studies.

Sullivan, J. P. 2006. "Maras Morphing: Revisiting Third Generation Gangs." *Global Crime* 7, nos. 3–4: 489–92.

Sullivan, J. P., and A. Elkus. 2009. "Global Cities—Global Gangs." *openDemocracy* (blog), December 2. http://opendemocracy.net/

Suttles, G. D. 1968. *The Social Order of the Slum: Ethnicity and Territory in the Inner City.* Chicago: University of Chicago Press.

Thrasher, F. 1927. *The Gang: A Study of 1,313 Gangs in Chicago.* Chicago: University of Chicago Press.

Tilly, C. 1985. "War Making and State Making as Organized Crime." In *Bringing the State Back In,* edited by P. B. Evans, D. Reuschmeyer, and T. Skocpol, 169–87. Cambridge: Cambridge University Press.

USAID. 2006. *Central America and Mexico Gangs Assessment.* Washington, D.C.: USAID.

van Gemert, F., D. Peterson, and I.-L. Lien, eds. 2008. *Street Gangs, Migration, and Ethnicity.* Cullompton, U.K.: Willan.

Venkatesh, S. A. 2000. *American Project: The Rise and Fall of a Modern Ghetto.* Cambridge, Mass.: Harvard University Press.

———. 2006. *Off the Books: The Underground Economy of the Urban Poor.* Cambridge, Mass.: Harvard University Press.

———. 2008. *Gang Leader for a Day: A Rogue Sociologist Takes to the Streets.* New York: Penguin.

Venkatesh, S. A., and R. Kassimir, eds. 2007. *Youth, Globalization, and the Law.* Stanford, Calif.: Stanford University Press.

Vermeij, P.-J. 2006. "That's Life: Community Perceptions of Informality, Violence, and Fear in Two Spontaneous Human Settlements in Managua, Nicaragua." Master's thesis, Utrecht University.

Vigil, J. D. 1988. *Barrio Gangs: Street Life and Identity in Southern California.* Austin: University of Texas Press.

Whyte, W. F. 1943. *Street Corner Society: The Structure of an Italian Slum*. Chicago: University of Chicago Press.

Winton, A. 2004. "Young People's View on How to Tackle Gang-Violence in 'Post-conflict' Guatemala." *Environment and Urbanization* 16, no. 2: 83–99.

Wolf, S. 2012a. "El Salvador's Pandilleros Calmados: The Challenges of Contesting *Mano Dura* through Peer Rehabilitation and Empowerment." *Bulletin of Latin American Research* 31, no. 2: 190–205.

———. 2012b. "Mara Salvatrucha: The Most Dangerous Street Gang in the Americas?" *Latin American Politics and Society* 54, no. 1: 65–99.

Wolseth, J. 2011. *Jesus and the Gang: Youth Violence and Christianity in Urban Honduras*. Tucson: University of Arizona Press.

World Bank. 2011. *Word Development Report 2011: Conflict, Security, and Development*. Washington, D.C.: World Bank.

Yablonsky, L. 1963. *The Violent Gang*. New York: Macmillan.

Zaluar, A. 1983. "Condomínio do Diabo: As Classes Populares Urbanas e a Lógica do 'Ferro' e do Fumo." In *Crime, Violência e Poder*, edited by P. S. Pinheiro, 249–77. Sao Paulo: Brasiliense.

———. 1994. *Condomínio do Diabo*. Rio de Janeiro: Editora Revan/UFRJ.

Zdun, S. 2008. "Violence in Street Culture: Cross-Cultural Comparison of Youth Groups and Criminal Gangs." *New Directions for Youth Development* 119:39–54.

Zilberg, E. 2011. *Spaces of Detention: The Making of a Transnational Gang Crisis between Los Angeles and San Salvador*. Durham, N.C.: Duke University Press.

PART I. GANG FORMATION AND TRANSFORMATION

1

Intimate Connections: Gangs and the Political Economy of Urbanization in South Africa

STEFFEN JENSEN

Gangs and gang culture have occupied central positions in the imaginaries and anxieties of mainstream society in South Africa for more than a century. In Cape Town, gangs, both yesterday and today, are said to constitute one of the most serious threats to the fabric of society. To some extent, the fears and anxieties are warranted, but the phenomenon of gangs must be explored in more detail to understand both when and how gangs are a problem and when the problems emerge from elsewhere. To sift through these issues, I explore three sets of related questions: first, how and why did youth gangs emerge as major social factors in Cape Town? Second, how have youth gangs in Cape Town evolved over time, and what are the reasons for their particular path of evolution? Finally, how are youth gangs situated within a wider panorama of violence in the city? What are their links with other armed actors, both state and nonstate? These questions beg the analysis of genesis, development, and relations with other violent networks. To that end, I explore how these questions are played out in the intimate sphere of township lives.

A brief caveat is necessary before I begin exploring these issues. The gangs that I analyze in this chapter have emerged out of what in apartheid terminology were colored areas.[1] However, South Africa is a testimony to the diversity in gang cultures, and gangs exist in many other areas as well, where they take on quite a different outlook. The diversity of gangs and gang culture should be attributed to the apartheid regime and its racialization of economy and society. African gangs are different from colored gangs, not because they are racially different, but because Africans and coloreds were inscribed differently in the political economy of South Africa (Jensen 2008). Hence, throughout this chapter, I also discuss how gangs in Cape Town are different and have different histories separate from the African gangs of, especially, Johannesburg.

GENESIS: THE EMERGENCE OF GANGS IN CAPE TOWN

Gangs have a long history in Cape Town, beginning around the time of the Second World War. Thousands of impoverished rural residents migrated to the city. In the area where Cape Town is located, migrants mostly came from farms around the city and were either impoverished white farmers or colored farm workers. Both ended up in the urban sprawl of Cape Town. The city authorities watched this development with growing fear and anxiety, first because of the sheer multitude and increasing poverty of the urban fringes, especially in the area called District Six. Their second concern was with issues of race. As whites and nonwhites were equally impoverished, they all ended up in the poorer sections of the city, bringing into sharp relief the dangers of miscegenation and dilution of "white blood" and the precarious white right to rule. It is from around this period that issues of separation of races and racially based betterment schemes became paramount political questions, eventually resulting in the passing of apartheid's spatial segregation laws and separate development.

Apart from being based in fears of racial miscegenation, responses to the urban question were animated by racial stereotypes of, especially, colored men, not least the uncouth rural cousins, derogatorily termed *plaas jappies* (farm boys). These stereotypes drew on historical and racial understandings of the coloreds as happy-go-lucky, physically and emotionally weak, promiscuous, prone to drink, and almost inherently criminal (Western 1996). These stereotypes were embodied in the abstract figure of the *skollie,* the scavenger lurking in backstreets and dark alleys, terrorizing hardworking people of all colors (Salo 2004). Although the *skollie* was and is an abstraction, he animated government interventions, and as argued elsewhere, many coloreds internalized the abstract figure as a real, existing figure against the backdrop of which coloreds had to stake their claim to morality, residents and gangs alike (Jensen 2008).

The first known gang in Cape Town dates back to the 1940s, when the Globe gang was formed as an anticrime, anti-*skollie* initiative. However, economic need and state police pressure led Globe members to criminal activities,[2] and soon the gangs began to constitute a problem in their own right. Pinnock (1984) argues that strong neighborhood webs of social and personal ties countered the gangs' negative impact on communities and their ability to secure safe livelihoods. As the predominantly colored people of the older neighborhoods were forcibly removed and resettled on the Cape Flats, the web of social control broke down. As there were no new forms of control, the new colored areas on the Cape Flats became inherently dangerous. The dislocation led young men "to build something coherent out of the one thing they had left—each other" (30). Thus gangs in Cape Town emerged out of the breakdown of social controls in the old inner city, crippling unemployment, and social marginalization.

In Pinnock's analysis, gangs were the creation of the apartheid regime and forced removals. Clive Glaser (2000) disagrees and argues that Pinnock fails to explain why "defensive" youth gangs emerged in the Cape Flats only around 1980, a considerable time lag given that the bulk of relocations took place between the mid-1960s and the mid-1970s. His analysis of the gangs in the Johannesburg area from 1930 to 1976 indicates that in the decade following the destruction of old urban areas like Sophiatown (i.e., the 1950s), gangs as recognized structures did not emerge to any significant degree. Only after 1968 did a resurgence of gangs take place in Soweto's new townships. Evidence from Cape Town supports this point. In a panel discussion on security problems in Cape Town townships Manenberg and Bonteheuwel in 1975—today both gang hot spots—gangs were only mentioned once (see National Institute for Crime Prevention and the Re-integration of Offenders 1975, 7–10). For the most part, the panel discussants lamented the presence of the *skollie,* the *robies,* and other criminals lurking in the backstreets. This suggests that gangs, along with communities in general, suffered from the dislocations wrought by the forced removals. Hence the gangs that emerged from the beginning of the 1980s were of a new, Cape Flats breed.

Despite these differences, it would seem that we need to locate the genesis of the gangs in both Cape Town and Soweto in the large societal transformation relating to urbanization and its management. Gangs emerged as a response to urbanization; they were sometimes structures of social control but often developed into being part of the problem for struggling residents—according to all accounts, gangs were a constant feature of the old urban neighborhoods of Cape Town and Johannesburg. Along with the rest of the urban population, gangs suffered quite significantly from apartheid, and they only reemerged in a new and transformed nature after a decade in the new townships of Cape Flats and Soweto. But gangs also became a way by which government made sense of life in the urban fringes; as a category, the gang became a tool of government (Greenhouse 2003; Alexander 2000). In the categorization of particular forms of life as gangs, the Cape authorities drew implicitly on the stereotypes of the colored man. This also made Cape Town gangs different from their cousins in Johannesburg.

These gangs might be called the township-based gangs. However, other ganglike structures developed, especially in the Johannesburg area, around the mining sector. These gang structures were often ethnically based and organized and emanated out of the single-sex mining compounds that housed different ethnic groups, especially Basotho, Shangaan, and Zulu, that had managed to maintain or wanted to maintain a rural base. Often they were formed as direct responses to the urban, township gangs, which scavenged on miners for their livelihood. The Marashea, a Basotho gang, was a case in point (Kynock 2005). The apartheid regime and the mining sector actively sought to promote such ethnic factionalism by delegating particular work to particular groups (Moodie 1995). The process of urbanization also affected the formation of different kinds of gangs. In certain parts of the country, the rural areas were so overly populated that migration could not, to the same extent, be circular. Hence, in the townships, a more permanent urban population developed that was at odds with the migrants, maintaining a stake in the rural areas. This was later to develop into intense factional fighting between the African National Congress (ANC) (township) supporters and the Inkhatha Freedom Party (hostel) supporters (Jensen and Buur 2007; Mamdani 1996).

In conclusion, gangs in South Africa emerged as a result of urbanization and the political economy of the specific city. They were often responses to real social and political pressures, but often they

became part of the problem for an already struggling nonwhite population. In Cape Town, gangs emerged to confront the *skollie* menace,
but often they came to incarnate that very menace. They developed
in at least two distinct phases. First, gangs emerged in the inner city
of pre-apartheid Cape Town. These gangs roamed the intensely over-
populated districts with equal amounts of swagger and danger and
became part and parcel of the popular culture. After the forced removals to the sprawling suburban Cape Flats, they took a knock and only
reemerged a decade later in a new form and shape that was distinctly of
the Cape Flats.

DEVELOPMENTS: PRACTICES AND NARRATIVES
OF THE GANGS ON THE CAPE FLATS

When the gangs reemerged, they did so with a vengeance; from the relatively isolated phenomenon occurring in the inner city, the Cape Flats
witnessed an almost exponential growth in gangs. They were to be found
in every township (see Figure 1.1). In Grassy Park, for instance, Pinnock (1984) reported the presence of almost twenty gangs. This meant
that hundreds of gang structures emerged around the Cape Flats. The
New Yorker gang in Heideveld provides an illustration of the process.
During more than a decade, from the middle of the 1980s to the end of
the 1990s, the New Yorker gang was one of the strongest in Heideveld.
At the height of its influence, the gang commanded great respect from
many people, especially young boys, in its territory. At the same time,
the gang was expanding into drug dealing and was employing increasing levels of violence. As with other gangs, the New Yorkers began as
a means of defending themselves against harassment. The Naughty
Angels, a few years their senior, embodied their personal nightmare.
As Gerard, a long-standing member of the New Yorkers, explained in
April 1999, "We were like kids in their eyes. They were fooling with us,
sending us around. We were scared of those guys." But the Naughty
Angels also had their adversaries in the older Pipekillers. This hierarchy
of age was played out in fights. As Michael, who had a brief fling with
the New Yorkers, explained in April 1999, "The Pipekillers decided to
go and beat up the Naughty Angels to re-establish their authority. But
now the Naughty Angels were going to do to the New Yorkers what the

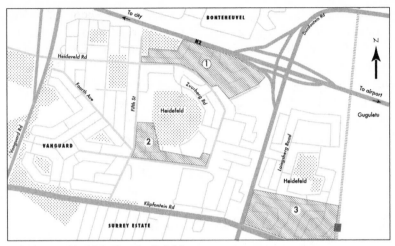

Key 1 Americans   2 New Yorkers and Cat pounds   3 Junky Funkies

Figure 1.1. Gang territories in Heideveld after 1995. 1. American territory; 2. New York/Cat Pound territory; 3. Junky Funky Kids territory. Map from Jensen (2008). Reproduced by permission of James Currey/Boydell and Brewer Ltd. Woodbridge.

Pipekillers were doing to them." This harassment came to a halt when the New Yorkers decided to strike back.

The New Yorkers' main economic activity was drug dealing, particularly among the gang leaders. With fights over drug turfs, guns became an increasing part of New Yorker activity. This appears to be a general trend in the beginning of the 1990s. With the introduction of guns, gang fights changed character, and guns became part of the paraphernalia of masculinity. Although the New Yorkers fought other gangs, their prime antagonists were the Asbestos Boys from the station side. The Asbestos Boys ended badly, while some of them left before it was too late for Nazeem, who headed the Asbestos Boys. He was killed in another township. Another member of the Asbestos Boys was killed at a drinking party. Dickey from the New Yorkers killed two others later in 1995. The last incident proved to be not only the end of the Asbestos Boys but also the beginning of the end for the New Yorkers.

The war with the Asbestos Boys provided the backdrop for the almost mythological construction of the strength of New York. For instance, the apartment block whence the leaders came was called "New York" and was the place of warriors. In these constructions, the role of the hero was crucial. With the New Yorkers, Dickey filled this role with brutal efficiency. As Gerard put it, "Dickey was always in front. The rest of us just filled the holes." Although Gerard considered Dickey his friend, it was with a great deal of ambiguity that he talked about Dickey's almost legendary capacity for violence. Regardless of his reservations, it was this capacity for violence, coupled with his ability to inspire the other members, that earned Dickey his leadership in the New Yorkers.

In the end, Gerard decided to get out of the gang, but as he continued to stay in the courts, he could not leave the gang entirely, and his house was used as a storage place for guns and drugs. He also occasionally fought together with the New Yorkers. Gerard was one of the first to leave. This slow drainage to polite society of the older New Yorkers was one reason for the decline of New York. The other reason related to an incident touched on earlier. In November 1995, after a drinking spree, Dickey killed three people, wounded around ten, and, on top of this, fired at the police. He and one of his friends were arrested, and three years later, Dickey received a long prison sentence for murder.

The New Yorkers were reduced in number after this incident, but their style and presence in the courts changed, as did their main opponent. In the post-1995 conflicts, the Americans became the main antagonist. Anthony, one of the few remaining original New Yorkers, took over leadership. He tried to reduce the levels of violence and fighting, but his control was far from absolute—especially when it came to Rocco. The first incident happened in 1997, when Rocco killed an American. After months of relative quiet, violence flared up again, following an argument between Rocco and another American over a girl. This led to retaliation after retaliation, leaving more than ten young men dead and several others wounded. Although Anthony tried to control Rocco and the emerging new gang, the Cat Pounds, he, in the end, was also caught in the violence and killed in late 1998.

Four months after Anthony's death, Rocco was shot dead. The gang at their heels, the Cat Pounds, was drawn into the conflict because of Rocco, who had become the patron of the Cat Pounds, and because they were youngsters living in the lower courts, and hence legitimate targets for American violence. In the first five months of 2001, several different gang wars simultaneously engulfed the city, leaving 103 dead on the Cape Flats, 18 of whom were from Heideveld. Around that time, I received a letter from a friend summing up the destiny of the Cat

Pounds: "The Cat Pounds have involved themselves with the fight and are busy dying."

The story of the rise and fall of New York illustrates a number of points: gangs are peer groups that last a particular span of time; they are partly economic, partly identitary, partly protective entities; and they are replies to particular pressures of the street and domination. First, with regard to the generational issue, New York came at the heels of the Naughty Boys, who, however, never developed into a full-blown gang, as they were taken over by New York. Figure 1.2 illustrates schematically how some of the gangs in Heideveld around the New York territory developed over time.

This figure, however, obscures many of the complications and intricacies: Terrible Pipekillers fathered both Americans and New Yorkers. The Asbestos Boys were followed by their younger siblings, the Junky Funky Kids, who were aligned with New York in the struggle against the Americans. Furthermore, dozens of smaller groups emerged and disappeared to the extent that Heideveld at no particular time only housed two or three gangs.

The account of New York illustrates also that there are clear hierarchical differences within the gang, especially in relation to economic activities. Throughout the decade of New Yorker dominion, the drug trade was the domain of the leaders, first Dickey and his brothers, then Anthony and his brothers. They were subordinates to the drug-dealing business of the "biggest china" in the township, Kelly, original founder of the Sexy Boys. As I have explored elsewhere (Jensen 2000), Kelly's biography from street gangster to drug dealer suggests that we need to distinguish between drug dealers (called merchants) and street gangs like New York. Street gangsters and merchants differ on a number of counts. They use violence differently, they have a different relationship to the state, and they have quite a different relationship to territory. Crudely, we might say that the street gangsters often use violence in relationship to the identitary questions of the gang fights and confrontation with the police, whereas the merchant's violence seems to be subordinated to his economic interests. Contrary to the street gangsters' wish to confront the police, the merchant would also want a different, corrupt relationship with the police. In the last section, I return to relationships with the police. Finally, merchants are more translocal than street gangs, which are often confined to a few blocks. This translocality is often the result

Approximate Year	Inside Territory	Main Opponent
1970s and 1980s	Sexy Boys	Terrible Pipekillers
Mid-1980s to mid-1990s	New York	Asbestos Boys
Mid-1990s to 2000	New York / Cat Pounds	Americans

Figure 1.2. Heideveld gang evolution.

of prison, where the merchants established links to other would-be merchants in other areas. As a consequence, residents in the gang territories have very different, but equally ambiguous, relationships with the gangs and the merchant. Young men's gang-related practices were often rendered invisible by residents, who saw them as good sons and respectable fathers (Salo 2004), while recognizing that the young men were uncontrollable. The merchant's drug-dealing practices were also frowned on, while residents recognized the ability of the merchant to control the young men and even assist people in times of need. On the night of his death, residents contemplated the life of Kelly: "In the townships there are no banks, only the merchant!" Distinguishing between the structural positions of merchants and drug dealers, respectively, should not obscure that there are important relations between the two. Street gangsters are, for instance, both front pushers and the main consumers of drugs. However, as we return to later, media reports and policies incorrectly conflate the two.

What pushed young men into gangs? To survive on the streets, young men sought protection in groups that were invariably interpreted through the lens of the gang. Furthermore, for many colored men, prison was not a far-fetched possibility but a likelihood for which they needed to prepare to survive, and prison lore was transmitted through numerous accounts and stories of ex-convicts. On top of this, owing to economic and social marginalization, many colored men of the township, formally declared "unemployable" by the state (Republic of South Africa 1976), needed to engage in informal and illicit activities, as the formal labor market was often closed to them. These illicit, informal or illegal practices became part of the pattern of criminality that made up the gang. Finally, gangs in prison and outside provided the means through which to cope with racial stereotypes and systemic mortification. Through gangs, stereotypes could be deferred elsewhere in the construction of a marginal masculinity, proto-revolutionary (Jensen and Rodgers 2009) in opposition to dominant polite (white) society. However, tragically, marginalization was reproduced on a higher level, as their acts confirmed for dominant society that members of gangs were bad people. This was true not only for those who engaged in gang-related practices but also for coloreds in general, confirming the perception of colored men as dangerous.

Earlier, I outlined some of the push factors that see young men end up in gangs. However, this approach takes as its only point of departure the objective existence of the gang. Empirical evidence from Cape Town suggests that gangs are more fluid forms than such a view would allow. Gangsters are not gangsters all the time, and their practices—although criminal—might not relate to their gang membership, which often does not appear particularly relevant. The Homeboys, a group of young men on the border of American and New York territory, illustrates some of these complexities.

In 1999, the Homeboys gained a reputation as a group or gang. Its status was intensely negotiated, but through 1999, a number of developments—a territory-like hangout, a fight with a neighboring group who had friends with big guns, police attention, imprisonment, their own ritual performances of gangster style, the promenading of guns, and so on—seemed to settle the question. Although there were very ganglike reasons for many of these events, the Homeboys were increasingly seen and acted on as a gang to the anguish of their parents and the adults around them. In particular, their struggle with a rival group, the Junior Mafias, was serious. The Junior Mafias were related to one of the Terrible Pipekillers, who traded in drugs and was well connected with the police. Thus, when a community activist called the police to stop the fight, the police officer from the elite gang unit turned out to be the very one with Junior Mafia connections. The people opposing the Homeboys bragged about how much it had cost to have the charges against the Junior Mafias dropped. The Homeboy was subsequently charged with attempted murder. Ironically, the case against the Homeboy proceeded at least partially because the Homeboys did not have criminal connections to the police. On the streets of Cape Town, it can be dangerous to be law abiding or incorrupt.

Whether or not the Homeboys would travel the route taken by older gangs was still unsettled in 1999. One of their older relatives, himself a longtime inmate of Pollsmoor Prison and a member of the Terrible Pipekillers, stated in March 1999, "If you got a name, you're a gangster. I warned them—if they begin with this gangster-shit, they gonna end up dead or in prison." When I returned in 2003 at the back of yet another gang war, except for one Homeboy, all had managed to find their way into polite society, and the Homeboys no longer existed as a gang structure. This reminds us that gangs are quite transient but also that "gang" is a category that allows particular forms of action and inaction. As Carol Greenhouse (2003, 276) asserts, talking of crime, "interests of authority and its needs for self-legitimization determine crime, then, not the nature of the acts in question."

Hence what was defined as a gang and especially who was defined as a gangster was not only a matter relating to the practices of young men. "Gangs" emerged in the intersection between young men's practices, governmental development intervention and policing, and the practices of township residents. In this light, gangs became the polyvalent antithesis to polite society; the marginalization of the former traced the outer boundaries of the latter—and polite society was, of course, as unstable and constructed as the gang. This constitutes "antipolicy" (Walters 2008) or "governing through crime" (Simon 2007), where polite society defers all that is bad to a parasitical entity outside an otherwise healthy society. In the final section, I continue this line of thought as I explore how the state has acted in relation to the gangs as well as how gangs relate to other violent networks like political organizations and vigilante groups.

VIOLENT NETWORKS: GANGS, VIGILANTE POLITICS, AND THE STATE

Contrary to the gangs in Johannesburg, gangs in Cape Town have always had a tenuous relationship to politics. Around 1976, gangs in Johannesburg, the *tsotsies,* transformed famously into *com-tsotsie*—a hyphenation of *comrade* and *tsotsie* (Glaser 2000). Gangs in Cape Town participated only to a limited degree in the struggle against apartheid. In their own minds, however, especially prison gangs were at the forefront of the struggle, fighting institutionalized apartheid every day in the cell blocks (Steinberg 2004). Contrary to these proto-revolutionary claims, colored activists suggested that the gangs were used against them. One activist had been deliberately put into a cell with gangsters to be beaten up. Nonetheless, it is fair to say that the gangs were primarily in hostile contact with the police, both before and after apartheid.

Gangs were targeted violently by the apartheid state in the same torturous way as the activists (Fernandez 1991). Gang units were established, as was the infamous Belville Murder and Robbery unit. In 1994, the new government thought that when apartheid broke down, much of the crime and the gangs in the townships would disappear as government entered into a new social contract with the townships. The ANC government continually revised its analysis; after 1998, the gangs and the township increasingly became the main obstacle to transformation, and something needed to be done. This rethinking emerged out of the dual process of increased attention to crime among ordinary South Africans and the violent challenge from several local or regional vigilante groups (Jensen 2005). Consequently, the state embarked on a radical revamping of police and criminal justice systems, not least of which were the legal provisions enabling the state to wage a war on the gangs on the Cape Flats.

In his suggestive account, André Standing (2006) analyzes the fundamental assumptions behind the legal and criminal justice reforms in South Africa to identify what he calls the *parasitic model*. This model is derived from American mainstream criminology. Gangs are distinct and isolated entities whose main objective is the commissioning of crime, with a leadership organized either as a bureaucracy or as a network. They infect the economy and undermine democracy. They are in all matters equal to a tumor, the removal of which will heal an otherwise healthy social body. According to this model, the solution consists in harsher sentences, criminalizing association, targeting gang-related economic activities through asset forfeiture, and targeting the gangs specifically through the introduction of gang courts and gang units. Many of these steps have been taken over the past decade. In 1998, the U.S. Racketeer Influenced and Corrupt Organizations (RICO) Act, influenced by the Prevention of Organized Crime Act (POCA), was passed, which criminalized criminal gangs. The gang definition of the acts was lifted almost unchanged from a Californian act (the Street Terrorism Enforcement and Prevention [STEP] Act of 1988). Gang courts were introduced in 2003, and mandatory sentencing was introduced in the late 1990s. However, most of the assumptions on which interventions are based are faulty.

First, gangs are not the distinct entity the parasitic model would have us believe they are. Their sole purpose in life is not economic, and they are far from the organized outfit they are made out to be, and to which they themselves subscribe. The criteria for gang membership in the legislation are so broad that virtually all young, male residents could fall under the definition. Finally, the South African state is, unsurprisingly, not a healthy body that is corrupted by the gangs. As the story of the Homeboys illustrates, it is rather that the state corrupts the people in the townships. Elsewhere I have explored the relationships between the young men and their mothers (Jensen 2008, 2009; see also Salo 2004). Suffice it to say that in these women's minds, the police constitute the problem, not the boys. Fifty-year-old Faudilla exclaimed about the police, "Oh, they are corrupt!" She continued,

> The police came here one day and they searched here for drugs and so forth and they took this one guy. Right now I'm shouting at the police to leave him alone. Then one of the police said I'm interfering with their work! The more they want to grab him the more I fight them. Then this cop stands there with a gun to my head and tells me that I am interfering with his work!

"Corrupt" stood for the collective category encompassing the different negative, broadly immoral traits attributed to the generic police officer. To work with the police could never be positive; in fact, it would constitute something close to treason. This perception was based in everyday experiences of the police. However, even Faudilla did not hesitate to work with the police when doing so suited her interests. When one of the main drug dealers of her area was killed, she did not hesitate to volunteer her advice about from where the violence emanated, that is, from across the road in American territory. This suggests that the relationship between the police and the gangs is complex. To understand this, we need to pay attention to the police.

As described previously, gangs have a different relationship to police than do drug dealers. However, the police cannot be reduced to a monolithic organization. We can identify at least two different groupings in the police in terms of their relationship with the townships. First there are the uniformed (shift) officers. Most of the corruption is attributed to them, not only among the township residents but also within the police. Detectives and the Crime Prevention Unit frequently referred to their investigations being compromised by shift officers. Rather than understanding it as an illustration of a lack of morality, I suggest that we need to understand shift corruption in terms of shift officers' structural and operational position.

Each shift consisted of six police officers and a shift commander, but often they were off sick or a van was broken down. The shift officers had to cover a large area with some of the highest crime rates in South Africa. The shift officers also worked in an environment in which their relation to the people they policed was often very tense. To make up for their structural disadvantage, the shift officers navigated the townships through the use of "safe bases," where their authority was not questioned and where they were relatively safe. In an ironic twist, these safe bases often included merchants. When I went on patrol with the shift officers, they invariably took me past some of the merchants with whom they appeared to be on amicable terms. The shift officers introduced me to two of the drug dealers who had been raided by the Crime Prevention Unit during the weekend. In one case, a shift officer stopped the patrol van, honked his horn, and called the merchant to the car, who was subsequently introduced as "one of the biggest drug dealers and richest men in the area." Whether this particular officer took money from this particular dealer is impossible to know, and it is beside the point, which is that shift officers and drug dealers had no particular interest in antagonizing each other. The rapport helped both sides. The drug dealer affirmed what the shift officer had said and showed his privileged access to state authorities toward rivals within the townships as well as people who might report him, and the police officer confirmed his relationship with the drug dealer, who had at least a measure of control over the street gangsters. This control translated into an equal measure of security for the shift officers, working alone in a hostile environment.

However, far from all police corruption emanated from the shift officers. As the case of the Homeboys illustrated, a prominent police officer and spokesperson for a gang-busting special Operation Good Hope was affiliated with the people within one of the gangs. Through an interview, it emerged that particular gangsters and merchants develop relations with particular police officers. These relations develop as both police and merchant move up in the world. As an indication, one of the prominent merchants, Rashied Staggie, met with the provincial head of the police in a restaurant. Eminent criminologist Wilfried Schärf suggests that these relations develop over time, implicating colleagues of the police officers as well, and that these relationships are used in internal struggles among police officers and gangsters (W. Schärf, pers. comm., 1999). Analyzing the police in Johannesburg, Julia Hornberger (2004) captures the relationship with the phrase "my police, your police."

The corrupt relationship between the police and the merchants has led to much violence in the townships. It was also the trigger in relation to establishing the last violent network that I present, the People against Gangsterism and Drugs, better known as Pagad. Pagad entered the national consciousness when the organization burned, shot, and killed a merchant in front of rolling cameras. Pagad was a response to a need on the Cape Flats to confront gangs. Sometimes the need was born of personal experiences, sometimes of a more general fear for personal security or that children might become involved with drugs. Initially Pagad gave many residents on the Cape Flats a sense of power vis-à-vis drug dealers and gangsters, who had hitherto been untouchable. Although not all drug dealers heeded Pagad's warnings, some did. The state was initially quite ambiguous, but it implicitly endorsed Pagad, and the main body of Islam in Cape Town, the Muslim Judiciary Council, likewise supported the anticrime organization. The initial successes caused a groundswell of support among the general population, if not for Pagad, then at least for collective, extrastate action.

Pagad was always strongest in Muslim middle-class areas such as Surrey Estate next to Heideveld, but the organization could initially field considerable support in the townships too. However, for various reasons, support for Pagad began to wane in 1997. Splits between a radical Muslim group, Qibla, and groups concerned primarily with safety began to appear not only in discourse but also in violent encounters between the different groups. As Qibla asserted itself increasingly within Pagad, the organization also lost the support of the Muslim Judiciary Council. Finally, despite its earlier endorsement of Pagad, the state came to view Pagad in an increasingly critical light. Pagad reciprocated the hostility with a pronounced antistate rhetoric, and during 1997, Pagad and the state became each other's prime enemies. By the end of 1997, Pagad had lost virtually all support by the state and among the inhabitants of Cape Town. The state tried its utmost to pin acts of violence on Pagad, and it reconfigured anticrime violence as urban terrorism. For three years, the police attempted to obtain convictions, but they did not manage to secure lengthy prison sentences for Pagad members until 2000. When the state succeeded, the penalty was harsh.

These three violent male networks were locked in a mutual battle, but it was a war without clear frontiers. Gangs were in bed with the police, and some factions of Pagad were rumored to be in alliance with some of the gangs. Furthermore, residents on the Cape Flats had divided allegiance to the extent that families might even be in internal conflict, as some family members were members of gangs, whereas others supported Pagad and/or the police. This is the real tragedy: while gangs, police, and vigilante groups slug it out among and against each other, ordinary residents' lives are endangered and compromised.

CONCLUSION: THE INTIMACY OF VIOLENCE

In this chapter, I set out to explore the genesis of gangs, their development, and their relationship to other violent networks in Cape Town's colored townships as well as how the colored gangs in Cape Town compared to other gang structures in South Africa, notably in and around Johannesburg. I argued that we must understand the emergence of gangs as a result of urbanization and the political economy of the specific city from where they come. In Cape Town, this was linked to the migration of colored farm workers *and* poor whites to the city. The *skollie* menace became the medium through which to understand race relations and maintain notions of white superiority despite the objective existence of thousands of poor whites, lacking in culture and education. The colored Cape Town gangs developed in two distinct phases. The first took place in the inner city, while a second, new breed of gangs emerged after the forced removals of the 1960s and 1970s. Gangs in Johannesburg were likewise the result of political economy and urbanization, but here gangs were much more closely related to the capitalist mining industry and the single-sex hostels.

As to the development of gangs in Cape Town, I argued that the push factors related to the need to survive the streets of the city and the influences of prison gangs, and it became a way in which to emerge as strong men in a world where the odds were stacked against masculine assertion. However, this, I argued, only forms part of the story, as it takes as its point of departure the objective existence of gangs. We also need to see the gang as a governmental category that allows certain state interventions, for instance, the present war on gangs (Jensen 2010).

In this way, gangs emerge in the intersection between the practices of young men, governmental interventions, and the ideas and perceptions of other township dwellers.

If we then look at other violent networks in the city, it becomes clear that they are often the same, that is, state governmental action, especially among the police and other township dwellers in the form of vigilante groups. These three violent networks—the police, the gangs, and the vigilante groups—were locked in battle during the latter part of the 1990s and early 2000s. However, this essay argues that the boundaries between these groups were in no way fixed or permanent. Gangs were in bed with the police; police officers belonged to Pagad; and Pagad became another gang structure on the Cape Flats, while retaining links to some gangs and fighting others. Often these conflicts were fought out (or managed) within the intimate sphere of families.

In the final paragraphs of this chapter, I focus on this issue of intimacy and violence in the townships. In much policy literature and in many interventions against gangs, it is assumed that gangs are aberrations to sociality—that they prevent the possibility of community. As such, policy understands gangs through what André Standing (2006) suggestively calls the parasitic model: a tumor on society, the removal of which can restore society to health. My analysis suggests otherwise. As the discussion of the police illustrates, the police and the state are often the corruptors rather than the corrupted ones. Pagad's membership emerged out of Muslim middle-class families, but its links to the gangs were quite evident in many cases, often through family relations. One example will illustrate these intricate and intimate relations. In one family, the oldest daughter was active in Pagad when it emerged in friendship and activist circles close to her. Simultaneously, she was a member of several policing initiatives, despite that the police and Pagad were becoming mortal enemies. In her family, several of her brothers were using drugs; they were close to the gangs, and one of them had killed a neighbor but had seemingly been "forgotten" by the police, who did not take action, while the family anxiously awaited whether the state would prosecute.[3] Several of the members of the broader family were imprisoned on drug charges. I could mention other families in which similar or parallel configurations were present. They would all speak to how seemingly insurmountable enmity would be negotiated—successfully or not—inside the domestic intimacy of families.

How do we understand this, and what are the implications? Das,

Ellen, and Leonard (2008) usefully suggest that the family should not necessarily be seen as one domestic sphere divorced or separate from the outside. Rather, the family is a place in which competing domestic spheres that extend from the family and out are negotiated. These domestic spheres include the household and, for instance, the street, the welfare office, the police, and the prison. They have to be reconciled in different ways inside the household, which then becomes the battleground for all conflicts. In this way, the family is far from the sanctuary of kin and intimate relations. Rather, it is the central battlefield of the different violent, male networks. As I have argued elsewhere (Jensen 2009), women often manage to successfully allay some of the conflicts to emerge as legitimate local leaders exactly because the family is a central point of contestation.

However, this intimacy is fraught with risks and vulnerabilities when, for instance, a young man is accused of a crime that subjects his police-cooperating mother to trouble with the state. This speaks to what we, drawing on Peter Geschiere (1997), can call "the dark side of intimacy." As Sharika Thiranagama (2010, 135), analyzing treason among Tamils, suggests, "the family which ideally is premised around trust, solidarity and amity, is often equally filled with jealousy, inequality, conflict and aggression." Hence intimacy is not only what suffers from onslaught on the family; intimacy is also potentially the source of dispute. In both my and Thiranagama's analyses, intimate danger is often the result of outside violent networks reaching into the family and demanding allegiance (the state, the Tamil Tigers or the police, the gang or the vigilante group). In Cape Town, the family manages most of the time to negotiate successfully and even to allay some of the conflicts that would otherwise be much harder to resolve between, for instance, gangs and vigilante groups. However, this comes at a high price, as the pressure on the family is enormous and continuous. Any strategy to combat gangs and their violence will fall short if it does not take into account these pressures and how they are negotiated in the intimate sphere of township lives. Only by exploring the intimate nature of violence may we understand why gangs are so hard to defeat and why violence is so intractable in places like the colored townships on the Cape Flats.

NOTES

1. The term *colored* refers to one of four racial categories of the apartheid regime (*black, white, colored,* and *Indian*). It is generally considered to refer to individuals of "mixed race." Although it is clearly a constructed category, it has maintained its importance as a self-referential identity for most people in the townships as well as in general South African public discourse.

2. For further elaboration on the history of gangs in Cape Town, see Pinnock (1984, 23–30).

3. Twelve years down the line, the son has still not been prosecuted, and the case seems forgotten entirely. He now has four kids and a wife and no longer worries about the charges that potentially loom over him.

REFERENCES

Alexander, Claire. 2000. *The Asian Gang: Ethnicity, Identity, Masculinity.* London: Berg.

Das, Veena, Jonathan Ellen, and Lori Leonard. 2008. "On the Modalities of the Domestic." *Homes Cultures* 5, no. 3: 349–72.

Fernandez, Lowell. 1991. *Police Abuses of Non-political Criminal Suspects: A Survey of Practices in the Cape Peninsula.* Cape Town: Institute of Criminology.

Geschiere, Peter. 1997. *The Modernity of Witchcraft: Politics and the Occult in Post-colonial Africa.* Charlottesville: University of Virginia Press.

Glaser, Clive. 2000. *"Bo-Tsotsi": The Youth Gangs of Soweto, 1935–1976.* Cape Town: David Philips.

Greenhouse, Carol. 2003. "Solidarity and Objectivity: Re-reading Durkheim." In *Crime's Power: Anthropologists and the Ethnography of Crime,* edited by Philip Parnell and Stephanie Kane, 269–90. New York: Palgrave Macmillan.

Hornberger, Julia. 2004. "My Police—Your Police: The Informal Privatization of the Police in the Inner City of Johannesburg." *African Studies* 63, no. 2: 213–30.

Jensen, Steffen. 2000. "Of Drug Dealers and Street Gangsters: Power, Mobility and Violence on the Cape Flats." *Focaal* 36:105–16.

———. 2005. "Above the Law: Practices of Sovereignty in Surrey Estate, Cape Town." In *Sovereign Bodies: Citizens, Migrants, and States in the Postcolonial World,* edited by Thomas Hansen and Finn Stepputat, 218–40. Princeton, N.J.: Princeton University Press.

———. 2008. *Gangs, Politics, and Dignity in Cape Town.* Oxford: James Currey.

———. 2009. "Gendered Connections: Politics, Brokers, and Urban Transformation in Cape Town." *Critique of Anthropology* 29, no. 1: 47–64.

———. 2010. "The Security–Development Nexus: War on Gangs, Counterinsurgency, and Citizenship in Cape Town." *Security Dialogue* 10, no. 1: 77–98.

Jensen, Steffen, and Lars Buur. 2007. "The Nationalist Imperative: South Africanisation, Regional Integration, and Mobile Livelihoods." In *The Security-Development Nexus: Expressions of Sovereignty and Securitization in Southern Africa,* edited by Lars Buur, Steffen Jensen, and Finn Stepputat, 63–84. Uppsala, Sweden: NAI.

Jensen, Steffen, and Dennis Rodgers. 2009. "Revolutionaries, Barbarians, or War Machines? Gangs in Nicaragua and South Africa." *Socialist Register* 45:220–38.

Kynock, Gary. 2005. *We Are Fighting for the World: A History of the Marashea Gangs in South Africa, 1947–1999.* Athens: Ohio University Press.

Mamdani, Mahmoud. 1996. *Citizens and Subjects: Contemporary Africa and the Legacy of Late Colonialism.* Princeton, N.J.: Princeton University Press.

Moodie, Dunbar. 1995. *Going for Gold: Men, Mines, and Migration.* Berkeley: University of California Press.

National Institute for Crime Prevention and the Re-integration of Offenders. 1975. "Living in Manenberg and Bonteheuwel." Proceedings from a Workshop on Living Conditions in Some Coloured Townships on the Cape Flats and Their Implication for the Incidence of Deviant Behaviour, Cape Town.

Pinnock, Don. 1984. *The Brotherhoods: Street Gangs and State Control in Cape Town.* Cape Town: David Philips.

Republic of South Africa. 1976. *Commission of Inquiry into Matters Relating to the Coloured Group.* Pretoria: Theron Commission, Government Printer.

Salo, Elaine. 2004. "Respectable Mothers, Tough Men, and Good Daughters: Producing Persons in Manenberg Township, South Africa." PhD diss., Emory University.

Simon, Jonathan. 2007. *Governing through Crime: How the War on Crime Transformed American Democracy and Created a Culture of Fear.* New York: Oxford University Press.

Standing, André. 2006. *Organized Crime: A Study from the Cape Flats.* Pretoria: Institute for Security Studies.

Steinberg, Jonny. 2004. *Nongoloza's Children: Western Cape Prison Gangs during and after Apartheid.* Johannesburg: Centre for the Study of Violence and Reconciliation.

Thiranagama, Sharika. 2010. "In Praise of Traitors: Intimacy, Betrayal, and the Sri Lankan Tamil Community." In *Traitors: Suspicion, Intimacy, and the Ethics of State-Building,* edited by Sharika Thiranagama and Toby Kelly, 127–49. Philadelphia: University of Pennsylvania Press.

Walters, William. 2008. "Editor's Introduction: Anti-policy and Anti-Politics: Critical Reflections on Certain Schemes to Govern Bad Things." *European Journal of Cultural Studies* 11:267–88.

Western, John. 1996. *Outcast Cape Town.* Berkeley: University of California Press.

2

Cholo!: The Migratory Origins of Chicano Gangs in Los Angeles

JAMES DIEGO VIGIL

Waves of migration since the 1850s have brought Mexican immigrants to the streets of Los Angeles in large numbers. The limited opportunities available to the new arrivals led to the emergence of segregated neighborhoods and increased poverty and marginalization of the Chicano population. Poverty further reduced traditional social controls on youth and schools, and law enforcement proved incapable of providing external controls on youth behavior. Instead, street socialization provided a guide to those growing up on the streets. Street socialization took over as a form of social control, and conformity to new street gang rules and regulations emerged. Street gang subculture was rife with values and norms that encouraged nonconformity and an antisocial lifestyle. Most youths from the new immigrant waves had to contend with this gang street subculture in addition to the Anglo American culture and lifestyle. This made for an even more confusing and problematic adaptation to the United States.

This persistence of gangs can be attributed, in large part, to the continuous immigration of Mexicans into southern California and their continuing confrontation with the problems associated with adaptation and adjustment to urban society, especially the marginalization that so often affected the second and subsequent generations (Waters 1999). These gangs would not follow the paths of earlier ethnic gangs, such as the Irish gangs in Boston and New York at the turn of the twentieth century, which disappeared as the arrival of new immigrants diminished and as the more established immigrants assimilated into mainstream American society. The Chicano gangs of Southern California, by contrast (Moore, Vigil, and Garcia 1983, 183),

> are long-lasting, not transitory phenomena.... With few exceptions, the Chicano communities of Los Angeles have never been invaded by another ethnic group, nor has another ethnic group succeeded them, nor has there been total cultural disintegration. Instead, there has been more or less continuous immigration of yet more Mexicans, with a reinforcement of some of the traditional culture.

This chapter builds on earlier work on multiple marginality (Vigil 2002, 2007) and provides an integrated framework for considering the complexity of social phenomena and the role of many factors in social processes. The framework addresses ecological, economic, sociocultural, and psychological factors that underlie the creation of street gangs and youth participation in them (Vigil 1988a, 1988b, 2002; Covey, Menard, and Franzese 1992). The influences of family, school, and law enforcement are particularly important in examining how youth learn to adjust and conform to modern, urban society. By focusing on socialization experiences, we can gain a better understanding of how and when family structures unravel, schools fail, and law enforcement disconnects from low-income communities. We can also investigate other factors that influence youth development, and in the case of gangs in particular, how and when multiple-aged peer group and street socialization begins to dominate the life of a youth.

The chapter focuses on the origins of Chicano gangs in Los Angeles, paying particular attention to the roles of immigration, adaptation, poverty, and socialization in the emergence and persistence of youth gangs in Los Angeles. It is divided into three sections. The first section identifies important dynamics during immigration and the subsequent adaptation to a new homeland. The second section reveals the negative impacts of maladaptation, such as poverty, segregation, and the breakdown of traditional family structures. The third section emphasizes the role of "choloization" and the street in socializing youth and creating the context for the emergence of gangs.

IMMIGRATION AND ADJUSTMENT

Los Angeles in the middle of the nineteenth century was a Mexican pueblo of roughly ten thousand people, mostly native Mexicans (Griswold del Castillo 1980). However, the flood of Anglos in the late nineteenth century began the urbanization process, and by 1900, the city had grown to more than one hundred thousand residents, with Anglo American newcomers becoming the majority.[1] During the Anglo influx, the Mexican section of town, the old pueblo near modern-day Olvera Street, became a *barrio*,[2] as Anglos developed areas to the south and west and began to move toward a segregated city. Later, poor Mexican immigrants were enticed to Los Angeles as workers but segregated residentially from the rest of the city and pushed into barrios along the eastern margin of the town center (Camarillo 1979), in an area now known as greater East Los Angeles. Their makeshift residences were often built on undesirable land, such as the ravines and hollows and low hills that were easily flooded or inaccessible and had therefore been bypassed by urban developers.

In the early decades of Mexican immigration and adjustment, the settlement pattern resulted in the creation of isolated, insulated urban enclaves. These original barrios were segregated, overcrowded, and devoid of many of the amenities found in the Anglo sections of town (Ranker 1958). A definite spatial separation existed between the low-income immigrant population and the higher-income Anglo population. This separation was only reinforced by the visual distinctiveness of the barrios when compared to the more prosperous sections of town. Substandard, even dangerous, housing facilities prevailed in the barrio. Homes were older, smaller, and poorly constructed. One such barrio was El Hoyo Maravilla, which translates literally as "the Wonder Hole." Established in the 1930s, the area had been described as one where "lots in the tract were very cheap; its most conspicuous feature was its unsuitability for houses. . . . El Hoyo became a barrio inside an area of barrios. There was no water service, no sewer, no pavement, and no gas main" (Moore 1978, 56; 1991). A relatively more recent set of barrios was created in the Pico-Union area just west of downtown Los Angeles. Rows and rows of four-story apartment complexes that once housed lower-level Anglo clerical and sales workers began in the 1970s to become home to more and more Mexican immigrants. This process accelerated when

Central American refugees subsequently flooded the neighborhood.

Mexicans, like immigrants of other ethnicities, often chose to live in the barrios because of their preference to reside in communities that helped soften the culture shock of migration and provided a sense of ethnic security (Romo 1983). Similar language, religion, values, and other customs and habits make for a more comforting environment. Although some immigrants chose the barrios, it was also clear that other choices were extremely limited. Historically, Chicano immigrants have been subject to extreme pressure to stay in the barrio: houses were prohibitively expensive elsewhere, and Anglos would refuse to sell or rent residences in Anglo neighborhoods to Mexicans, even if the Mexicans could afford to do so (Bogardus 1934). These restrictions have since been relaxed largely because of civil rights laws and regulations enacted since the 1960s. Despite advances in legal rights, however, Mexican homeowners in Huntington Park and South Gate have reported that Anglo residents in those neighborhoods attempted to exclude them from the area well into the 1970s and 1980s (Vigil 2007).

Since the 1970s, the settlement pattern has been different. Almost all the open spaces have been filled, and building and safety restrictions prevent establishing squatter-like settlements. Service occupations now dominate the job market, as custodial, gardening, restaurant, and garment-related industries attract and keep immigrants in Los Angeles. As new immigrant families move to the area, they take up residence in the older, run-down neighborhoods from which earlier residents have resettled. What was once housing for Anglos in south and southeast Los Angeles, and for blacks in the south central area, is now inundated by Mexicans and Central Americans. Even white, middle-class strongholds on the western side of the city, such as Venice and Santa Monica, now have sizeable Mexican populations.

Living in inferior ecological situations and conditions has undermined the adjustment and integration of large numbers of Mexicans into the fabric of the United States. Acculturation, assimilation, and other cultural adjustment strategies were strongly affected and reshaped by the social segregation and discrimination barriers of the past century. Large-scale immigration has also tended to harden attitudes and practices toward Mexican newcomers. Along with an inferior and socially distant environment, the Mexican population has had to contend with a life of poverty and low income status. Mexicans have historically been used as a cheap source of labor and, because of discrimination, have also been barred from higher-income employment and educational opportunities (Gomez-Quinones 1994). As I noted in an earlier work, "poverty, discrimination, and group choice helped to create the Mexican barrios, but urbanization and the concomitant poor city planning and neglectful and uncaring authorities make the barrios an ecologically inferior place in which to raise a family" (Vigil 1988a, 24).

An early result of immigration was the emergence of gangs. The second wave of Mexican migration in the 1940s led to the widespread emergence of Chicano gangs in the Los Angeles area. These gangs early on organized into a number of age-graded cliques, with two or three such affiliated cliques typically active in each neighborhood. In the older barrios of the city, more than a dozen cliques had succeeded one another by the late 1970s (Moore 1978). The gangs have shown remarkable persistence and longevity and have even come to include some second- and third-generation gang families. Indeed, it is probably fair to say that a gang subculture is a street fixture with which all new immigrant youths must contend (Vigil 1988a; Klein 1971).

A number of different gangs now dot the densely populated barrio landscape. One of the largest and perhaps most threatening gangs in the area is the Eighteenth Street Gang, with an alleged membership of twenty thousand members (Vigil 2002). However, because residents settled into an already built-up area, the Eighteenth Street Gang has been less completely defined by territorial boundaries than by its population, which is more dispersed socially, with cliques and affiliates radiating in all directions from its place of origin. These new types of settlements, although still spatially distanced from white areas and dilapidated in appearance, have resulted in a more sprawling urban barrio that includes areas that share many of the same marginalization experiences that often generate street gangs. These conditions are exacerbated by the presence of the many nearby street gangs in the surrounding area, which have spurred the creation of the new gangs (Klein 1995).

POVERTY AND THE BREAKDOWN OF SOCIAL CONTROLS

A social reality of want and limited opportunity begins when a people set foot on a new land. The consequences of these beginnings go beyond generations over time. The severe and widespread social and economic problems experienced by the Mexican immigrant population contributed to a significant percentage of the immigrants falling victim to a cycle of persistent and concentrated poverty. Through time, matters improved for many subsequent generations of immigrants' descendants who managed to move out of the barrio and move up in socioeconomic status. However, the poverty rate among Mexicans in Los Angeles remains high, and the overall average income level has remained low. The effects of poverty are enhanced by the ecological conditions of the barrio and have an insidious impact on the psychological well-being of barrio dwellers, particularly youths. Knowing that they live in physically inferior and necessitous neighborhoods contributes to a sense of being social outcasts, pariahs. Venturing out of the barrio to see and compare what others have makes young immigrants feel unwanted and restricted in what they can reach for in terms of life goals. A psychological state of bitterness and resentment often becomes another burden, adding to the sense of inferiority that weighs them down. Perhaps not surprisingly, a recent study (Vigil 2007) in a public housing project in East Los Angeles provided findings that support the premise that the poorest families are more likely to have children in gangs. At the same time, there emerges a multiple marginality that results in the breakdown of normal socialization processes and the reduced effectiveness of the three principle socializing agencies for youth: family, school, and law enforcement. The poor families surveyed in the previously mentioned study also had a higher incidence of single-parent households and the additional burden of personal emotional and psychological problems.[3]

Generally, the Mexican family has a strong tradition of cohesiveness and stability. However, the effects of long-term poverty, social discrimination, and cultural conflict have undermined this tradition. With the passage of time in the United States, and marginalization of all sorts taking its toll, the status of some members of this community has progressively worsened. A particularly important element in this respect is the fact that many families are mother centered with an absent father figure (Vigil 1988a; Moore and Vigil 1987). The father is traditionally the head in the Mexican family, and his stable presence engenders a great deal of social control and security in the family. Thus, when the father is absent, for whatever reason, the results can be traumatic. When, in addition, fathers in some cases were themselves former gang members and/or involved in criminal activity, most commonly drug dealing, a double influence results. Absent, and unable to provide proximate direction and supervision to his children, the father's chosen lifestyle and behavior provide symbolic sources of antisocial identification for his children to emulate.[4]

With the breakdown of the family—which traditionally has been the strongest form of social control in the Mexican community—the burden of providing goals, direction, and sanctions to youths has shifted to the schools and law enforcement. However, for a variety of reasons, both these institutions have also failed to exert a mitigating influence on youths who might be impelled toward gang membership. Mexicans in the early twentieth century were subjected to the prejudice of their teachers and to programs such as "ability tracking," which placed Mexican students on an inferior educational course of study (Bogardus 1934). Similar practices persisted throughout most of the past century, such as academic tracking (which placed Mexican students in remedial classes); biased counseling and testing practices that steered Mexican students into vocational training and lower-income career paths; and hiring practices that resulted in teachers who were unable or unwilling to understand the minority student's culture, the challenges of adaptation, or the special needs of immigrant children (U.S. Civil Rights Commission 1971).

Historical factors and events have also had lingering effects. Many people affected by racism and poverty lived in deteriorating neighborhoods and crowded conditions, and their children attended schools that had crumbling infrastructures, insufficient staff, and no resources to fix these problems. These, and other deprivations, resulted in the marginalization of these populations. After the 1924 Immigration Act, which restricted immigration from Southeast Europe, the United States turned south to encourage even more Mexican immigration, as the need for free but cheap "exploitable, expendable, redeemable" labor accompanied free market thinking and an open border. From this juncture, an array of educational practices began to negatively affect the academic performance of the Mexican American school-aged population. Racist attitudes and housing covenants had already segregated the populations (Almaquer 1994), and separate and unequal schooling practices and facilities were well in place (Alvarez 1988). Not surprisingly, Chicano students typically fared poorly in these circumstances.[5]

Another issue for Chicano gang youth concerns law enforcement and the whole criminal justice apparatus. Like the family and the schools, law enforcement has also failed to exert social control over the growing gang problem. Community–police relations have been marked more often by hostility than by respect. As immigration grew and became an important factor in the changing nature of the Chicano population, the preexisting negative attitude Anglo authorities had toward Mexicans was sharpened by an antiforeign, anti–illegal alien campaign. Police often continue to discriminate in their treatment of barrio residents. Moreover, immigration officials have mounted one offensive after another to rid neighborhoods of Mexicans, sparking incidents that have attracted public attention. Thus barrio residents are made to feel that they are perceived as being deviant and criminal. They have come to resent the extra police attention that they receive just by living in the barrio (Morales 1972; U.S. Civil Rights Commission 1971).

CHOLOIZATION AND STREET SOCIALIZATION

While intense poverty and neighborhood ecological effects altered social control networks over youth within immigrant communities, gradually changing them for the worse, other social and cultural reverberations also accompanied adaptation (or maladaptation) to American life. Two major transformative influences were *choloization* and *street socialization* (see Vigil 1988a). The former is an age-old phenomenon fundamentally linked to marginalization and cultural ostracism from mainstream, dominant society. Street socialization refers to the main arena where youth learn the routines and rhythms of the street subculture of gangs.

Choloization is the cultural attribute that goes hand in hand with the pressures and influences of the street in Latino immigrant communities. It makes for commonality of upbringing and purpose. Choloized individuals can come from different types of barrios (i.e., urban, rural, suburban; classic, modern; each with its own name, e.g., White Fence, El Hoyo Maravilla, Eighteenth Street). Gang members also differ in the intensity and duration of their involvement, depending on the variation in neighborhood histories and influences and personal proclivities. Street socialization and choloization, with the concomitant breakdown in social control, might compel a youth to join a gang before he has reached his teen years. For example, a nine-year-old from an old barrio, White Fence, was raised in a gang household, had many relatives (including his parents) as street role models, and, by the time he reached fourteen years, was an active and recognized leader of the younger clique. Such youths have been pre–gang socialized by older brothers and sisters or other relatives who were gang members.

Cholo is a label that Americans and Mexican Americans have used to refer to the poorest of the poor, marginalized Mexican immigrants. The term itself is several hundred years old and was used in various areas of Latin America where Indian populations are concentrated. The label describes an indigenous person who is halfway acculturated to the Spanish ways—in short, a person marginal to both the original and the more recent European culture. In the contemporary U.S. cultural context, it is used to denote individuals who are marginally associated with both Anglo and Mexican culture. Thus cholo is a term that, since early times, has been associated with culture change and has designated people caught between two cultures (Vigil 1988a, 1990). The use of the term cholo has continued and persisted in the United States. Chicano street populations who have undergone intense culture change embrace and use this label with pride to denote their speech, dress, and other customs and habits as well as themselves.

Because of these culture contacts, conflicts, and changes, the choloization (marginalization) of the Mexican population has increased the risk that some youth will become gang members. It is important to note that cholo applies to a larger subset of the Mexicans who have undergone extreme and destabilizing marginalization. From such cultural dynamics gangs emerged, comprised principally of the marginalized who were even poorer and more isolated. Thus a gang member is always a cholo, but a cholo is not always a gang member. Instead, the processes of marginalization and cultural adaptation has created the subset of the cholo and, within this, a smaller subset, the gang, which has become thoroughly and completely street socialized.

Continual Mexican immigration in this century has added new elements to the cholo historical phenomenon. Many immigrants already considered cholo in their native country underwent further—if different—marginalizing experiences in the United States to add a binational dimension to the word and to the process of becoming a cholo (Chavez 1992). Others who were less marginalized in Mexico became cholos in the United States through a secondary process of choloization and in response to conditions in the United States. What this means is that a steady stream of cholos arrive and/or are produced in each generation. This is especially true for the second generation, for whom culture change can be more intense and whose backgrounds increase their risk of becoming gang members. In earlier decades, cholos struggled to keep afloat on the environmental fringes and economic margins of American society; as the American social and economic systems underwent transformation, so did the cholos.

Through all of these developments, some families were unable to become socially mobile. Instead, they experienced one setback after another and thus became rooted in long-term poverty. Although most immigrant families were subjected to economic shifts and culture change, some of the families were burdened even more. When status change is impeded across generations, choloization is intensified. In time, this tended to change the conditions in the barrios, with the less successful families being left behind. With less hope and inspiration shaping the future of the new generations, a budding incipient underclass began to form.

In this context of wide and deep choloization, social control networks unraveled, such as families, schools, and police relations, and a second transformation entered the picture: street socialization. A number of factors contributed to children spending more time on the streets, under the purview and guidance of a multiple-aged peer group. Street socialization is a result of the failure of home and school influences and a life on the streets for the most marginalized youths. A consequence of the loosening of family control engendered by tension and stress is that youths spend an inordinate amount of time outside of the home with street peers, thus creating primary connection bonds that reflect deviant and unconventional roles. These peers thus became major agents of socialization, filling the void that the absent or inattentive parents have created. This shift to secondary connections often places the peer group (gang) in the role of a surrogate family to substitute for the broken or disorganized family. This dynamic goes back to the 1930s and 1940s, when the paths of immigrants were particularly difficult and social control networks were weak, and there emerged a critical mass of street-raised immigrant youths.

In various Los Angeles ethnic communities, this peer group often takes the form of the street gang. It is a variable process, however, as the rate and depth of street socialization determine the type of gang (Klein 1995) and gang member (Vigil 1988a), some being more violent and longer lasting and others merely experiencing a passing fancy. For girls as well as boys, the street becomes a haven, and gang life is romanticized as a subculture of last resort. However, this attraction often ultimately brings youths trouble and, for girls, additional victimization. What established gangs in the neighborhood have to offer is nurture, protection, friendship, emotional support, and other ministrations for unattended, unchaperoned resident youths. In other words, street socialization fills the voids left by inadequate parenting and schooling, especially inadequate familial care and supervision. This street-based process molds the youths to conform to the ways of the street. On the streets, the person acquires the models and means for new norms, values, and attitudes. The "ought-to" (values) and "blueprints for action" (norms) often substitute for the voids left by conventional social control institutions. I have heard many times during interviews with gang members, "These guys are like a family and take care of me."

Thus the gang is a source of attraction that provides many family-type functions. This "spontaneous" street social unit reflects a group of youths whose lives were neglected. Some parents and other family members failed to make an early connection. Thus this void forced many marginalized youths to seek an alternate bonding source. The street gang group has arisen as a source of familial compensation where all else has failed. Clearly the group represents a ready source of nurturance and acceptance and helps to provide a sense of structure to the youth who has been raised under familial disconnected circumstances. In short, there appears to be a close association between family stress and disruption and the personal tendency of some youths to seek another source of emotional comfort and safety in the street gang, thus completing a shift from primary to secondary connections. The culmination of all the street experiences is the shaping of a mind-set of *locura*. This is an attitude that is deeply internalized by some gang members, especially the regular ones, who have had particularly traumatic lives and are "crazy-like," but is equally instrumental as an attitude that can be adopted as circumstances dictate. Thinking and acting *loco* is like playing with insanity, moving in and out of crazy, wild events and adventures, showing fearlessness, toughness, daring, and especially unpredictable forms of destructive behavior.

There are many other symbolic features to the gang subculture, such as sights, sounds, and images that characterize the street and the cultural identity of gang members. The dress, walk, talk, and body language are distinct and assert a streetwise sense of control and a command of life's challenges and threats. A gang member's walk is affected and perfected to mask insecurity and evince "machismo in motion." Gang members entertain themselves (i.e., party) with alcohol and drugs and fix their cars up as lowriders, slung low to the ground and driven slow, with the driver acting accordingly, alongside his equally "cool" chola. However, gangs and gang members gain most of their attention from the mayhem and violence associated with gang conflicts and homicides. Although this latter unconventional, destructive activity constitutes only a small percentage of their time, they attract an inordinate amount of media and public attention. Alcohol and drugs check the rational processes, guns accelerate acts of aggression, and cars make it easier to effect a getaway.

Making a distinction between the industrial and postindustrial periods since the 1970s, John Hagedorn maintains that the latter period has brought more violence because of the collapse of the industrial economy and, in the resulting vacuum, the rise of street enterprises like drug sales (Hagedorn 1998, 369–70). There is no doubt that during the past few decades, street gangs in impoverished neighborhoods have increasingly turned to the informal and illicit economy. Ways of making money and spending it have changed dramatically. What once was a penny ante drug sale has evolved into drug trafficking enterprises; bad check signings have grown into identity theft and credit card fraud; and other street-level criminal practices, such as "taxing," have been introduced as new money-making ventures. These deviant activities have led to another level of conflict and violence among street gangs and added to the mayhem and aura of aggression that are found in the streets. To magnify matters, in the last fifteen years, prison gang rhetoric and influences have been spilling over onto the streets, as have various forms of organized crime. For example, Eme (the Mexican Mafia prison gang originally founded in the 1950s) initially focused on drug sales and other illicit activities, and Mexican drug cartels have begun to make inroads into poor cholo barrios.

CONCLUSION

Despite numerous acculturation strategies developed both endogenously within immigrant communities and exogenously by the U.S. state authorities, the marginalization of sizeable segments of the Latino immigrant population in the United States has continued with each new wave. There is a long history of racism and poverty in the United States that has had significant repercussions and lingering effects on how, even whether, family life is structured and organized to effectively participate in immigrant societies, including, in particular, Latino ones. Moreover, the state of schooling for minority youths and relations with law enforcement in general have affected family life insofar as poor people often receive short shrift from authorities. Such processes of multiple marginalization have led to the emergence of a persistent cholo subculture. In contrast to earlier years, and combined with a more assertive Chicano ethnic identity inculcated by the civil rights movement of the 1960s and 1970s, in the contemporary period, this has become widely associated with "Mexicanization." This transformation has increased the possibility and utility of a bilingual–bicultural identity for many Mexican immigrants and Mexican Americans. At the same time, however, many Anglicized Mexicans, third and fourth generation, remain caught within an entrenched cholo street subculture that has become rooted in many areas of Southern California.

This cholo street subculture has played a significant role in institutionalizing street gangs as a standard element of new immigrant youths' acculturation experience. At the same time, the street gang phenomenon has worsened over time. Violence today is easier to carry out because of the sophisticated weaponry that is available to ensure that deadly injuries are meted out to the victim. Gang violence from low-income adolescent and youth populations is but a reflection of the aggression and violence that surround and shape their lives. The type of emotional despair that exists and the range of frustration and rage that stems from it are clearly triggered by the poverty, financial instability, and otherwise disquieting life of poor people. For newcomer youths and the children of immigrants, it is doubly so, in large part because there is a rooted gang subculture that is an urban fixture. There have always been gangs and gang members who have gone beyond the neighborhood violence, as these groups and individuals move up the criminal chain and network.

More common on the East Coast of the United States, especially at the inception of gangs among white ethnics (i.e., Irish, Italians, etc.), there was a career ladder setup. In recent decades, however, the gangs of Los Angeles, especially among cholo Mexican immigrants from border towns where drug cartels flourish, have emulated this pattern as some individuals and/or gang members have joined the drug trafficking industry in one capacity or another. These illicit entrepreneur activities mark current gang street life, and the streets themselves have become a place of economic enterprise and activity and a context for competition and rivalry rather than for the camaraderie and surrogate kinship that they previously marked.

NOTES

1. *Anglo Americans* refers here to a varied group of whites from the eastern and midwestern United States.

2. *Barrio* translates literally into "neighborhood." However, it is often understood in the United States to refer to a Mexican enclave, or neighborhood, in particular.

3. As a result, they typically lack readily available social capital, that is, people living nearby (e.g., relatives) whom they could usually expect to help them in a crisis.

4. The lack of a father figure may be particularly detrimental during a youth's adolescent period, as he begins to form his sexual identity (Boyle 2010). Gang members usually have been, in the absence of effective parental oversight, largely socialized in the streets by peers and slightly older youths. Those from mother-centered households have to adjust to a male-dominated street gang. Thus they may experience some role confusion as they try to mediate their self-identity. Some youths may attempt to resolve this conflict by overemphasizing their "male" qualities, acting aggressively and modeling themselves after the "street warrior" role models (Vigil 1988b).

5. The very high dropout rates among high school–aged barrio Chicanos indicate the persistence of major problems in barrio schools and can often be linked to parental problems, including, for example, when the parents of children belong to gangs themselves—something that also contributes to the children being more at risk of involvement in gangs. More generally, gang members have had particular difficulty in adjusting to school, and by the age of sixteen, most have dropped out of the educational system (Vigil 1988a, 1988b, 1997, 1999; Thornberry 2001).

REFERENCES

Almaquer, T. 1994. *Racial Fault Lines: The Historical Origins of White Supremacy in California.* Berkeley: University of California Press.

Alvarez, R. R., Jr. 1988. *Familia.* Berkeley: University of California Press.

Bogardus, Emory S. 1926. *The City Boy and His Problems.* Los Angeles, Calif.: House of Ralston, Rotary Club of Los Angeles.

———. 1934. *The Mexican in the United States.* USC Social Science Series 8. Los Angeles: University of Southern California Press.

Boyle, Gregory J. 2010. *Tattoos on the Heart.* New York: Free Press.

Camarillo, Albert. 1979. *Chicanos in a Changing Society: From Mexico Pueblos to American Barrios in Santa Barbara and Southern California, 1848–1930.* Cambridge, Mass.: Harvard University Press.

Chavez, L. 1992. *Shadowed Lives.* Ft. Worth, Tex.: Harcourt Brace.

Covey, H., C. S. Menard, and R. J. Franzese. 1992. *Juvenile Gangs.* Springfield, Ill.: Charles C. Thomas.

Gomez-Quinones, Juan. 1994. *Mexican American Labor: 1790–1990.* Albuquerque: University of New Mexico Press.

Griswold del Castillo, R. 1980. *The Los Angeles Barrio, 1850–1890.* Los Angeles: University of California Press.

Hagedorn, John M. 1998. "Gang Violence in the Postindustrial Era." In *Youth Violence,* edited by M. Tonry and M. H. Moore, 364–420. Chicago: University of Chicago Press.

Klein, Malcolm W. 1971. *Street Gangs and Street Workers.* Englewood Cliffs, N.J.: Prentice Hall.

———. 1995. *The American Street Gang: Its Nature, Prevalence, and Control.* New York: Oxford University Press.

Moore, Joan W. 1978. *Homeboys: Gangs, Drugs, and Prison in the Barrios of Los Angeles.* Philadelphia: Temple University Press.

———. 1991. *Going Down to the Barrio: Homeboys and Homegirls in Change.* Philadelphia: Temple University Press.

Moore, Joan W., and James Diego Vigil. 1987. "Chicano Gangs: Group Norms and Individual Factors Related to Adult Criminality." *Aztlan* 18, no. 2: 27–44.

Moore, Joan W., James Diego Vigil, and Robert Garcia. 1983. "Residence and Territoriality in Chicano Gangs." *Social Problems* 31, no. 2: 182–94.

Morales, A. 1972. *Ando sangrando.* La Puente, Calif.: Perspectiva.

Ranker, J. E., Jr. 1958. "A Study of Juvenile Gangs in the Hollenbeck Area of East Los Angeles." MA thesis, Department of Sociology, University of Southern California.

Romo, Richard. 1983. *East Los Angeles: History of a Barrio.* Austin: University of Texas Press.

Thornberry, Terence P. 2001. "Risk Factors for Gang Membership." In *The Modern*

Gang Reader, 2nd ed., edited by Jody Miller, Cheryl L. Maxson, and M. W. Klein, 32–43. Los Angeles, Calif.: Roxbury.

U.S. Civil Rights Commission. 1971. *The Mexican American Education Study.* Washington, D.C.: U.S. Government Printing Office.

Vigil, James Diego. 1988a. *Barrio Gangs: Street Life and Identity in Southern California.* Austin: University of Texas Press.

———. 1988b. "Group Processes and Street Identity: Adolescent Chicano Gang Members." *Ethos* 16, no. 4: 421–45.

———. 1997. *Personas Mexicanas: Chicano Highschoolers in a Changing Los Angeles.* Ft. Worth, Tex.: Harcourt Brace.

———. 1999. "Streets and Schools: How Educators Can Help Chicano Marginalized Gang Youth." *Harvard Educational Review* 69, no. 3: 270–88.

———. 2002. *A Rainbow of Gangs: Street Cultures in the Mega-City.* Austin: University of Texas Press.

———. 2007. *The Projects: Gang and Non-gang Families in East Los Angeles.* Austin: University of Texas Press.

Waters, Tony. 1999. *Crime and Immigrant Youth.* Thousand Oaks, CA: Sage.

3

Capitalizing on Change: Gangs, Ideology, and the Transition to a Liberal Economy in the Russian Federation

ALEXANDER L. SALAGAEV AND RUSTEM R. SAFIN

During the 1960s and early 1970s, youth crime rates in the Soviet Union were widely reported to be declining, alongside a general decrease in the number of crimes committed by organized delinquent groups. This trend led Soviet officials to formally proclaim the end of "banditry." This situation did not last, however, and by the late 1970s, youth gangs had become quite widespread in the Soviet Union. Their spread was clearly linked to the gradual transformation that the USSR underwent from the 1970s onward. Most notably, the introduction of elements of a market economy by the Soviet government during this period created spaces for illegal economic activity, which helped the gangs institutionalize, to the extent that the youth gangs of the 1970s can in many ways be seen as the direct predecessors of contemporary Russian youth gangs.[1] The latter emerged as major social actors following the collapse of the Soviet Union in the mid-1990s and the wholesale introduction of free market economics in Russia. A new wave of youth gangs rapidly established themselves as powerful actors in a booming illegal economy, competing for control over economic resources and gradually dividing the illegal and semilegal spheres of the new post-Soviet economy among themselves. This chapter looks at the origins of youth gangs in both the Soviet and Russian contexts in an effort to better understand the driving forces behind gang formation and focuses in particular on the similarities and differences between the Soviet gangs of the 1970s and today's Russian gangs. The first section focuses on the emergence of youth gangs in the Soviet period, whereas the second section addresses the development of youth gangs in the post-Soviet, or Russian, period. The third section assesses the similarities and differences between gangs of these two eras. Although the emergence of gangs in both periods can be linked to economic transformation, it is clear that contemporary Russian youth gangs have become more professionalized and are increasingly being integrated into adult gangs. To this extent, the analysis presented in this chapter offers a strong case for considering economic factors as significant drivers of both gang formation and transformation.

THE ORIGINS OF SOVIET YOUTH GANGS

Prior to the 1970s, there only existed what one might call "proto-gangs" in the Soviet Union. During the 1920s and 1930s, for example, there were frequent cases of group hooliganism, characterized by various degrees of delinquency and violence ranging from obscene language to group rapes and assaults, which operated mainly in the large cities of the USSR. These had mostly disbanded by the late 1930s, however, owing to strict measures taken by authorities (Stepakov 1998; Panin 2003). Another type of youth group that existed prior to the 1970s was the *besprizorniki*, groups of primarily homeless and unattended children and youngsters that emerged mainly during the Russian civil war (1917–23) and in some regions during World War II. These groups, however, disappeared as soon as normal living conditions returned after these wars (Rudov 2002; Gizatulin 2008). Although there was some rise in juvenile delinquency following the 1953 political amnesty and in subsequent years, this generally remained rather unorganized, even if many of the antistate protests in the USSR during the 1950s and 1960s tended to involve youths under the age of twenty-five (Kozlov 2006, 97–99).

Increasing ideological disappointment with the Soviet regime and youth-led social protest in the 1970s did, however, lead to the widespread emergence of neighborhood peer groups. One of the primary features of Soviet culture was ideological indoctrination. Children raised in Communist families were brought up in an atmosphere of constant ideologically correct education. The Soviet system consisted of nursery schools (up to age seven), primary schools (ages seven to ten), secondary schools (ages eleven to sixteen), and higher education in institutes and universities (age seventeen and older). With the exception of nursery school, youngsters were expected to join a Communist organization at each phase of their educational growth. They would be *oktyabryata* (in reference to the October 1917 revolution) in primary school, *pionery* (pioneers) and *komsomoltsy* (members of Komsomol, the Communist Union of Youth) in secondary school, and as youths, they generally faced the need to join the Communist Party if they wanted to move upward in their careers. Strong Communist ideology was present not only in schools but also in other spheres, including the army, leisure clubs, and the like. As a result, the only ideology-free space for youths was the neighborhood, where most undirected juvenile socialization would occur. Most typically, youths would spend their time informally playing football, hockey, and other outdoor games. As they grew older, they also acquired new interests—love, film, music, dancing, and so on. Generally, youths coalesced in peer groups, and it is out of these that the Soviet gangs of the late 1970s grew.

A peer group is a collective unit in which members share the same characteristics, such as age or ethnicity (Abercrombie, Hill, and Turner 1994). The basic features of such a group include a high degree of intragroup social solidarity and a code of behavior often based on the rejection of mainstream (adult) values and experiences (Abercrombie, Hill, and Turner 1994). Youth peer groups are not necessarily deviant, but they can provide an avenue to a delinquent career (Sutherland 1934) and can often constitute the nucleus for the emergence of youth gangs, which are (peer) groups characterized by territoriality, unfinished primary socialization, an orientation toward delinquent activities, and a rigid hierarchical structure, which includes role differentiation, regular meetings, payment to a common money fund, and so on (Salagaev 2001). Part of the reason for the transformation of neighborhood peer groups into youth gangs during the 1970s was that under the Soviet regime, any behavior that appeared ideologically counter to Soviet culture met with a strong reaction on the part of Soviet officials. This was, for example, very frequent with regard to countercultures that imitated Western subcultures, such as the *hippari*, who imitated Western hippies. Although, more often than not, the individuals involved in such subcultures were not delinquent, even the slightest appearance of a foreign lifestyle met severe opposition, and this would inevitably in turn provoke a reaction against the authorities among youths.[2]

In many ways, youths in the Soviet Union can be said to have lived with the constant feeling of being in two worlds, or what psychologists call *cognitive dissonance*. The sharper the contrast between constructed and witnessed reality, the more youths refused to stick to the proposed model of the Soviet citizen. Certainly, the Soviet researcher Kara-Murza (2001), whose research focuses on the reasons for the Soviet Union's collapse, argues that the Soviet system was unable to provide the necessary "social imaginary" for Soviet citizens. He explains that although many Soviet citizens clearly felt "hungry" for an imaginary beyond the Communist one, Soviet propaganda declared that this was not necessary, and those who failed to conform to mainstream Communist lifestyle were marginalized (another example beyond the *hippari* were the members of the *stilyagi* subculture[3]). At the same time, however, Kara-Murza argues that another factor contributing to dissatisfaction with the Soviet system was paradoxically its high level of social security, insofar as living in such a definite and stable society often led to Soviet citizens feeling a need for a "bit of adventure." In Western countries, according to Kara-Murza, this problem was solved through high levels of competition in every sphere of life, freedom of entrepreneurship, and social stratification. But there were no such forms of competition in the USSR. Kara-Murza notes that it was not surprising in such circumstances that the demand for sporting activities grew among youngsters enormously, as sport was one of the few competitive outlets available.

To this extent, it could be argued that one of the main reasons for the appearance of Soviet youth gangs was systematic boredom—disappointment with the Communist ideology and Soviet lifestyle. Certainly the lack of leisure opportunities for youths can be seen as having been another influential factor in the transformation of youth peer groups into youth gangs in the USSR. For example, Kazan City, a working-class city in which numerous youth gangs emerged during the early 1970s—to the extent that the phenomenon was in fact named the *Kazan phenomenon*—very visibly lacked leisure facilities such as cinemas, discos, and affordable cafes. Teplokontrol, a district of Kazan, which gave birth to the famous Tyap-Lyap gang discussed later, had one two-hundred-seat cinema for 150,000 inhabitants (Pirovich 2004). Indeed, Makarov (2007), who studied moral panics surrounding the Kazan phenomenon, notes that the lack of leisure infrastructure was often cited as a reason for deviant behavior by youths themselves. Without other outlets for social interaction and entertainment, they argued that they were only left with the option of hanging out in the streets and finding entertainment in delinquency.

At the same time, another important factor driving the transformation of youth peer groups into gangs was the rapid industrialization of the USSR during the 1950s and 1960s (Salagaev and Shashkin 2005). Many of the Soviet cities that saw gangs emerge during the 1970s—such as Kazan, Naberezhnie Chelny, Lyubertsy, or Ulyanovsk—were among those where large plants and factories were constructed (e.g., the KAMAZ truck plant in Naberezhniye Chelny, a number of military plants in Kazan and Ulyanovsk). These new factories encouraged the mass migration of people from rural areas to the big cities for employment. According to official Soviet data, in 1951, the urban population of the USSR consisted of 55 percent of the population; by 1970, this had increased to 62 percent, and by 1981, to 70 percent (Pivovarov 2001, 103). The rural population moving to the growing cities and newly built towns of the Soviet Union in the 1960s and 1970s often preserved their norms, values, and traditions when they came into their new urban environments. Among these traditions were traditional forms of intervillage ritualized feuding in which the majority of the male populations of these villages generally took part (Schepanskaya 2001). This became transformed in the cities into intra-youth fighting over turf between different neighborhoods and streets affiliated with rival villages. This helped cement territory-based unity as the basis for gang identity.

However, perhaps the most important factor that contributed to promoting the transformation of youth peer groups into youth gangs was the economic reform of 1965—the so-called Kosygin–Lieberman reform—without which most youth peer groups would not necessarily have transformed into youth gangs. These reforms provided a certain level of autonomy to a substantial number of state economic enterprises, which in turn led to the widespread production and circulation of unregistered goods in Soviet society and created numerous opportunities for profitable illegal economic activity. Indeed, according to Kozyrev and Sokolova (2009), up to one-third of the Soviet population became engaged in underground market activities during the 1970s and 1980s. Certainly a special social class known as *tsekhoviki* (illegal enterprise managers or underground entrepreneurs) emerged, both producing and selling goods outside of the state distribution system. Individual *tsekhoviki* rapidly developed extensive networks with corrupt state officials and also with groups of young men, whom they hired to provide protection and ensure the smooth operation of illegal transactions. These youths were often boxers and wrestlers belonging to a sports club and would carry out acts of violence on demand for the *tsekhoviki* in exchange for money, generally against traditional adult criminals, who would frequently target *tsekhoviki,* because the latter would never report them to the police owing to their own illegal activities (Latov 2001). This *tsekhoviki* demand for security and protection drove the widespread transformation of youth peer groups into gangs; by the end of the 1980s, such gangs had appeared in approximately forty cities of the former Soviet Union (Salagaev 2001). One of the most famous was the Tyap-Lyap gang in Kazan.

Case Study: The Tyap-Lyap Gang

The famous Tyap-Lyap gang demonstrates well how the aforementioned factors contributed to the appearance of youth gangs in the Soviet Union, insofar as its origins lie in a youth peer group clearly associated with the city's industrialization during the 1960s. At the same time, the case also shows how this youth peer group's transformation into a youth gang ultimately led it to a further transformation into a more powerful criminal gang that become widely known for its violence and a broad scope of criminal activity. The Tyap-Lyap gang originated from a youth peer group in a neighborhood inhabited by the workers of the Teplokontrol plant in Kazan. This was associated with a boxing club organized by an individual called Sergey Antipov. He proved to be a charismatic leader and, by the early 1970s, had a group of thirty to forty devoted youth to whom he gave boxing lessons. Connection with local *tsekhoviki* gradually drew the group into criminal activities and led to it becoming the backbone of the Tyap-Lyap gang. Initially, gang members were simply employed as hired muscle, but over time, they became increasingly involved in brain work, that is to say, their own independent criminal activity.

Certainly by the mid-1970s, gang members were involved in a range of different violent criminal activities, including racketeering. As the profits of this business mounted, the Tyap-Lyap gang became the first gang in Kazan to embark on a policy of territorial expansion by absorbing local neighborhood peer groups into a federated Tyap-Lyap structure. In some cases this occurred peacefully, with many local youth peer groups glad to unite with the increasingly powerful and therefore attractive Tyap-Lyap gang. In other cases the Tyap-Lyap forcefully recruited local groups, despite often fierce resistance to such efforts. Those youth groups that successfully resisted being integrated into the Tyap-Lyap in fact also transformed themselves into gangs, expanding the numbers of "fighters" they had, engaging in systematic involvement in criminal activities, and becoming large-scale organizations with a strong sense of discipline. These gangs then entered into competition with the Tyap-Lyap and other gangs, which fostered numerous conflicts in Kazan during the 1970s.

In the late 1970s, the Soviet police and the Supreme Court of Tartarstan opened proceedings against the Tyap-Lyap gang and convicted its members of committing more than sixty crimes, including robbery, armed robbery, extortion, racketeering, assault, and murder. This was likely the tip of the iceberg, however, as the majority of the Tyap-Lyap's victims were criminals themselves and thus unlikely to report their troubles to the police. Most of the gang members were sentenced in 1978, which meant the end of the gang, although following the disbandment of the original Tyap-Lyap, there rapidly emerged a more secretive reorganized version of the gang, and more significantly, the Tyap-Lyap gang institutionalized certain practices and social functions that continued to produce youth gangs. The period of the 1980s through the early 1990s was characterized by increased youth participation in gang activities in Kazan, which in turn led to high levels of street violence (Salagaev 2001; Salagaev and Safin 2008). This further coincided with a second period of economic liberalization, commonly referred to as Perestroika, which further influenced youth gang formation. The liberalization process aimed to encourage business initiatives, broaden the possibilities to improve people's well-being, and stimulate economic growth in the country. In 1986 and 1987, the government implemented several laws on individual labor, cooperatives, and joint enterprises with foreign capital. These laws aimed at facilitating economic stabilization and growth. The introduction of market economy principles together with the general sociopolitical crisis in the USSR, however, provoked a massive growth of gangs in the USSR and led to their gradual transformation into new-era Russian gangs.

THE ORIGINS OF RUSSIAN YOUTH GANGS

According to most researchers, although the origins of contemporary Russian youth gangs can clearly be traced to the rise of Soviet youth gangs in late 1970s (Salagaev 2001; Stephenson 2006), the fundamental event that triggered their explosion in the early 1990s was the collapse of the USSR, which left contemporary Russia in chaos. Indeed, the events of this period are best characterized as a systemic crisis. State authorities were very weak, and the country was in a state of social and economic crisis and disorganization. Changes in the political regime together with complete economic liberalization opened up an uncontrolled space into which a new wave of youth gangs emerged. These macro-level changes were reinforced by several other factors, including the fact that youth gangs had existed previously. Certainly, by the time the Soviet Union collapsed, many gang members had developed a fair amount of criminal experience, especially compared to the first era of youth gangsterism in the late 1970s, when most members did not have anything in the way of a criminal background. During the 1980s, many gang members were imprisoned for possessing weapons or for "hooliganism" and gained further criminal experience in prison. As many of these gang members were released in the early 1990s, they found that they had a certain prestige and charisma that attracted both their peers and a younger generation of gang members. They introduced these to prison norms and values, including the *vory* (thief) subculture that emphasized disobeying social norms; placed a low value on earning money through hard work; and raised criminal activity, conspicuous consumption, and the manipulation of power as primary aspirations.

Partly as a result, the new wave of youth gangs that emerged in 1990s Russia seized on new illegal economic opportunities with an enthusiasm and a degree of single-mindedness that previous Soviet gangs had not had (Salagaev 2001; Salagaev and Shashkin 2005). In particular, the official introduction of a free market completely changed the economic opportunities available to youths. Changes to the economic system included a total shift to private entrepreneurship and the possession of private property as well as a rejection of state-based price controls, which meant that there were greater possibilities for both legal and illegal activities than before. Moreover, prior to the late 1980s, private entrepreneurship had been considered a crime according to Article 153 of the 1960 Criminal Code of the USSR and was punishable by three to five years in prison and property confiscation. Following the abrogation of this law and the creation of several new laws, the number of people engaged in the private sector grew exponentially. By 1991, some 110,000 cooperatives were functioning in the former Soviet Union (Kaufman and Hardt 1993). This massive growth of the private sector attracted involvement by youth gangs, as these were contracted to provide protection services to new businessmen in a context of legal flux and weak contract enforcement, in a manner very similar to the 1970s *tsekhoviki*. At the same time, however, the more professional nature of gangs meant that many businessmen also began to have to pay protection money to gangs instead of taxes to the Russian state, as the former often decided that it was more profitable to extort money for themselves than it was to protect businesses from extortion (Salagaev and Shashkin 2005). Not surprisingly, perhaps, the period of economic liberalization in post-Soviet Russia coincided with a particularly rapid growth in crime rates—during 1989–1990, the overall crime rate increased 20 to 25 percent.

At the same time, however, the new Russian youth gangs were not just more professionalized criminal gangs. They also represented a transformed socialization mechanism for youths who often faced significant gaps in other areas of their lives. Although Russia's liberalization was accompanied by processes of democratization that proved very popular with the youth population, this was often imperfect in nature, and the fact that neither the new economic nor political situation offered them opportunities for upward mobility rapidly emerged as a major source of dissatisfaction, especially in the face of visibly rising inequality in post-Soviet Russian society. This made engaging in criminal activities an attractive alternative career option for many youths, with gangs rapidly emerging as the principal institutional vehicles through which to successfully achieve it (Salagaev and Shashkin 2005). To this extent, gangs were—and, to a certain extent, remain—not only economically motivated groups but also cultural arenas for a particular form of socialization of young Russians.

Case Study: Khadi-Taktash

The particular evolution of contemporary youth gangs in Russia is well exemplified by the case of another famous gang from Kazan: the Khadi-Taktash, which originally appeared in the 1980s as an offshoot of the Tyap-Lyap gang but rapidly evolved into a more organized criminal gang during the 1990s (Salagaev and Safin 2008). The original Khadi-Taktash gang was little more than a street-based youth gang made up of younger members of the Tyap-Lyap gang who were not imprisoned in the late 1970s. This changed in the early 1990s when one individual called Radik Galiakberov, also known as Rajah, rallied a subgroup of youths within Khadi-Taktash to challenge the gang's aging leadership. During the ensuing power struggle, played out in 1992 and 1993, Galiak-berov's followers killed the existing leadership but also much of the rest of the gang, which, as a result, became smaller, leaner, and meaner, with the gang in fact consolidated around kinship ties—for instance, the group included two brothers, an uncle, and a nephew. This new structure allowed Khadi-Taktash to become more efficiently involved in a range of criminal activities beyond simply hiring out as muscles on demand. These included drug trafficking, weapons trading, large-scale racketeering, and the trafficking of women. Not surprisingly, this led to clashes with rival groups, including a rival gang called Pervaki. The Khadi-Taktash, however, proved very effective in its ability to control its territory and, during the course of a war during the latter half of the 1990s, managed to kill a majority of the members of the Pervaki gang and forced those remaining, including its leader, to flee the city and live outside of Kazan. This widespread violence, however, brought the Khadi-Taktesh to the attention of the Russian state, and senior members of the gang were brought to justice in 2001 after several years of investigation, their convictions bringing an end to the gang.

ASSESSING SIMILARITIES AND DIFFERENCES BETWEEN SOVIET AND RUSSIAN GANGS

Although there is a clear filiation between Soviet and Russian gangs, there also exist a number of important differences between them. Con-temporary Russian gangs are generally more organized compared to the gangs in the Soviet period, and their internal structures are often more complicated. Russian gangs also tend to be more secretive than Soviet gangs were, partly because the latter developed in opposition to the authorities. Russian gangs also do not use forceful recruitment mechanisms. More generally, although the origins of both Soviet and Russian youth gangs lie in economic factors, Soviet gangs were clearly less engaged in economic activities than Russian gangs, which are nothing but illegal economic actors. This section discusses in more detail the differences and similarities in structure and activity between Soviet and Russian youth gangs.

The Structure of a Gang

Although both Russian and Soviet youth gangs are organized on the basis of age cohorts—of members joining the gang in the same year rather than their actual ages—the Russian gangs display a more complicated structure than Soviet gangs.[4] Whereas the latter recruited new members during regular initiation periods that took place once every one or two years, the former display much less strict initiation practices and allow gang members to join the gang in between formal acceptance periods. Soviet gangs were also structured on the basis of age cohort division only, but in Russian youth gangs, a second stratification also takes place: gang members belonging to a single age cohort (*vozrast*) are further divided into brigades. Brigades are generally formed on the basis of where one resides or on previous friendship ties. Russian gang age cohorts are thus divided into several brigades. This secondary stratification of members began at the end of the 1980s, just before the collapse of the USSR, during a time of rapid gang growth.

Age cohorts can aid in determining the difference between youth gangs and adult criminal groups, but this is not always the case. Although youth gangs often have young members (ages thirteen, fourteen, and fifteen) in the lower cohorts, they can also have members in their thirties and forties in the upper cohorts.[5] Age cohorts generally do not mix with one another and tend to have separate criminal activities. For example, in Soviet gangs, senior members were the ones engaging in more organized criminality (e.g., racketeering), whereas junior members were just "button-men," that is to say, happy-go-lucky small-time delinquents who were often more associable with moral panics than any real criminal activity. The main difference between Soviet and Russian gang age cohorts is that the latter tend to be much better organized and disciplined, especially in terms of criminal activities. For example, semi-anarchic fighting between gang groups was very common in the USSR, but after the USSR's collapse, this fighting decreased tremendously as gangs began to channel their violence more instrumentally toward il-legal and semilegal activities.

Leadership

In terms of leadership roles, youth gangs have not changed much since the collapse of the USSR. The top of the organizational structure is the gang leader, who is not very well known to the junior members of a gang. Below the leader are a number of age cohort leaders (*smotryas-hchie za vozrastom*). These act as "gang executives," telling youth gang members what to do, when and how, and are chosen from members of the upper age cohort. They are expected to be very well acquainted with gang norms and rules and to be responsible for the activities of junior gang members and ensure that they follow the code of the gang. Another important role within age cohorts is that of the manager of the common fund (*smotryashchiy za obshchakom*). Each age cohort has a common fund (*obshchak*), which is replenished by regular monthly payments by members as well as by a percentage of the profits made on criminal activities conducted by gang members. During the Soviet era, the common fund manager was called the *kassir* (cashier), but this role was often taken on by the gang leader. Delegating the responsibility for the *obshchak* to a specially appointed gang member became common practice after the beginning of the 1990s. The reason behind this change was to protect the gang's money from being seized by law enforcement agencies in case of the leader's arrest.

Recruitment of New Members and Leaving the Gang

The recruitment practices of the Soviet and Russian gangs are signifi-cantly different. Forced recruitment was quite common in Soviet gangs, especially once these began to become institutionalized. In the early and mid-1980s, youths were frequently forced into the gang through constant humiliation by existing gang members. Certainly it was a common practice for gang members to intimidate non–gang member youths, beat them up, and extort money from them. The harassed youths faced two options: either become gang members to end the harassment and obtain gang protection or continue being humiliated. There was also a third alternative, which was to pay the gang members a protection fee, but there was no guarantee that another gang wouldn't continue the pattern of harassment. In the 1990s, however, recruitment patterns changed. As Russian youth gangs became increasingly professionalized and critically involved in illegal economic activities, mass recruitment ceased, partly because too many new members would have reduced existing gang members' share of illegal profits. Forced recruitment was thus abandoned in favor of more selective recruitment through familial and friendship ties, although there continues to be some formal form of assessment of a candidate member's suitability for gang life. Whereas physical strength was an important member characteristic in Soviet gangs, contemporary Russian gangs tend to seek new gang members who will first and foremost be capable of conducting illegal and semi-legal affairs in a manner that benefits the whole gang. In this respect, it is considered paramount that a candidate not have a record of breaking trust or displaying behaviors contrary to the fundamental gang norms and values (e.g., snitching, cooperating with the authorities, or being a victim). To a certain extent, this change in recruitment patterns can also be attributed to the active action of state authorities against gang activities in the post-Soviet era.

Gangs in the Soviet era were very close-knit and based on shared life experiences, which made leaving the gang very difficult. Indeed, there are numerous reports that those who wanted to leave these gangs often had to pay a significant ransom or face severe beatings as a penalty for doing so. This was no doubt because of the fundamentally opposi-tional nature of Soviet gangs, which depended very much on members bonding against a common enemy. The more business-like nature of contemporary Russian gangs makes them much easier to leave. A gang member simply needs to produce a significant reason for leaving the gang (e.g., illness of parents, moving to another location, necessity to work to earn one's living), and he is normally given permission.

Norms and Values

Soviet youth generally displayed a number of common norms and values, known as *ponyatiya,* which had their roots in the Soviet prison subculture. The violation of any norm was considered *stremno,* an unacceptable act, including:

- never surrendering gang members to outsiders (i.e., being a snitch or *kozlit*)
- never letting anyone take advantage of a fellow gang member (e.g., stealing money, clothes, or other goods)
- never lying *(shalobolit),* although it is, of course, not prohibited to lie to the police
- never answering the question "Where are you from?"—meaning "Which gang do you belong to?"—with the words "From nowhere; I am on my own," if the person asking you the question belongs to your gang
- never expressing fear or running away *(lomitsya)*
- never displaying a lack of reaction when somebody is rude to you or insults you to your face
- never carrying out economic activities for your own personal enrichment *(baryzhnichat)*
- never selling drugs
- never letting younger gang members drink
- never engaging in "unjust behavior" *(bespredel,* which means more or less not recognizing any moral limits)

Although contemporary Russian gangs continue to follow some of these norms, many of them are now ignored. The most prominent example concerns the ban on drug dealing and on alcohol consumption. Whereas there had been a zero-tolerance policy among gangs for drug dealing and alcohol consumption by younger gang members during the Soviet era, most contemporary Russian gangs do not follow such strict rules, partly because drugs and alcohol have become important elements of fundamental gang economic activity. To this extent, it can be argued that the moral imperatives of Soviet gang behavior patterns have given way in the face of economic imperatives in the contemporary era.

Gang Names

Both Soviet and Russian youth gangs often named themselves after the district of the city or town in which they lived and considered this area their turf. Quite often, especially in the case of Soviet gangs, abbreviations were used, for instance, DSK (Dvadtsat' sed'moy kvartal, or "Twenty-seventh Block"). Abbreviations often included additional signifiers, such as "K" (for *koroli*, or "kings"), "S" (for *sila*, or "power"), or "VS" (for *velikaya sila*, or "great power"). This resulted in names such as MVS (Mirnyi—*velikaya sila!*, i.e., "District Mirnyi [is a] great power!") and TDK (Tatarskiy Dvor—*koroli!*, i.e. "Tatar Yard [are] the kings!"). Another very common pattern of naming the gang was to use the name of a street or a special place on the gang's turf, quite often a factory or a manufacturing plant associated with gang members' families. Each gang name implied a certain attachment to a particular territory. The Russian gangs in the 1990s were often much more mobile than their Soviet predecessors, and this affected naming patterns. When a gang moved to a new city or reorganized on a new territory, it no longer used its original name but adopted a new one. This was particularly the case when regional gangs in the mid-1990s moved to Moscow. Such gangs commonly renamed themselves after the home region of their leader (e.g., the Tambovskiye gang in Saint Petersburg or the Kazanskiye gang in Moscow) or after the ethnic group to which the majority of gang members belonged (e.g., Azerbaijanskaya, Chechenskaya). To this extent, local identity can be said to have been much less of a factor in post-Soviet gangs, although these did retain a more diffuse link to identity considerations.

Clothing

The decline in the importance of identity for youth gangs in the post-Soviet era can also be seen in changing clothing patterns. During the 1980s and early 1990s, youth gang members often wore special uniforms, for example, special worker coats *(telogreiki)*, caps, and boots *(proshyaiki)*. Russian gangs, however, abandoned this practice and, in some cases, prohibited it for practical reasons, such as ensuring a low profile and preventing being profiled. Having said that, members of Russian gangs in the 1990s often wore leather coats and jeans and generally had short hair, although such features were shared with many members of the more general youth population. In the early 2000s, the situation changed, and youth gang members today tend to wear very much the same clothes as the youth mainstream to completely avoid suspicion. Certainly it is now no longer possible to clearly distinguish between an ordinary non–gang member youth and a gang member based on his or her appearance. Once again, this particular evolution can be linked to the gangs' movement from identity-based organizations to institutional vehicles for economic activity.[6]

RUSSIAN GANGS: "TO BE OR NOT TO BE"

Our comparison of Soviet and Russian youth gangs clearly suggests that economic factors are critical drivers of their origins and development over time. The economic reforms of 1965 stand out as a particularly important force that tipped what had until then been youth peer groups into youth gangs, namely, by creating a demand for their violent services on behalf of illegal economic actors. When considered against other factors that contributed to the emergence of youth gangs, this had the most impact and can be seen as a turning point. Other factors, such as a countercultural moment or opposition to a staid Soviet imaginary, while contributing to gang formation, would not necessarily have led to youth peer groups becoming gangs, and even less to youth gangs becoming involved in criminal activities. Ideological disappointment and social protest just as often led to various social and nonviolent movements (e.g., so-called dissidents) or subcultures (hippies, heavy metal fans, etc.), whereas other factors, such as the rural tradition of intervillage feuding brought into the urban environment, would very likely have disappeared had they not been adopted by the gangs that emerged precisely because of economic factors. Certainly gangs had to be capable of much more than just ritualized feuding to become a power in the criminal world, capable of causing moral panic through constant fighting, controlling their turf, and forcibly expanding their gangs by violently recruiting local youths. Gangs, in other words, had to develop a reputation in a delinquent underworld that went far beyond such preexisting patterns of violence.

After the collapse of the USSR, youth gangs became even more powerful. They transformed from street gangs used as foot soldiers of the illegal economy into full-fledged actors in this illegal economy (Volkov 2005). The economic context, completely changed by the wholesale shift to market economy principles and universal privatization, encouraged this transformation. The ability to cause moral panic was no longer necessary to gain prestige and respect. Instead, gangs began to compete for the capture of economic resources. This competition has been marked by constant gang warfare since the mid-1990s. The wars last until there is some acceptance of the distribution of economic resources among both legal and illegal economic actors. At that point, gangs become more interested in preserving their economic resources and preventing further redistribution to new gangs but also to younger gang members. This has resulted in gangs taking two paths: legalizing their activities and becoming legitimate businessmen or restricting illegal activities to the senior members of the gang. As gangs have reduced the opportunities available to younger members to get involved in profitable illegal activities, the lower age cohorts of contemporary Russian youth gangs have developed a more fluid character, with gang members coming and going and, ultimately, most young members leaving the gang to seek economic opportunities elsewhere. To this extent, contemporary Russia can be said to be seeing a decline in youth gangs and the sedimentation of more professional criminal gangs.

NOTES

1. To ensure clarity, two terms are used in this chapter: *Soviet youth gangs* refers to youth gangs of the 1970s and 1980s, and *Russian youth gangs* refers to youth gangs since the 1990s.

2. It is not surprising that some researchers described delinquent youth peer groups during the Soviet era—sometimes known as *shpana*—as forms of anti-Communist rebellion and a proto-protest movement (e.g., Kozlov 2006).

3. A youth subculture that was widespread in the USSR from the late 1940s through to the early 1960s, *stilyagi* idolized the Western lifestyle. Its main features included political indifference, negative (or indifferent) attitude toward Soviet morality, gaudy clothing, a slang of Russianized foreign words (e.g., *shuzy* for "shoes," *lukat* for "looking," *drinkat* for "drinking"), and a great interest in Western music and dance.

4. There exists a range of special names for gang age cohorts that differ from one region to another as well as between eras. Contemporary Russian gang cohorts have names such as *molodej (yangstaz), superz* (supers), *molodye* (smallies), *srednie* (middies), *starshie* (oldies), *drevnie* (ancients), or *avtoritety* (guvs). During the Soviet period, age cohort names were different: *sheluha* or *skorlupa* (nutcases) and *stariki* (oldies)—although *superz* and *molodye* were also used.

5. In Soviet gangs, the upper age of gang members was generally under thirty.

6. It should be noted that tattoos, common to many gangs worldwide, are not a common feature of either Soviet or Russian gangs. Rather, tattoos *(nakolki)* are a specific feature of the prison-based, "traditional" criminal subculture of *vory* (thieves) and are used as a means of displaying criminal status (e.g., the reason for imprisonment, the length of sentence, and the individual's fidelity to criminal values).

REFERENCES

Abercrombie, Nicholas, Stephen Hill, and Bryan S. Turner. 1994. *The Penguin Dictionary of Sociology.* London: Penguin Books.

Gizatulin, Sh. 2008. "Prestupnost v rossiyskoy provintsii i bor'ba s ney v oktyabre 1917–1922 g. (na materialakh Samarskoy gubernii)" [Delinquency in the Russian province and the fight against it in October, 1917–1922]. PhD diss., Institute of History of Tatarstan Science Academy, Kazan, Russia.

Kara-Murza, Sergei. 2001. *Sovetskaya Tsivilizatsiya: ot Velikoi Pobedy do nashih dnei* [Soviet civilization: From the Great Victory to today]. Moscow: Algoritm.

Kaufman, Richard F., and John P. Hardt. 1993. *The Former Soviet Union in Transition.* New York: M. E. Sharpe.

Kozlov, Vladimir A. 2006. *Neizvestnyi SSSR. Protivostoyaniye naroda i vlasti. 1953–1985* [Unknown USSR: Confrontation between the people and the regime, 1953–1985]. Moscow: Olma Press.

Kozyrev, Mikhail, and Anna Sokolova. 2009. "Okhota na chastnika" [Hunting the "private-man"]. *Forbes,* May, 242–49.

Latov, Yu. V. 2001. "Osobennosti natsional'nogo reketa: istoriya i sovremennost" [Peculiarities of the national racket: History and the present]. *Mir Rossii* 3:153–82.

Makarov, A. S. 2007. "Konstruirovanie sotsial'noi problemy podrostkovoi delinkventnosti v pechatnyh izdaniyah Respubliki Tatarstan" [Construction of the social problem of juvenile delinquency by the Tatarstan Republic's press]. PhD diss., NNGU, Nizhniy Novgorod.

Panin, S. E. 2003. "Hozyain ulits gorodskih': Huliganstvo v Sovetskoi Rossii v 1920-e gody" [Masters of the urban streets: Hooliganism in Soviet Russia during the 1920s]. *Vestnik Evrazii* [Acta Eurasica] 4:135–54.

Pirovich, V. 2004. "Kazanskiy fenomen molodejnoi prestupnosti" [The Kazan phenomenon of youth delinquency]. *Pervaya Krymskaya* 54.

Pivovarov, Yu. L. 2001. "Urbanizatsiya v Rossii v 20 veke: predstavleniya i real nost" [Urbanization in Russia during the twentieth century: Conception and reality]. *Obshestvennye nauki i sovremennost* 6:101–13.

Rudov, A. 2002. "Besprizornaya Rossiya" [Unattended Russia]. *Index* 17.

Salagaev, Alexander L. 2001. "Podrostkovo-molodejnoe territorialnoe soob-shchestvo delinkventnoy napravlennosti kak ob'ekt teoreticheskogo issledo-vaniya" [The delinquent orientation of youth territorial communities as an object of theoretic study]. PhD diss., Saint Petersburg State University, Russia.

Salagaev, Alexander L., and Rustem R. Safin. 2008. "Organized Criminal Gangs in Tatarstan Republic of Russia: From Dawn to Dusk." Paper presented at the Conference on Subcultures and Lifestyles in Russia and Eastern Europe, Salford, U.K.

Salagaev, Alexander L., and Alexander V. Shashkin. 2005. "After-Effects of the Transition: Youth Criminal Careers in Russia." In *Youth—Similarities, Differences, Inequalities: Reports of the Karelian Institute*, edited by Vesa Puuronen, Jarna Soilevuo-Grønnerød, and Jatta Herranen, 154–72. Joensuu, Finland: University of Joensuu.

Schepanskaya, T. B. 2001. "Zony nasiliya (po materialam russkoy selskoy i sovre-mennykh subkulturnikh tradiciy" [The zones of violence (on the materials from Russian rural and contemporary subcultural traditions]. In *Antropologiya nasiliya* [Anthropology of violence], 115–77. St. Petersburg: Nauka.

Stepakov, V. 1998. "Peterburgskaya shpana" [St. Petersburg's Riffraff]. *Neva* 7:220–26.

Stephenson, S. 2006. "Kazanskii Leviathan: Molodyozhnie Territorialnie Grup-pirovki i Problema Sotsialnogo Poriadka" [The Kazan leviathan: Youth street gangs and the problem of social order]. *Otechestvennie Zapiski* 30, no. 3: 97–110.

Sutherland, Edwin H. 1934. *Principles of Criminology.* Chicago: J. B. Lippincott.

Volkov, Vyacheslav V. 2005. *Silovoe predprinimatel'stvo: ekonomiko-sotsiologicheskiy analiz* [Power-related entrepreneurship: Economic and sociological analysis]. Moscow: GU VSHE.

4

Of Marginality and "Little Emperors": The Changing Reality of Chinese Youth Gangs

LENING ZHANG

Youth gangs and gang-related crime in China were rare and were not considered a social problem during the 1950s and 1960s. The nation had very low crime rates and was even viewed as a "crime-free" society (Fairbank 1987; Rojek 1996). Official statistics indicate that China had only five to six criminal cases per one hundred thousand inhabitants annually during this time period (Dai 2001). However, since the nation implemented economic reform in the late 1970s, the situation has changed dramatically. The crime rate climbed to 356 per 100,000 inhabitants in 2005 (Zhang, Messner, and Liu 2008). As total crime rose significantly, so did youth offenses. According to official statistics, offenses among youths aged fourteen to twenty-five years old accounted for about 20 percent of total crime in 1952 but reached 74 percent in 1989 (Bakken 1993; Wong 2001). Chinese studies have also indicated that gang-related crime accounts for between 60 and 70 percent of the total youth offenses in recent years (Wang 2005; Wang 2006; Zhen 2001; Zhang and Tu 2005).

China's Department of Justice reported that Chinese police forces cracked down on about thirteen thousand gangs involved in some one hundred thousand gang-related criminal cases nationwide during the three-year period from 2004 to 2006 (*People's Daily* 2009). At a more local level, the police department of Zhejiang Province reported that a crackdown on 567 youth gangs involved 2,265 gang member arrests in 1985; this increased to 3,150 youth gangs and 11,845 gang member arrests in 2002 (Zhang and Tu 2005). Chinese studies furthermore suggest that youth gangs in China are becoming more violent, more organized, more sophisticated, and involved in a broader range of criminal activities than in the past (Wang 2005; Zhang 2001; Zhang and Tu 2005). Not surprisingly, perhaps youth gangs and gang-related crime have widely come to be perceived as a social problem of public concern in contemporary China.

This chapter first examines the formation and characteristics of Chinese youth gangs, in particular, relative to Chinese legal statutes, and explores a range of possible explanations for gang formation and evolution linked to the particular social context of contemporary Chinese society. Using available information, the chapter further discusses possible future trends, more specifically in light of China's continuing economic reforms, which have grown deeper and broader since the late 1990s. It concludes with a discussion of China's control strategies regarding youth gangs.

YOUTH GANGS IN CHINA

Although the colloquial Chinese phrase for "youth gangs"—*qing shao nian fan zui tuan huo,* which literally translates as "youth crime gangs"— is generally understood to refer to loosely connected groups of youths aged between fourteen and twenty-five who engage in collective criminal activities,[1] the legal categorization is much more vague. There are three related but distinct conceptions of collective crimes in the Chinese criminal justice system (Guo and Ma 1981; He 2002; He 1993; Wei and Guo 2000). The first is *co-offense,* which refers to crimes committed jointly by at least two persons. The second is *organized crime,* which refers to crimes committed by a group of persons characterized by well-defined organizational structure and rules, definite organizational objectives, and relatively permanent members. The third is *gang crime,* which refers to crimes committed by three or more persons and by youths in particular.

The gang differs from the criminal organization in several respects. Compared to groups responsible for organized crime, a gang is characterized by less organization, limited cohesion, impermanence, shifting membership, and diffuse role definition.[2] In the Chinese legal definition of a gang, two criteria must be met: (1) it must be a group consisting of at least three people and (2) it must be involved in illegal activities. This latter requirement of criminal involvement is consistent with the widely accepted conception of gangs in the United States (Esbensen and Huizinga 1993; Spergel 1990). As Spergel explains, "the principal criterion currently used to define a 'gang' may be the group's participation in illegal activities" (179).

A number of studies have addressed some common characteristics of Chinese youth gangs (Guo and Ma 1981; He 1993; Wang 2005; Wang 2006; Wen and Zhang 2003; Zhang 2001; Zhang and Tu 2005; Zhou, Liu, and Wang 2004). These characteristics can be summarized along four dimensions. The first is the degree of sophistication in criminal organization. The organizational level of most youth gangs in China is fairly low, although organizational level varies across gangs in different regions. Nevertheless, some youth gangs have clearly defined leadership, differentiation between core and peripheral members, and a division of labor in engaging in illegal activities. A second dimension is membership status, which is generally impermanent and changeable. A third dimension is the basis of membership. Youth gangs are likely to be age graded, territorial, and occupational. Youth gangs often consist of classmates, neighbors, or coworkers who are linked through stable patterns of association and interaction. Finally, gang crime involves almost all types of crimes against property and persons; although some youth gangs specialize in property or sexual crimes, most others engage in multiple criminal activities.

Chinese studies have identified several reasons for the formation of youth gangs in China (Guo and Ma 1981; He 1993; Lin 2000; Liu 2004; Wen and Zhang 2003; Xiu and Wu 1984a; Zhou, Liu, and Wang 2004). First, youths enjoying common interests and hobbies bond together to engage in antisocial behaviors to meet certain personal psychological needs. Second, potential delinquents associate with one another and form a group to increase the probability of finding a suitable target for crime. Third, youths join together to commit crimes to show loyalty to their friends. Fourth, potential delinquents join together to commit crimes in an attempt to decrease their fear in committing crime or to lessen their responsibility for a particular offense. Finally, youths jointly commit crime primarily by chance.

Among these five possibilities, common interests and being loyal to friends are considered to be the key factors. Certainly being loyal to friends is a primary moral standard in the Chinese cultural tradition— one that governs interpersonal interaction and association and is an especially important rule among youths. This moral imperative for loyalty is expressed in such phrases as "sacrifice yourself for your fellow friends even when a knife is stabbed into your belly" and "share bitter and sweet in times of trouble or reward" (Guo and Ma 1981; He 1993; Pi 1984). Zhou, Liu, and Wang's (2004) 2002 survey of inmates in the Chinese city of Tianjin indicates that about 60 percent of the youth respondents reported that being loyal to friends was the main reason for joining a gang and engaging in gang crimes. About 20 percent reported common interests as a major factor in the formation of their gangs.

Chinese studies also indicate that a large percentage of gang members are recidivists (Xiu and Wu 1984b; Zhang and Huang 1984; Zhang and Tu 2005; Zhang et al. 1997; Zhou, Liu, and Wang 2004). For instance, Zhang and Huang (1984) investigated recidivism among one hundred youth gangs in Guangzhou, China, and found that about 49 percent of the gang members were recidivists and that most of the recidivists were core gang members. Their analyses suggested that these recidivists play an important role in organizing gang-related activities, overseeing gang recruitment and training, and maintaining gang solidarity. Zhou, Liu, and Wang's (2004) surveys of inmates in the city of Tainjin offer similar findings, suggesting that most core members of youth gangs are recidivists who are the recipients of either criminal sanctions by courts or administrative sanctions by police agencies. These core gang members have both criminal experience and accrued ability to control gang activities and therefore benefit most from these. These findings support the notion that offenders who have criminal records are more likely to seek out gangs to commit crime collectively (Zhang et al. 1997).

POSSIBLE EXPLANATIONS FOR THE EMERGENCE OF CHINESE YOUTH GANGS

There are various explanations for the emergence of youth gangs in China. They may not be unique to China, as similar gang-related issues have been observed in many other countries around the world. At the same time, however, China has undergone extraordinary social and economic change since the late 1970s, and this change has clearly affected the emergence and development of youth gangs and gang-related crime, both of which are part of the broader changing patterns of crime that China is undergoing as a result of its contemporary economic modernization.

China since the late 1970s has embarked on an ambitious program of economic reform that has profoundly altered many features of Chinese society and that has had many unanticipated consequences for individual behavior patterns. These transformations can be observed at the level of the society's social stratification system, housing patterns, population distribution across regions, and cultural values, for example.[3] Particularly disruptive and disintegrative processes include increased inequality (Cao and Dai 2001), changing cultural beliefs and norms (Rojek 2001), the disruption of traditional social control mechanisms (Deng and Cordilia 1999; Feng 2001; Rojek 2001), decreased social integration (Lu and Miethe 2001), massive migration of the rural population into urban areas (Curran 1998; Ma 2001), and an altered age structure of the population (Flaherty et al. 2007; Rosenberg 2006; Zhang and Goza 2006).

As many researchers have observed (e.g., Deng and Cordilia 1999; Rojek 2001), getting rich has been becoming a new and dominant tenet in Chinese society as the nation moves toward a market economy. Striving for personal wealth and material possessions has gradually become a nationwide fad that drastically departs from the old Communist ideology and largely weakens the political and social control exercised under Mao's regime. Given the dramatic movement to a new social and economic system, the phenomenon of anomie has become widespread (Cao and Dai 2001). The economic transition has also resulted in a significant increase in economic inequality within urban areas as well as between urban and rural areas (Cao and Dai 2001). A clear division between the rich and the poor is emerging in Chinese society (Bian 2002), which is leading to significant resentment and unrest among the poor and underclass (Deng, Zhang, and Leverentz 2009). Given this changing social and economic context, it is perhaps not surprising that more people have been involved in illegal activities, especially property-related illegal activities. China's official statistics have consistently reported that offenses against property, such as larceny, theft, and burglary, have generally accounted for about 70 percent of the total crime nationwide since the statistics were first published in 1987 (Press of China 1987–2006). Findings from Chinese studies also indicate that youth gangs are most likely to get involved in property crime such as larceny, theft, or robbery (Zhang 2001; Zhou, Liu, and Wang 2004).[4]

Prior to economic reform, ideological and political forces greatly shaped Chinese lifestyle. Under Mao's regime, Chinese were expected to live in a working-class style with similar material resources and supplies (Davis 2000). Any individual pursuit of wealth was viewed as nonsocialist or bourgeois. The Communist regime fostered a common, poor lifestyle with little individual differentiation. It greatly facilitated social control of individual behaviors and largely contributed to the very low crime rates in China. Since China began implementing a policy of economic reform, the political–ideological expectations and control are fading. The development of a market economy has opened up a public sphere for the freedom of individual choice, and Chinese have gradually begun to enjoy personal expression and privacy (Davis 2000). Consequently, individuals have become much more diverse in their routines and lifestyle than they were in the past. Individualism is rising, and traditional forms of communalism are falling by the wayside.[5] Such changes are much more evident among youths, who quickly adapt to Western individualism and materialism in a way not so easily accepted by their parents or by the authorities (Anderson and Gil 1998). When the lifestyle young people pursue is met with significant opposition and opprobrium, they may form interest groups or gangs to achieve their life aims through illegal means (Lin 2000; Mei 2001; Wang 2005).

Another dramatic change in China has involved the breakdown of the dual system of citizenship. After the Communists assumed power, China implemented a system of rural and urban citizenship. Rural citizens usually could not become urban citizens. The control mechanism was the urban registration system referred to as *hukou*. Each urban citizen had a registration card that was held by the neighborhood police station (Cheng and Selden 1994; Solinger 1999). This dual system of citizenship effectively limited population mobility from rural to urban areas and contributed to social control in urban areas. However, economic reform has placed great pressure on this dual system of citizenship due to the large labor surplus in rural areas and the need for a more open labor market in growing cities (Oi 1999). In response to this pressure, the Chinese authorities have loosened restrictions on population mobility from rural to urban areas. The result has been the movement of a large number of rural residents to cities (Keister and Nee 2000; Ma 2001). This so-called floating population has significantly changed China's population patterns and raised concerns about poverty and crime in neighborhoods where rural migrants are concentrated (Curran 1998; Ma 2001; Situ and Liu 1996; Solinger 1999).

A large number of the rural migrants are young people who want to pursue a better life in urban areas. Chinese studies indicate that gang-related offenses account for over 70 percent of the total crime among migrants and that most of the offenses are property related (Lin, Yu, and Zhang 2008; Mi 2008). Members in these gangs commonly come from the same province, county, town, or village (Lin, Yu, and Zhang 2008; Mi 2008; Zhang et al. 1997; Zhou, Liu, and Wang 2004) where they were born and raised, and where several generations of their families have lived. They are "fellow provincials" *(Tongxiang)* and are bound together by local regional ties. These young rural migrants often experience a clash between their hopes for a better life and the reality in urban areas. They migrated to cities with high expectations, but they face a situation of poverty and limited options and often experience discrimination in cities. Consequently, many young rural migrants live in very poor conditions and suffer greatly. To cope, some young rural migrants use their local regional ties to form gangs to engage in illegal activities, especially property-related illegal activities, to gain the resources needed for living in cities.

When China first carried out its economic reform in the late 1970s, the nation also implemented the (in)famous one-child policy, widely viewed as "the most aggressive, comprehensive population policy in the world" (Short et al. 2001, 1). The implementation of this policy has resulted in many unanticipated consequences, such as a sex imbalance in the population and a ratio imbalance between elderly parents and adult children (Flaherty et al. 2007; Rosenberg 2006; Zhang and Goza 2006). One particularly significant consequence is the dramatic change in family and household structures. Traditionally, Chinese had large extended families with many children. However, since the nation implemented the one-child policy, the size of families and households has reduced dramatically, particularly in urban areas. Such a change in combination with the nation's movement toward a market economy has had a profound impact on parenting practices and adolescent development and behavior.

The rapid decrease in the birthrate because of the implementation of the policy, combined with a stable or improving life expectancy, has also led to an increasing proportion of elderly people and an increase in the ratio between elderly parents and adult children in China (Flaherty et al. 2007; Zhang and Goza 2006). Given China's poor social welfare system, the aging population and the rising ratio of dependents to wage-earning adults may have had a tremendous psychological impact on parents raising their only child. In the minds of Chinese parents, children's futures are closely connected to their own futures. Thus parents tend to have extraordinarily high expectations for their only child and do whatever they can to instill in their only child an elite consciousness and aspiration to an elite status, even though few can attain it (Fong 2004). They hope that their only child will be better off in the future and that they will be able to count on the child's bright future after their retirement. Such high expectations and aspirations are likely to foster unrealistic life goals and lead to increased competition and stress for adolescents (Liu, Munakata, and Onuoha 2005). When life goals conflict with reality, adolescents are likely to develop behavioral problems.

High parental expectations for their only child are reinforced by the rapid development of China's market economy. This development has led to a significant shift in the locus of economic planning from the state to families and individuals (Cornia 1994; Guthrie 1998; Zuo 2003). The government is no longer the main guarantor of food, shelter, education, and employment opportunities. Therefore parents have a deep concern for their only child's future because it is intimately tied to their own future. They try to utilize every possible resource to help their only child be successful. Studies indicate that Chinese parents traditionally tend to be more controlling of their children compared to Western parents (Chao 1994; Chao and Sue 1996). This traditional parenting style has become intensified and reinforced in one-child families. At the same time, parents are likely to make every effort to satisfy their only child's desires and needs to ensure that the child can enjoy the best resources available to maximize the chance of subsequent success. Studies have observed a significant surge in parental indulgence in one-child families (Chen, Liu, and Li 2000; Tao and Jing 1985). Parents pour almost all of their family resources into every aspect of the child's life, such as education, meals, and transportation. Many parents are willing to sacrifice anything, including their own diets, to meet their child's needs and demands (Chow and Zhao 1996; Fong 2004). The only child is viewed as a "little emperor" in the family and is likely to be spoiled by his parents (Zhang and Messner 1995). This unique mix of authoritarian and permissive parenting practices is not likely to create a healthy environment for the child's development. Consequently, children who grow up in this kind of family environment are likely to be impulsive, aggressive, and selfish, although there are no systematic studies to substantiate this.

Under the tremendous pressure of high parental expectations and aspirations, the only child sacrifices almost all of her leisure time and friendships to try to obtain good school grades and compete for limited places at top universities. Being educated in a prestigious university is believed to be the sole means of accessing elite status given the Chinese political and economic structure (Fong 2004). For the Chinese, child achievement is not only an individual matter but is also closely linked to a family's reputation. The only child is often instilled with a belief that any failure in social and academic performance will bring disgrace to his parents and to the whole family (Chen, Liu, and Li 2000; Luo 1996). As a result, the child is likely to feel pressure from his parents, relatives, peers, and other relevant individuals to achieve success, which may lead to mental and behavioral problems (Liu, Munakata, and Onuoha 2005).

The Chinese have become increasingly concerned with the development and growth of these "little emperors," and it is widely hypothesized that there is a link between such unhealthy parenting practices and problematic adolescent behaviors. Official statistics indicate that during the 1950s, 1960s, and 1970s, the percentage of juvenile offenses compared to the total number of crimes committed ranged from 0.2 to 3 percent. By contrast, this percentage increased to between 15 and 30 percent during the 1990s (Wong 2001). Chinese studies have linked youth gangs and gang-related crime directly to unhealthy parenting practices (Lin 2000; Liu 2004; Wang 2005; Zhen 2001). The nature of the link between the one-child policy, unhealthy parenting, and youth gang activities is unclear because of a lack of systematic empirical studies. However, typical gang cases reported in China indicate that those who are involved in gang organization and activities in some large urban areas (e.g., Beijing and Tianjin) are likely to be socially marginalized young people. These young people failed to meet their parents' high expectations to study in prestigious universities and have been looked down on by their relatives and old classmates. They had to enroll in vocational or labor training schools, which are often referred to as a "low" social category with no bright future. As a result, their parents are likely to ignore them or no longer intervene in their behavior and daily activities. Facing distinctive social pressure and discrimination as well as a lack of parental care and monitoring, these marginalized young people are likely to form their own groups or gangs to demonstrate their existence and power and gain a sense of collective identity and self-protection.

POSSIBLE FUTURE TRENDS

As the scope and depth of the market-oriented economic reform in China have gained momentum and the nation has become increasingly more open since the 1990s, a number of Chinese studies have explored the progression of youth gangs and gang-related crime. Using data collected from a 1991 survey of inmates in the city of Tianjin, Zhang et al. (1997) found that the organizational level of Chinese youth gangs was low, that youth gangs were typically oriented to a single rather than multiple purposes, and that the number of relatively permanent gang members tended to be very small. They also found that gang-related crimes were unlikely to be more violent and serious than non-gang-related crimes. They concluded that these patterns might be comparable to those found in the United States during the time period of the 1930s to the 1960s, which might imply that "China is in an early stage of gang development" (Zhang et al. 1997, 299).

However, recent Chinese studies show that youth gangs in China have become more organized, larger, more violent, involved in multiple types of offenses, and mobilized across much larger territories (Wang 2005; Zhen 2001; Zhang and Tu 2005; Zhou, Liu, and Wang 2004).[6] For instance, Zhou, Liu, and Wang (2004) compared data collected from inmates in the city of Tianjin from 1990 to 2002 to explore the changes in gang characteristics over time. They found that in 1990, some 49 percent of gang-related offenders reported that their gangs were relatively stable rather than a spontaneous grouping. This percentage increased to 59 percent in 2002. Another change concerned the structure of the gang, including in particular the status of gang members. In 1990, about 20 percent of gang-related offenders were identified as gang leaders who controlled their gangs, and about 30 percent were core members who played major roles in gang-related offenses. By 2002, the number of gang leaders and core members had dropped to 5 percent and 20 percent, respectively. Zhou, Liu, and Wang (2004) concluded that this structural change might have implied that the organizational level of youth gangs had increased, with, notably, an increased centralization of power in the hands of a few core members. As the organizational level increases, it is possible that young gangs may become more powerful and have more influence in Chinese society and that their activities may spread into more areas.

Zhou, Liu, and Wang (2004) also found that the reported level of internal agreement and cohesion among members in the same gang increased over the time period. Some 51 percent of the gang-related offenders reported that there were no disputes and conflicts in their gangs in 1996. The percentage increased to about 79 percent in 2002. When the offenders were asked whether they used weapons such as knives during the course of their gang-related offenses, 41 percent reported yes in 1996, compared to 59 percent in 2002, which may indicate that youth gangs are becoming more violent. Gun involvement, on the other hand, is relatively rare because China has strict gun control. Some youth gangs were reported to use hand-made firelocks, but the common weapons used by Chinese youth gangs are hardwood clubs, knives, or other metal devices. The Chinese National Congress adopted a legal statute titled Gun Control Measures in 1996. It is an administrative law that is enforced by police agencies. According to the statute, no Chinese residents are allowed to possess guns, except individuals who have gun permits, which are only issued to specific professions. The 1997 revised Chinese Criminal Law also has several articles that define criminal liability and penalties for possessing, selling, transporting, and manufacturing guns. Article 128 of the law stipulates that violation of the Gun Control Measures and possession of a gun shall be punishable with a sentence term of no less than three years in prison.[7] Article 136 states that anyone who carries a gun without official permission and endangers public safety and security shall be punished with no less than three years' sentence or detention, depending on the specific circumstances. China's official statistics reported 6,307 gun-related criminal incidents handled by police agencies nationwide in 2005, equivalent to 0.1 incidents per ten thousand inhabitants (Press of China 2006).

Although gun control in China is very strict, gun-related crimes are increasing in number, and Chinese authorities have serious concerns about them (Chen 2004; Deng and Cao 2001; Yang 2002). These gun-related crimes and concerns are commonly associated with criminal organizations and organized crime. As China is becoming more open to the outside world, Chinese authorities have a constant fear that criminal organizations are internationalizing, including, in particular, those involved in illicit drug operations in other countries. They worry that these cross-national organized crime cartels may penetrate into China's territory and establish connections with "native" Chinese criminal organizations. However, neither official reports nor Chinese academic studies have (yet) found a clear link between youth gangs and criminal organizations, although some Chinese scholars have expressed concerns about a possible link (e.g., He 2002; Wei and Guo 2000).

Finally, youth gang involvement in drugs has been a major public concern in the United States since the crack cocaine epidemic began flourishing in the mid-1980s (Klein 2002; National Drug Intelligence Center 2009). Youth gangs there have been involved in the wholesale trafficking of drugs nationwide and have come to be intimately connected to organized drug-trafficking syndicates. Although similar drug-related problems have begun to emerge in China in recent years, so far no official reports or academic studies have indicated that Chinese youth gangs are becoming actively involved in drug trafficking. However, the Chinese government has shown caution and concern over the possible spread of illicit drug use to the youth population. China's 2006 Annual Drug Control Report indicated that there were more than one million registered drug addicts (China National Drug Control Commission 2006), and the Chinese National People's Congress adopted a Drug Control Law in 2007, the first such piece of legislation since the Chinese Communists took power in 1949.

CONCLUSION

Chinese authorities tend to regard youth gangs as special crime-related social entities and gang-related offending as an especially serious form of crime. This is because gangs involve groups of individuals and gang-related crime is by definition a collective action. As such, youth gangs influence more young people and have more harmful consequences for the community and society than individual offenders. They represent a greater challenge to the social and political order than isolated, individual criminal acts. At the same time, political authorities have been relatively free to sanction gang behavior more or less severely, depending on the perceived needs of society at a given point in time.

As is the case in most societies around the world, a common official practice in response to the social threat of youth gangs and gang-related crime in China has been to launch campaigns to "strike back" or "crack down" on gangs nationwide or in specific regions. Such a response reflects the traditional deterrence philosophy in Chinese society and can be viewed as a continuation of Mao's "mass" line in criminal justice (Tanner 2005; Zhang and Tu 2005). These campaigns have mobilized not only police forces and other legal agencies but a variety of social sectors. The basic principle of these campaigns is that crime control is not only the duty of police and other legal agencies but also a necessary responsibility of citizens (Feng 2001). Although official reports indicate that several such campaigns have been implemented since the 1980s, the actual effectiveness of these campaigns is open to question. There have been no independent, academic studies in China to assess the effectiveness of these massive efforts to mobilize police forces and other social agencies to fight against gangs.

Moreover, official punishment of gang-related crime tends to be in practice based on either the codes for collective offenses or those for organized crimes. Indeed, criminal justice officials are often inclined to punish gang crime based on the codes for organized crime because these allow for more severe punishment than do codes for collective offending. This particular practice has emerged much more prominently during social campaigns against gangs and gang-related crime, with the criminal justice system commonly pursuing fast processing and severe punishment of gang-related cases during such periods. Western scholars frequently challenge the legality of such criminal justice practices (Tanner 2005; Trevaskes 2007), and certainly, using data collected from inmates in China, Zhang et al. (1997) found that gang-related crime increased the severity of official punishment when other important variables, such as the seriousness of offenses, were controlled. Similarly, it is unclear whether such punitive legal practice has any measurable effect on deterring the development of youth gangs and gang-related offenses.

In sum, although youth gangs are widely seen as having emerged as a significant social problem in China as a result of the nation's rapid social and economic changes, the extent to which this is a real or perceived issue is unclear. An important task to undertake to get to grips with the youth gang phenomenon is uncovering the extent to which the characteristics and patterns of Chinese youth gangs are unique. Although some Chinese youth gangs are comparable to youth gangs in the West, others may be linked to China's unique context. Currently studies of youth gangs in China are fairly preliminary, and most are descriptive, with very limited application of theory and methodology developed in the West. Also, primary data on youth gangs are relatively rare. Most studies have relied heavily on official statistics or reports. Primary data collected by independent researchers are much needed and must constitute the next phase of Chinese youth gang research.

NOTES

1. In China, the definition of a gang is based on the public's perceptions and investigations of gang members' perceptions. It is fairly similar to many scholars' views on the definition of a gang in the United States (e.g., Hagedorn 1988; Klein 1968, 1971).

2. According to the Chinese definition, the difference between co-offending and gang crime is complex. An offense jointly committed by two people is a co-offense but not a gang crime. But when an offense is jointly committed by three or more people, but there is no formal organization among offenders, the notions of co-offense and gang crime may overlap. How the offense is defined is basically at the discretion of criminal justice agencies. Generally, an offense committed jointly by three or more youths is defined as gang crime. Different Chinese terms are used to describe these three types of collective crime: *Gongtong Fanzui* for "co-offense," *Jituan Fanzui* for "organizational crime," and *Tuanhuo Fanzui* for "gang crime."

3. Such patterns have also been observed in other countries that have experienced rapid social and economic changes (Karstedt and Bussmann 2000; Liu and Messner 2001).

4. Robbery is defined as property crime in the Chinese legal statute.

5. For a detailed description of these changes, see Davis (2000) and Tang and Parish (2000).

6. These findings must be interpreted with caution because they commonly rely on official records or statistics to explore the development and progression of youth gangs in China. Systematic and independent data collections are relatively rare.

7. If the situation is deemed more serious, the offender shall receive a prison sentence term between three and seven years.

REFERENCES

Anderson, Allen F., and Vincent E. Gil. 1998. "China's Modernization and the Decline of Communitarianism: The Control of Sex Crimes and Implications for the Fate of Informal Social Control." *Journal of Contemporary Criminal Justice* 14:248–61.

———. 2005. "Comparative Perspectives on Crime in China." In *Crime, Punishment, and Policing in China,* edited by Borge Bakken, 57–88. Oxford: Rowman and Littlefield.

Bakken, Borge. 1993. "Crime, Juvenile Delinquency, and Deterrence Policy in China." *Australian Journal of Chinese Affairs* 30:29–58.

Bian, Yanje. 2002. "Chinese Social Stratification and Social Mobility." *Annual Review of Sociology* 28:91–116.

Cao, Liqun, and Yisheng Dai. 2001. "Inequality and Crime in China." In *Crime and Social Control in a Changing China,* edited by Jianhong Liu, Lening Zhang, and Steven F. Messner, 73–88. Westport, Conn.: Greenwood Press.

Chao, Ruth K. 1994. "Beyond Parental Control and Authoritarian Parenting Style: Understanding Chinese Parenting through the Cultural Notion of Training." *Child Development* 65:1111–19.

Chao, Ruth K., and Stanley Sue. 1996. "Chinese Parental Influence and Their Children's School Success: A Paradox in the Literature on Parenting Styles." In *Growing Up the Chinese Way: Chinese Child and Adolescent Development,* edited by Sing Lau, 93–120. Hong Kong: Chinese University Press.

Chen, Caian. 2004. "China's Gun Control" [in Chinese]. *Journal of Fu Jian Police College* 79:25–29.

Chen, Xinyin, Mowei Liu, and Dan Li. 2000. "Parental Warmth, Control, and Indulgence and Their Relations to Adjustment in Chinese Children: A Longitudinal Study." *Journal of Family Psychology* 14:401–19.

Cheng, Tiejun, and Mark Selden. 1994. "The Origins and Social Consequences of China's *Hukou* System." *China Quarterly* 139:644–68.

China National Drug Control Commission. 2006. *2006 Annual Report of Drug Control.* Beijing: China National Drug Control Commission.

Chow, Esther Ngan-ling, and S. Michael Zhao. 1996. "The One-Child Policy and Parent–Child Relationships: A Comparison of One-Child with Multiple-

Child Families in China." *International Journal of Sociology and Social Policy* 16:35–62.

Cornia, Giovanni Andrea. 1994. "Income Distribution, Poverty, and Welfare in Transitional Economies: A Comparison between Eastern Europe and China." *Journal of International Development* 6:569–607.

Curran, Dean. 1998. "Economic Reform, the Floating Population, and Crime." *Journal of Contemporary Criminal Justice* 14:262–80.

Dai, Yisheng. 2001. "New Directions of Chinese Policing in the Reform Era." In *Crime and Social Control in a Changing China,* edited by Jianhong Liu, Lening Zhang, and Steven F. Messner, 151–58. Westport, Conn.: Greenwood Press.

Davis, Deborah S., ed. 2000. *The Consumer Revolution in Urban China.* Berkeley: University of California Press.

Deng, Guoliang, and Yuenqing Cao. 2001. "Gun-Related Crime" [in Chinese]. *Journal of Jiang Xi Police College* 64:32–38.

Deng, Xiaogang, and Ann Cordilia. 1999. "To Get Rich Is Glorious: Rising Expectations, Declining Control, and Escalating Crime in Contemporary China." *International Journal of Offender Therapy and Comparative Criminology* 423:211–29.

Deng, Xiaogang, Lening Zhang, and Andrea Leverentz. 2009. "The Dual System of Land Use Policy and Its Related Problems in Contemporary China." In *China in an Era of Transition: Understanding Contemporary State and Society Actors,* edited by Resa Hasmath and Jennifer Hsu, 79–102. London: Palgrave Macmillan.

Esbensen, Finn-Aage, and David Huizinga. 1993. "Gang, Drugs, and Delinquency in a Survey of Urban Youth." *Criminology* 31:565–90.

Fairbank, John K. 1987. *The Great Chinese Revolution: 1800–1985.* New York: Harper and Row.

Feng, Shuliang. 2001. "Crime and Crime Control in a Changing China." In *Crime and Social Control in a Changing China,* edited by Jianhong Liu, Lening Zhang, and Steven F. Messner, 123–32. Westport, Conn.: Greenwood Press.

Flaherty, Joseph Henry, Mei Lin Liu, Lei Ding, Birong Dong, Qunfang Ding, Xia Li, and Shifu Xiao. 2007. "China: The Aging Giant." *Journal of the American Geriatrics Society* 55:1295–1300.

Fong, Vanessa L. 2004. *Only Hope: Coming of Age under China's One-Child Policy.* Stanford, Calif.: Stanford University Press.

Guo, Xiang, and Jingmiao Ma. 1981. "Youth Gang Crime." In *Yearbook on Chinese Juvenile Delinquency Studies* [in Chinese], edited by the Association of Chinese Juvenile Delinquency Study, 374–88. Beijing: Chuenqiu.

Guthrie, Douglas. 1998. "Organizational Uncertainty and Labor Contracts in China's Economic Transition." *Sociological Forum* 13:457–94.

Hagedorn, John M. 1988. *People and Folks: Gangs, Crime, and the Underclass in a Rustbelt City.* Chicago: Lake View Press.

He, Bingsong. 2002. "Youth Gangs and Criminal Organizations" [in Chinese]. *Journal of Zhe Jian Normal University* 27:37–45.

He, Cheng. 1993. "Current Youth Gang Crime in China" [in Chinese]. *Studies of Juvenile Delinquency* 128:17–23.

Karstedt, Susane, and Kai-D Bussmann. 2000. "Introduction: Social Change as a Challenge for Criminological Theory." In *Social Dynamics of Crime and Control: New Theories for a World in Transition*, edited by Susane Karstedt and Kai-D Bussmann, 1–10. Portland, Oreg.: Hart.

Keister, Lisa A., and Victor G. Nee. 2000. "The Rational Peasant in China: Flexible Adaptation, Risk Diversification, and Opportunity." *Rationality and Society* 13:33–69.

Klein, Malcolm W. 1968. *From Association to Guilt: The Group Guidance Project in Juvenile Gang Intervention.* Los Angeles: University of Southern California, Youth Studies Center, and the Los Angeles County Probation Department.

———. 1971. *Street Gangs and Street Works.* Englewood Cliffs, N.J.: Prentice Hall.

———. 2002. "Street Gangs: A Cross-National Perspective." In *Gangs in America III*, edited by C. Ronald Huff, 237–54. Thousand Oaks, Calif.: Sage.

Lin, Peng, Fei Yu, and Tongxia Zhang. 2008. "Crime Problems among 'New Rural Migrants'" [in Chinese]. *Journal of Chinese Youth Study,* February, 29–34.

Lin, Qingshan. 2000. "Analysis of a Youth Gang." *Journal of Shan Dong Police College* 51:26–27.

Liu, Chenyng, Tsunetsugu Munakata, and Francis N. Onuoha. 2005. "Mental Health Condition of the Only-Child: A Study of Urban and Rural High School Students in China." *Adolescence* 40:831–45.

Liu, Cuihua. 2004. "The Characteristics and Causes of Youth Gang Crime" [in Chinese]. *Journal of ChangQiu Vocational and Technological College* 11:55–56.

Liu, Jianhong, and Steven F. Messner. 2001. "Modernization and Crime Trends in China's Reform Era." In *Crime and Social Control in a Changing China*, edited by Jianhong Liu, Lening Zhang, and Steven F. Messner, 3–22. Westport, Conn.: Greenwood Press.

Lu, Hong, and Terance D. Miethe. 2001. "Community Integration and the Effectiveness of Social Control." In *Crime and Social Control in a Changing China*, edited by Jianhong Liu, Lening Zhang, and Steven F. Messner, 105–22. Westport, Conn.: Greenwood Press.

Luo, Gang. 1996. *Chinese Traditional Social and Moral Values.* Beijing: University of People Press.

Ma, Guoan. 2001. "Population Migration and Crime in Beijing, China." In *Crime and Social Control in a Changing China*, edited by Jianhong Liu, Lening Zhang, and Steven F. Messner, 65–72. Westport, Conn.: Greenwood Press.

Mei, Fagen. 2001. "The Causes of Youth Gang Crime and Control" [in Chinese]. *Journal of Jiang Hui Law Study* 9:26–29.

Mi, Zhanqing. 2008. "Analysis of Rural Migrants' Criminal Activities" [in Chinese]. *Law and Economy* 179:40–49.

National Drug Intelligence Center. 2009. *National Drug Threat Assessment.* Washington, D.C.: U.S. Department of Justice.

Oi, Jean C. 1999. *Rural China Takes Off: Institutional Foundations of Economic Reform*. Berkeley: University of California Press.

People's Daily. 2009. "China's Anti-gang Drive Cracks 900 Major Organized Crime Cases." March 26.

Pi, Yijun. 1984. "The Characteristics of Delinquent Gangs." In *Yearbook on Chinese Juvenile Delinquency Studies* [in Chinese], edited by the Association of Chinese Juvenile Delinquency Study, 388–91. Beijing: Chuenqiu.

Press of China. 1987–2006. *China Law Yearbooks*. 20 vols. Beijing: Press of China Law Year Book.

Rojek, Dean. G. 1996. "Changing Directions of Chinese Social Control." In *Comparative Criminal Justice: Traditional and Nontraditional Systems of Law and Control*, edited by Charles B. Fields and Richter H. Moore Jr., 234–49. Prospect Heights, Ill.: Waveland Press.

———. 2001. "Chinese Social Control: From Shaming and Reintegration to Getting Rich Is Glorious." In *Crime and Social Control in a Changing China*, edited by Jianhong Liu, Lening Zhang, and Steven F. Messner, 89–104. Westport, Conn.: Greenwood Press.

Rosenberg, Jared. 2006. "An Unintended Consequence of China's One-Child Policy?" *International Family Planning Perspectives* 32:108–23.

Short, Susan E., Fengying Zhai, Siyuan Xu, and Mingliang Yang. 2001. "China's One-Child Policy and the Care of Children: An Analysis of Qualitative and Quantitative Data." *Social Forces* 79:913–43.

Situ, Yingyi, and Beizheng Liu. 1996. "Transient Population, Crime, and Solution: The Chinese Experience." *International Journal of Offender Therapy and Comparative Criminology* 40:293–99.

Solinger, Dorothy J. 1999. "Demolishing Partitions: Back to Beginnings in the Cities." *China Quarterly* 159:629–39.

Spergel, Irving A. 1990. "Youth Gangs: Continuity and Change." In *Crime and Justice: A Review of Research*, vol. 12, edited by Michael Tonry and Norval Morris, 171–275. Chicago: University of Chicago Press.

Tang, Wengfeng, and William L. Parish. 2000. *Chinese Urban Life under Reform: The Changing Social Contract*. New York: Cambridge University Press.

Tanner, Murray Scot. 2005. "Campaign-Style Policing in China and Its Critics." In *Crime, Punishment, and Policing in China*, edited by Borge Bakken, 171–88. Lanham, Md.: Rowman and Littlefield.

Tao, Kong, and Chiu Jing. 1985. "The Only-Child-per-Family Policy: A Psychological Perspective." In *Chinese Culture and Mental Health*, edited by Wen-Sheng Tseng and David Y. H. Wu, 153–65. New York: Academic Press.

Trevaskes, Susan. 2007. *Courts and Criminal Justice in Contemporary China*. Lanham, Md.: Lexington Books.

Wang, Guangshi. 2005. "Gang Crime, Its Causes, and Control Policy" [in Chinese]. *Journal of Hunan College of Science and Technology* 25:65–69.

Wang, Honglang. 2006. "A Sociological Analysis of Gang Crime" [in Chinese]. *Journal of Beijing Policy College* 5:59–61.

Wei, Tong, and Lirong Guo. 2000. "A Study of Legal Issues on Criminal Organizations" [in Chinese]. *Journal of Sichuan Police College* 47:46–52.

Wen, Jing, and Lianhuang Zhang. 2003. "Youth Gang Crime" [in Chinese]. *Police Education* 7:29–41.

Wong, Dennis S. W. 2001. "Changes in Juvenile Justice in China." *Youth and Society* 32:492–505.

Xiu, Deqi, and Zaide Wu. 1984a. "An Investigation of Gang Crime and Delinquent Association." In *Yearbook on Chinese Juvenile Delinquency Studies* [in Chinese], edited by the Association of Chinese Juvenile Delinquency Study, 179–87. Beijing: Chuenqiu.

———. 1984b. "An Analysis of the Characteristics of Gang Leadership." In *Yearbook on Chinese Juvenile Delinquency Studies* [in Chinese], edited by the Association of Chinese Juvenile Delinquency Study, 398–406. Beijing: Chuenqiu.

Yang, Yujuan. 2002. "The Characteristics of Gun-Related Crime" [in Chinese]. *Journal of Jian Xi Police College* 68:39–41.

Zhang, Baoyi. 2001. "The Characteristics of Youth Gangs" [in Chinese]. *Journal of Fu Jian Police College* 62:40–95.

Zhang, Lening, and Steven F. Messner. 1995. "Family Deviance and Delinquency in China." *Criminology* 33:359–87.

Zhang, Lening, Steven F. Messner, and Jianhong Liu. 2008. "A Critical Review of Recent Literature on Crime and Criminal Justice in China: Research Findings, Challenges, and Prospects (Introduction)." *Crime, Law, and Social Change: An Interdisciplinary Journal* 50:125–30.

Zhang, Lening, Steven F. Messner, Zhou Lu, and Xiaogang Deng. 1997. "Gang Crime and Its Punishment in China." *Journal of Criminal Justice* 4:289–302.

Zhang, Yingli, and Xiehua Tu. 2005. "The Trend of China's Gang Crime and Control Policy" [in Chinese]. *Development and Policy* 4:31–35.

Zhang, Yuanting, and Franklin W. Goza. 2006. "Who Will Care for Elderly in China? A Review of the Problems Caused by China's One-Child Policy and Their Potential Problems." *Journal of Aging Studies* 20:151–64.

Zhang, Zhongjiang, and Wenzun Huang. 1984. "The Role of Recidivists in Delinquent Gangs." In *Yearbook on Chinese Juvenile Delinquency Studies* [in Chinese], edited by the Association of Chinese Juvenile Delinquency Study, 175–79. Beijing: Chuenqiu.

Zhen, Binmei. 2001. "An Exploration of the Causes of Youth Gangs and Control Policy" [in Chinese]. *Journal of Guang Zhou Police Administration College* 3:33–36.

Zhou, Lu, Wengcheng Liu, and Zhiqiang Wang. 2004. *Contemporary Positivist Criminology: A Study of Crime Patterns* [in Chinese]. Beijing: Publishing House of People's Courts.

Zuo, Jiping. 2003. "From Revolutionary Comrades to Gendered Partners: Marital Construction of Breadwinning in Post-Mao Urban China." *Journal of Family Issues* 24:314–37.

5

From Black Jackets to Zulus: Social Imagination, Myth, and Reality Concerning French Gangs

MARWAN MOHAMMED

Youth gangs in France are frequently invoked in public debates but are arguably rarely coherently characterized.[1] On one hand, they are generally seen to constitute a critical social danger, one that inherently threatens the fabric of society owing to their intimate association with violence. At the same time, however, they are also considered to be fundamentally the "other"—spatially excluded social forms that are totally alien to the mainstream. Such a contradictory vision of things is to a certain extent due to a particular imagination of gangs pervading the French collective consciousness, one that owes much to North American movies such as *The Wild One* (1953), *Warriors* (1979), and *Boyz n the Hood* (1991) as well as to sensationalistic reporting that often explicitly draws on the violent and dramatized images offered by such films. The Hollywood lens is, however, extremely misleading, especially in the French context. In addition to moving contradictorily between personalized and alienating portraits of gangs, it generally portrays them as well-organized, ethnically homogeneous, and territorial social forms, with clearly defined leadership roles, behavior patterns, and social responses—or in other words, as well-structured social institutions.

Despite more than fifty years of empirical research suggesting that such gangs do not exist in France, this vision of things has had a profound impact on French gang studies. In particular, a recurrent theme of French gang studies has concerned distinguishing between the social forms that researchers have commonly reported on and supposedly more "real" gangs corresponding to the Hollywood model. The latter are generally claimed not to exist or else are associated with a highly mythologized past (see Monod 1968; Dubet 1987), whereas the former are depicted in very limited ways, and moreover, on the basis of a very small number of generally qualitative studies. To a certain extent, this situation reflects the general lack of data about gangs in France, but it is also a function of the particular ways in which gangs have been discussed in French society throughout the twentieth century. In particular, interest has waxed and waned according to broader social concerns, whether regarding youth, the poor, or, more recently, immigrants and minorities (see Muchembled 2008), or as governments have wanted to divert attention from such social concerns. In 2009, for example, French president Nicolas Sarkozy made a series of speeches specifically targeting gangs, at least partly to avoid discussing more pressing, polemical social issues such as the economic crisis or the reformation of the national pension system.[2]

The existence of a particular social imagination about gangs in France, as well as their contradictory and sensationalistic portrayal in both media and political discourses, has had a profound effect on French gang studies. Combined with the lack of reliable official data, these depictions have made sensible discussion of the existence of youth gangs extremely difficult. They have also obscured the fact that gangs in France have significantly evolved over time, something that is critical to properly understanding French gang dynamics. This chapter seeks to establish some of the basic parameters to take into account with regard to French youth gangs, focusing in particular on the way that broader social changes over the past several decades have affected them. It begins by exploring what is known about the youth gang phenomenon in France, drawing on the limited official and academic data available, before then framing this knowledge in relation to the main socioeconomic mutations that have affected French society over the last fifty years. It then considers the recent transformation of French youth gangs that has in many ways led them to correspond more to the Hollywood depiction of gangs. The chapter ends with some speculation on what this might mean for the future.

FRENCH YOUTH GANGS: A KNOWN UNKNOWN?

Gangs have never been properly quantified or geographically mapped in France. Although there has been sustained interest in the phenomenon, both real and imagined, until recently, public authorities made few efforts to implement any systematic data gathering, tailor legislation, or even simply adapt police or judiciary practices (see Mohammed and Mucchielli 2007). Since the beginning of the 1990s, however, the French interior intelligence services have been officially assigned the task of tracking gangs and enumerating their violence. Following riots in several peripheral neighborhoods of Paris in 1991, the French Central Intelligence Directorate (Direction centrale des renseignements généraux, or DCRG)[3] created a special unit dedicated to dealing with so-called sensitive neighborhoods.[4] This unit focused specifically on measuring levels of urban violence, and among the different forms of violence that it identified were a range characterized as gang-related, including "criminal gang violence," "gang brawls," and "gang-related revenge killings." The methodology and data underlying these classifications and the measurement of violence were never meant for the public domain, however, and except for some partial extracts from reports that have been discussed in an isolated and piecemeal manner by the media, they remain confidential and generally unknown.

The subjective nature of the unit's data collection eventually led to the project's abandonment in 1999. Data collection concerning urban violence was taken over by the Central Public Security Directorate (Direction centrale de la sécurité publique), which set up a "computerized urban violence analysis system" (Système d'analyse informatique des violences urbaines). According to an official explanatory note about the project, this aimed to "overcome the essentially quantitative perception of the phenomenon as it has been recorded until today" and relied principally on qualitative data gathered from "daily reports from Police stations and kiosks, Police and judicial registers, and other public records."[5] This complicated process was, however, abandoned in 2002 and replaced in 2005 by a "National urban violence indicator" (Indicateur national des violences urbaines, or INVU), which, among other things, aimed to measure and quantify the number of "gang fights," albeit still drawing on police reports. The content of these reports must be considered with caution, however. In 2005, for example, the INVU suggested that more gang fights were registered in the rural areas of the Gard Department than in Seine-Saint-Denis, despite the latter having the highest levels of recorded crime in France. Ultimately, this regular turnover of measurement approaches, sources, and databases clearly highlights the lack of definitional rigor, homogeneity, and reliability of the knowledge about youth gang activity in France.

Since 2008, however, the French Ministry of the Interior has been implementing a new approach. First of all, it began publishing unusually precise data about gangs, to the surprise of many researchers. In particular, it produced a study claiming that in 2008, there were 222 gangs in France, made up of about twenty-five hundred regular members and twenty-five hundred occasional members. Seventy-nine percent of these gangs were reported to be in or around Paris, and 48 percent of members were under age eighteen. The Ministry of the Interior subsequently made the claim at a press conference that the number of gangs increased to 511 gangs by the end of 2009, 85 percent of which were in Paris and its surrounding areas, and that they involved five thousand individuals.[6] In other words, in one year, the number of gangs doubled, although the number of gang members remained stable, a bizarre trend that the ministry conspicuously failed to explain. Even more troubling, the ministry also reported that 348 gang fights were recorded in 2009 and that these had resulted in 132 deaths and 185 serious injuries. According to the Ministry of the Interior's official statistics, a total of 682 homicides were committed in France in 2009,[7] so this figure suggests that some five thousand gang members, that is, 0.008 percent of the French population,[8] were responsible for 19.3 percent (132) of the nation's homicides in that year.

The lack of transparency regarding the methods used to obtain and calculate these data, as well as the massive—and unlikely—increases in the number of gang-related homicides, highlights the need for a proper analysis of the political economy surrounding the production of official statistics concerning gangs. Certainly it is striking that journalists rarely question the data and tend to report on them without actually checking the figures provided by the Ministry of the Interior.[9] At the same time, it is also obvious that the ministry's new communication strategy is very much part of a broader political project. The origins of this new strategy coincided with the "war on gangs" declared by President Nicolas Sarkozy prior to European elections in March 2009. The war was based on an explicitly stated but very vague definition of a gang: "a group made up of at least three teenagers or young adults. The structure of the gang can vary but it comprises a stable nucleus of members who consider themselves or are considered by occasional members as being a gang. They come together for social, cultural or other reasons, and deliberately or in a disorganized manner commit antisocial, offensive, or criminal acts. This definition de facto excludes all groups of youth that simply aim at 'hanging out'; every neighborhood and every building has such groups" (Observatoire National de la Délinquance 2010, 21).

This very general definition effectively ignores almost everything French gang studies has uncovered over the past fifty years. The number of firsthand empirical studies is relatively small, with only a dozen or so focusing specifically on gangs per se, namely, Carra (2001), Copfermann (1962), Duret (1999), Fize (1993), Lagrange (2001), Lagrée and Lew-Faï (1985), Lepoutre (1997), Marlière (2005), Mauger (2006), Moignard (2008), Mohammed (2007), Mohammed and Mucchielli (2007), Monod (1968), Robert (1966), Rubi (2005), and Sauvadet (2006). Nevertheless, each decade over the past fifty years is represented in the preceding list, and there has been a proliferation of such studies during the past ten years. A synthesis of these different studies is obviously beyond the purview of this chapter, but a number of key findings can be mentioned very quickly:

- gangs have generally concentrated in spatially marginalized, working-class, residential areas, especially those with socioeconomically vulnerable populations
- ethnic minorities are often overrepresented in these neighborhoods and sometimes in gangs, too
- gangs are deeply socially embedded institutions within their areas of origin
- the trajectories of individual gang members highlight the roles played by school-related difficulties and problematic postscholastic professional integration
- the offenses most commonly associated with gangs are vandalism, petty theft, group clashes, and conflicts with the police
- gangs are mainly associated with forms of public disorder rather than criminality per se, although drug trafficking is a growing activity

- gangs are informal and autonomous organizations that do not have links with other violent organizations, be they public or private
- whether gangs use firearms or other tools of violence constitutes a major information gap

Drawing on these insights, as well as on certain studies of impoverished youths and delinquency that touch on gang issues, the next sections attempt to link the more macro-level general transformation of French society over the past fifty years with the known evolution in gang dynamics, aiming to highlight general trends to allow for a better approximation of the underlying nature of gangs and their evolution.

SCHOOL AND WORK IN POSTWAR FRANCE: TWO CHANGING VECTORS OF YOUTH SOCIALIZATION

It is clearly not coincidental that the emergence of gangs as a social phenomenon in France has occurred during a half century of rapid and intense social change. Improvements in rates of schooling and the transformation of labor markets have had a deep impact on youth trajectories and ways of life, which have in turn affected the social ecology of gangs. In particular, the broader transformation of French society can be linked to a transformation of the "transition regime" of youth to adulthood (Bidart 2006; Van de Velde 2008) and to a mutation in social attitudes toward youth (Robert 2002), particularly among the working class.

Half a century ago, youth's social integration primarily played out in the labor market, and perhaps not surprisingly, youth gangs, such as the so-called Black Jackets (Blousons noirs), were frequently blamed on the lack of employment opportunities. At the same time, however, these gangs emerged in a generally favorable economic context, which partly explains why, overall, they were not considered a major social concern. During the 1950s and 1960s, France's economic growth rate averaged around 5 percent per year, and national wealth increased rapidly. This was the period known in France as the "Thirty Glorious Years" (les Trente Glorieuses). As Chauvel (2006) has demonstrated, generationally, it was much better to be a twenty-year-old in 1968, when the unemployment rate for those within two years of graduation from high school was 4 percent, than in 1994, when the rate was 33 percent. Perhaps not surprisingly, the proportion of unemployed Black Jackets was low—only about 8 percent for male members (Robert and Lascoumes 1974)—and indeed, work was an integral element of being a gang member. As Monod (1968, 295) described,

> in Sarcelles, I met a gang that had 30 members.... They are all working-class... [and] they all work in the suburbs, either in factories or in small workshops (locksmiths, glaziers, etc.).... They drive mopeds, and only meet on weekends in the snack bar near the only movie theater of their neighborhood.

Similarly, Tétard (1988, 212) noted that gang members at the time were "mainly... manual workers or apprentices, who earn the same income as their fathers.... Few are inactive."

Gangs such as the Black Jackets essentially emerged as institutional means through which youths collectively managed the end of their adolescence and transition to adulthood in a context where becoming a factory worker seemed preordained and inevitable. Youths would join these gangs to delay their full integration into the established social order, combining membership with temporary employment and sporadic periods of voluntary redundancy. This, however, changed during the 1970s, with deindustrialization and the tertiarization of employment. Increasing international competition resulted in the development of new technologies, which in turn led to a change in the nature of jobs and employment. The need for unskilled labor decreased, and there was a sharp rise in unemployment, from 3.9 percent in 1975 to 7.7 percent in 1982. Permanent employment declined, and the average duration of inactivity between temporary jobs increased. This led to a critical change in the nature of the labor market, as Lagrée and Lew-Faï (1985, 26) note in their pioneering study of deviant youth, describing how this fragmented into "the stable job market, the secondary job market that perpetuates insecurity and instability, and ... a kind of parallel, informal labor market for those who do not even have the ability to play the game of social and economic integration." Youths (and foreigners) were the first victims of this developing economic crisis, but these transformations fundamentally affected traditional forms of working-class youth social integration.

At the same time, over the course of the second half of the twentieth century, schooling also gradually emerged as an increasingly major factor in the organization of youths' time and identity, something that it had not been previously because of low enrollment rates, particularly among working-class youths. Enrollment in secondary schools, however, doubled between the end of World War II and 1958, before growing by an additional 65 percent through 1964, becoming quasi-universal a decade later (Terrail 2005, 32). Although working-class youths were the last to be included in the process of universal schooling, and moreover often ended their education earlier than other social classes, this had little impact on their employment outcomes during the 1950s and 1960s, insofar as it was relatively easy to obtain a stable job without qualifications in the generally booming French economy. Certainly the Black Jackets youth gangs that emerged during this period had little to do with schooling issues—whether educational difficulties, discrimination, or blocked opportunities—but tended to be related to workplace concerns instead. The wholesale transformation of youths' educational experience changed gang dynamics considerably, however.

Besides the number of pupils, the average educational level attained has also increased in France. During the early 1960s, less than half of all students reached secondary school, and only one in ten ended up graduating; today, all youths enter secondary school, nine in ten make it to the end of middle school, and more than half graduate (Terrail 2005, 97). The social consequences of these developments are important. The time spent in school and the—relative—social openness of these new experiences redefined notions of the future for the post–baby boom generation. Alongside the family and the street, school has become a key institution for youths' socialization, fully occupying their time and critically determining their future in the context of a new economy that demands ever more skills. To this extent, during the 1970s and 1980s, schools in France became spaces of sociability that acted as both producers and reinforcers of contradictory social norms, thereby defining both age- and class-based social objectives (see Chamboredon 1966). This has destabilized traditional working-class expectations. As Terrail (2005, 110) reports, the proportion of working-class parents aspiring for their children to graduate increased from 15 percent in 1962 to 76 percent in 1992. The emergence of such new aspirations owed much to the intensification of the link between education and employability, which conditioned a new regime of transition between childhood and adulthood, particularly for working-class youths.

More specifically, these changes reconfigured the modalities of "growing up" and, in doing so, redefined both the stakes and length of gang membership. Gang membership in the Black Jackets of the 1950s and 1960s was generally very short. Certainly the individuals interviewed for Michard and Sélosse's (1963) study of collective delinquency in France were all between fifteen and twenty years old, while Robert and Lascoumes (1974) described the majority of youth gang members they studied as being between fourteen and twenty years old. Generally, the studies of gangs during this period agree that gangs had something to do with helping certain youths bridge the period of transition to adulthood that they faced in their late teens and early twenties. Indeed, Monod (1968, 300) argues that older members tended to be much less numerous and were generally explicitly considered as "elders" who were delaying "maturing out" of the gang. A major issue that precipitated the process of transition, according to many of the gang members interviewed in the previously cited works, was mandatory military service, which in 1959 lasted for twenty-eight months. Enlistment marked an efficient rupture from being a youth. The military provided rules, customs, and obligations as well as an outlet for youthful passions, enthusiasm, and macho virility that were comparable to those associated with gang membership. Military service also disciplined youths, preparing them—at least those who did not return too damaged from the war in Algeria—for factory work and integration into law-abiding working-class society.

The social and economic transformations of the 1970s and 1980s fundamentally undermined this system, in which the ideal of a typical destiny of stable employment, marriage, children, and relative affluence that was expected in the past no longer appeared feasible. Increasingly, the options open to youths included unemployment, impoverishment, and uncertainty. They now finished their studies later, but professional insertion became harder, and they now left their parental homes and entered into long-term partnerships at a later stage in their lives. Indeed, mass unemployment increased youths' dependency on their parents as well as on public institutions. The contrast with the past was stark in this respect, as Galland (2000, 24) noted: "just 2% of men born in 1952–53 were not financially independent by the time they were 25," whereas 25 percent found themselves in this situation in 1970–71. Between these two periods, the median age at which those who do not graduate from high school ended their studies increased from seventeen to twenty-one years old, and concomitantly, the median age at which individuals obtained their first job (of more than six months) also rose, from seventeen to twenty-two. The trend was the same with regard to setting up an independent household: whereas "youth of the later generations leave their parental home very late—generally after 27 years old—this was the case of one youth out of five in 1997" (Galland 2002, 57).

IMMIGRATION, ETHNICITY, AND RACE

The end of the Thirty Glorious Years and the rise of mass unemployment also reactivated a historically rooted workers' nationalism in France (Noiriel 2004), which in turn led to immigration being a major social concern.[10] This was initially raised in relation to housing, sanitation, and general living conditions, but debates rapidly turned to security and delinquency. In particular, whereas in the past, race and ethnicity had rarely been discussed in relation to gangs—although the jackets of the Black Jackets were black, those wearing them were generally always white—from the early 1980s onward, both media reports and academic studies began to make increasing reference to the existence of ethnic and racial gangs (see Bachmann and Le Guennec 1996). For example, a July 7, 1981, article in the French newspaper *Le Figaro* claimed that popular neighborhoods all over the country were becoming subject to the rule of "Arab gangs."

As Macé (2002, 36) notes, debates about gangs in France during the 1980s and 1990s came to be framed principally in terms of the ethnicity and race of their members rather than in terms of their class background, as had previously been the case. The unity and collective behavior of gang members were seen to originate from their particular ethnoracial histories, including the common experience of marginality of immigrant communities in France. Yet there is evidence to suggest that ethnically heterogeneous gangs were by no means a new feature of French society. During the 1960s, Monod (1968, 295) had, for example, observed that there had been a (limited) number of foreign gang members in the gangs he studied. As Bacher (2000) has described, this multiethnic dimension was considered secondary and unimportant relative to the more traditional class-based imperatives commonly associated with gangs. This was even the case with the so-called multiethnic Loubard gangs that emerged during the late 1970s, despite their being widely described as the embodiment of a broader transition from "monoethnicity" to "pluriethnicity" within French society (Fize 1993).[11]

During the 1980s, a clear schism slowly emerged within French gang studies regarding ethnicity and gangs. On the one hand, social scientists, such as Dubet (1987), claimed that immigrant youth gangs did not exist in France, and certainly not in opposition to French youth gangs. He argued that the gang phenomenon was an encompassing one that drew in youths regardless of their origins. On the other hand, others, such as Esterle-Hedibel (1995), argued that youth gangs were more often than not ethnically and racially homogeneous and that this was a critical factor to take into account. Drawing on her study of Algerian immigrant youth in poor urban neighborhoods around Paris, she contended that these youth gangs were instances of "defensive ethnicity" resulting from the broader processes of stigmatization and exclusion experienced by the wider immigrant community in France. In particular, she argued that "ethnic segregation, experienced since childhood, is a powerful motive for the gang-group to emerge" (203).

This debate petered out by the beginning of the twenty-first century, when a consensus emerged within gang studies concerning the ethnicization of youth gangs, particularly with the emergence of a new type of gang in a general context marked by the increased ghettoization of popular neighborhoods in and around French cities and the repeated proliferation of—and concomitant public interest in—violent rioting in them. The new gangs were the so-called Zoulous, and they were the first gangs to aggressively and very publicly claim a racial identification. They principally involved black youths, especially in the Paris *banlieues* (suburbs). This new symbolic action was the product of three distinct dynamics: (1) cultural importation from North America, through the spread of black ghetto culture and especially hip-hop; (2) a response to the increasing activity of racist skinhead groups, particularly those associated with the right-wing National Front; and (3) the minority status of black youths within French society, including in particular vis-à-vis other ethnic minorities.

The Zoulous only lasted a few years as major social actors, but in many ways they represented the high point of ethnoracialization of French gangs. Although gangs in France continue to be marked by ethnic and racial characteristics, the association is first and foremost an expression of the deep social exclusion suffered by immigrant and minority communities in contemporary France and is not necessarily put forward as a major vector of identity. Rather, as Mohammed and Mucchielli (2006) highlight, it is the reflection of the fact that French society is very much built on an ethnic and racial social order. Certainly race and ethnicity determine how the accumulation of family, educational, economic, and political difficulties can play out, insofar as this is very much determined by the profound urban segregation that characterizes French cities, which in turn is intimately ethnicized and racialized. These inequalities and discrimination are the basis for residential segregation, differential access to housing and other state resources, and blocked opportunities in the labor market (Felouzis 2005). This, of course, affects the aspirations and employment prospects particularly of youths, but the consequences of this racial and ethnic order do not stop here. They also include increased exposure of such youths to policing as the French state authorities focus their patrolling and control on segregated areas, as well as their potential judicial treatment and the likelihood of being imprisoned at some point, the French judiciary having been shown to be highly racialized (Jobard 2006).

To this extent, the emergence of ethnicity and race as important facets of French youth gangs during the 1980s and 1990s is ultimately a reflection of a common condition of societal exclusion based on differential treatment on the basis of ethnicity and race, which is experienced as a denial of rights and citizenship (Castel 2007). As such, it is not necessarily completely different from the class-based rebellion with which gangs were associated previously, insofar as they are a function of the structural rather an individualized experience of race and ethnicity, and gangs are not actively and explicitly structured along racial or ethnic lines (Madzou and Bacqué 2008). Such an understanding of the new ethnic dynamic of contemporary French youth gangs is also supported by the fact that most studies have underlined that very few youth gangs define themselves or their foes according to criteria of skin color or origin but rather do so either in terms of local territorial dynamics or in opposition to authority, in particular, the state.

DRUGS AND GANGS: TOWARD NEW GANG DYNAMICS IN FRANCE?

One factor that has significantly changed French youth gang dynamics during the past quarter century or so, however, is the question of drugs.

Although drugs are by no means a new phenomenon in France—or elsewhere, for that matter—until the 1970s, they were the purview of a relatively restricted social group. As a result of the spread of North American hippy culture, but also the decline of the student movement and the resurgence of more doctrinal forms of political contestation, drugs became part of a trend of "countercultural consumption" (Duprez and Kokoreff 2000; Mauger 1984). Although initially underground, and linked to alternative ways of life, drug consumption rapidly became an element of working-class youth culture, a process that Duprez and Kokoreff (2000, 19) have labeled "the proletarization of drugs consumption." This initially mainly involved cannabis, but the last twenty years have seen the proliferation of harder drugs, such as cocaine and heroin.

The extent to which drugs have pervaded poor urban neighborhoods should not be underestimated. As a recent study highlighted, three in ten residents aged between fifteen and sixty-four years of age claim they have already consumed drugs, whereas four in ten claim they have been offered drugs (Observatoire français des drogues et des toxicomanies 2007, 18). This has had extensively negative public health consequences for poor neighborhoods but also fundamentally changed gang dynamics, insofar as, in a manner similar to alcohol, drugs became part of gang social practices associated with machismo and virility and affected gang violence and gang members' life expectancy. Beyond the obvious health consequences of consumption, the arrival of drugs in the gang universe fundamentally changed gang dynamics because drug dealing has important symbolic and economic stakes within broader street culture.

Drugs can, of course, be a means of capital accumulation, and in the broader context of economic decline in late 1970s France, drug dealing played a major role in absorbing the effects of the crisis and mitigating socioeconomic exclusion for a small minority of residents living in poor urban neighborhoods. In particular, it was "an alternative to exclusion and dishonor" for gang members, as Kokoreff (2007, 79) put it. Unlike other forms of profitable delinquency, which are sporadic and often quite random, drug trafficking is part of a long-term strategy, which involves quite definite rules, functions, and guaranteed markets. In particular, drug dealing requires a specialized labor force, including, in particular, violence specialists and others with intimate knowledge of how to deal with state authorities. Youth gang members are ideal in both respects, and gangs have become drug dealers' primary recruitment ground for collaborators in poor urban neighborhoods. At the same time, although a small number do become drug dealers subsequently, for most youths, involvement in the drug trade is less about enrichment than simply about ensuring their own regular consumption and avoiding insolvency. Moreover, drugs also have certain aspects that go beyond the economic, as the activity structures gangs organizationally, relationally, and symbolically. Drugs provide gang members with new roles and statuses and reinforce gangs as "poles of deviant sociability," symbolically "diffusing a culture of illegality that is transmitted over generations through family and peer relations" (Kokoreff 2000, 404).

CONCLUSION

Youth gangs in France are a misunderstood social phenomenon, shrouded by stereotypes and reporting that is often subject to political manipulation. Images of gangs and gang members such as those projected by Hollywood films dominate debates, despite the fact that most serious studies suggest that the typical gang member is likely to be between fifteen and twenty years old, a high school dropout with a poor schooling career, living in social housing in a poor, spatially segregated suburban neighborhood, and moreover well known to the police and other state authorities. Because these characteristics overlap with the condition of immigrant populations in France, contemporary youth gang members are likely to be of North or sub-Saharan African origin. The relatively recent proliferation of drug consumption in France has significantly changed gang dynamics, to the extent that they are arguably beginning to correspond more to the Hollywood version of gangs that French gang studies often decries. In particular, drug dealing has transformed gang culture, both in terms of practice and more symbolically.

The dominating actors of the drug trade constitute themselves as the central figures of their neighborhoods. They represent a social trajectory that is both accessible and lucrative, a form of local success that is particularly attractive to youths who are bearing the brunt of the consequences of the spatial, ethnoracial, and economic exclusion that affects the contemporary French working class. Their daily visibility and their ways of life constitute a significant positive endorsement for their activities but, moreover, also promote the belief held by youth gang members that their delinquent careers can be extended beyond the gang. While the members of past youth gangs, such as the Black Jackets, enjoyed relatively short deviant careers, which mainly involved minor offenses and were generally ended by their military service and the beginning of factory work, the transformation of the economy, high unemployment, and limited educational opportunities all mean that the transition to adulthood is either significantly delayed or blocked for the youths of today. Drug dealing offers a possible solution but at the same time significantly changes the dynamics of belonging to a gang, pushing youths toward greater violence and criminality, thereby institutionalizing social practices that have little to do with transition to adulthood and more to do with organized, armed brutality.

NOTES

1. This chapter was translated from French by Julie Mandoyan and Dennis Rodgers.

2. See, e.g., Sarkozy's speeches in Gagny on March 18, 2009, and in Nice on March 19, 2009.

3. The reorganization of French intelligence services in 2008 has meant that gangs are now dealt with by the Departmental Service of General Intelligence (Service départemental de l'information générale, or SDIG).

4. To a large extent, the DCRG's involvement in gang-related intelligence gathering can also be related to its desire to increase its institutional legitimacy in a changing context where "traditional" security threats were being overtaken by new ones (Bonelli 2008, 98).

5. Cited in Observatoire National de la Délinquance (2006, 455).

6. See http://www.interieur.gouv.fr/sections/espace-presse/porte-parole-ministere/contre-bandes-violentes/view.

7. According to a report from the Central Direction of the National Police, partially described in *Le Figaro,* August 2, 2010.

8. Calculated on the basis of the 2009 official French census figures (see http://www.insee.fr/fr/ppp/bases-de-donnees/recensement/populations-legales/france-regions.asp?annee=2009).

9. See, e.g., *Le Figaro,* March 5, 2010.

10. Moreover, 1974 marked an official transition in the French immigration regime from the promotion of temporary labor immigration to the acceptance of more permanent settler immigration.

11. Indeed, some social scientists even went so far as to characterize the Loubards as positive exemplars of the ethnoracial diversification of French society.

REFERENCES

Bacher, Claire. 2000. "Le phénomène 'Blousons noirs' vu par la presse." Master's thesis, Université de Clermont-Ferrand II.

Bachmann, Christian, and Nicole Le Guennec. 1996. *Violences urbaines. Ascension et chute des classes moyennes à travers cinquante ans de politique de la ville.* Paris: Albin Michel.

Bidart, Claire. 2006. "Crises, décisions et temporalités: autour des bifurcations biographiques." *Cahiers internationaux de sociologie* 120:29–48.

Bonelli, Laurent. 2008. *La France a peur.* Paris: La Découverte.

Carra, Cécile. 2001. *Délinquance juvénile et quartiers sensible: Histoires de vie.* Paris: L'Harmattan.

Castel, Robert. 2007. *La Discrimination négative citoyens ou indigenes: Citoyens ou indigènes?* Paris: Seuil.

Chamboredon, Jean-Claude. 1966. "La société française et sa jeunesse." In *Darras: Le partage des benefices*, 155–75. Paris: Les éditions de Minuit.

Chauvel, Louis. 2006. "Les nouvelles générations devant la panne prolongée de l'ascenseur social." *Revue de l'OFCE* 96, no. 1: 35–50.

Copfermann, Émile. 1962. *La génération des Blousons Noirs*. Paris: François Maspero.

Dubet, François. 1987. *La galère: Jeunes en survie*. Paris: Fayard.

Duprez, Dominique, and Michel Kokoreff. 2000. *Les mondes de la drogue*. Paris: Odile Jacob.

Duret, Pascal. 1999. *Les jeunes et l'identité masculine*. Paris: PUF.

Esterle-Hedibel, Maryse. 1995. "Le rite et le risque, la culture du risque dans les bandes de jeunes de milieu populaire à travers la conduite routière." PhD diss., Université René Descartes, Paris.

Felouzis, Georges. 2005. *L'apartheid scolaire*. Paris: Seuil.

Fize, Michel. 1993. *Les bandes*. Paris: Desclée De Brouwer.

Galland, Olivier. 2000. "Entrer dans la vie adulte: des étapes toujours plus tardives, mais resserrées." *Économie et statistique* 337–38:13–36.

Jobard, Fabien. 2006. "Police, justice et discriminations raciales." In *De la question sociale à la question raciale? Représenter la société française*, edited by Didier Fassin and Éric Fassin, 211–29. Paris: La Découverte.

Kokoreff, Michel. 2000. "Faire du *business* dans les quartiers." *Déviance et Société* 24, no. 4: 327–30.

———. 2007. *Economies criminelles et mondes urbains*. Paris: PUF.

Lagrange, Hugues. 2001. *De l'affrontement à l'esquive: violences, délinquances et usages de drogues*. Paris: Syros.

Lagrée, Jean-Charles, and Paula Lew-Faï. 1985. *La galère: Marginalisation juvénile et collectivités locales*. Paris: Les éditions du CNRS.

Lepoutre, David. 1997. *Cœur de banlieue, codes, rites et langages*. Paris: Odile Jacob.

Macé, Éric. 2002. "Le traitement médiatique de l'insécurité." In *Crime et sécurité, l'état des savoirs*, edited by Laurent Mucchielli and Philippe Robert, 33–42. Paris: La Découverte.

Madzou, Lamence, and Marie-Hélène Bacqué. 2008. *J'étais un chef de gang*. Paris: La Découverte.

Marlière, Éric. 2005. *Jeunes en cite: Diversité des trajectoires ou destin commun?* Paris: L'Harmattan.

Mauger, Gérard. 1984. "L'apparition et la diffusion des drogues en France, Bruxelles." *Contradictions* 40–41:131–48.

———. 2006. *Les bandes, le milieu et la bohème populaire*. Paris: Belin.

Michard, Henri, and Jacques Sélosse, eds. 1963. *La délinquance des jennes en groupe: contributions à l'étude de la société adolescente*. Paris: Cujas.

Mohammed, Marwan. 2007. "Les bandes: familles de substitution? La place des familles dans la formation des bandes de jeunes." PhD diss., Université Versailles-Saint-Quentin-en-Yvelines.

Mohammed, Marwan, and Laurent Mucchielli. 2006. "La police dans les 'quartiers sensibles': un profond malaise." In *Quand les banlieues brûlent. Retour sur les émeutes de novembre 2005*, edited by Laurent Mucchielli and Véronique Le Goaziou, 98–119. Paris: La Découverte.

———. 2007. *Les bandes de jeunes, des Blousons Noirs à nos jours*. Paris: La Découverte.

Moignard, Benjamin. 2008. *L'école et la rue: fabriques de délinquance—recherches comparatives en France et an Brésil*. Paris: Le Monde/PUF.

Monod, Jean. 1968. *Les Barjots*. Paris: Julliard.

Muchembled, Robert. 2008. *Une histoire de la violence—De la fin du Moyen-Age à nos jours*. Paris: Seuil.

Noiriel, Gérard. 2004. *Gens d'ici venus d'ailleurs*. Paris: Les éditions du Chêne.

Observatoire français des drogues et des toxicomanies. 2007. *Rapport annuel*. Paris: Ministry of the Interior.

Observatoire National de la Délinquance. 2006. *Rapport annuel*. Paris: Ministry of the Interior.

———. 2010. *Rapport annuel*. Paris: Ministry of the Interior.

Robert, Philippe. 1966. *Les bandes d'adolescents, une théorie de la segregation*. Paris: Les éditions ouvrières.

———. 2002. *L'insécurité en France*. Paris: La Découverte.

Robert, Philippe, and P. Lascoumes Pierre. 1974. *Les bandes d'adolescents*. Paris: Ouvrières.

Rubi, Stéphanie. 2005. *Les "crapuleuses": ces adolescentes déviantes*. Paris: PUF.

Sauvadet, Thomas. 2006. *Le capital guerrier: solidarité et concurrence entre jeunes de cite*. Paris: Armand Colin.

Terrail, Jean-Pierre, ed. 2005. *L'école en France. Crise, pratiques, perspectives*. Paris: La Dispute.

Tétard, François. 1988. "Le phénomène blousons noirs en France fin des années 1950—début des années 1960." *Révolte et société* 2:205–14.

Van de Velde, Cécile. 2008. *Devenir adulte, Sociologie comparée de la jeunesse en Europe*. Paris: PUF.

6

Maras and the Politics of Violence in El Salvador

JOSÉ MIGUEL CRUZ

Where does Mara Salvatrucha come from? How did the U.S.-born Eighteenth Street Gang become a powerhouse of the Salvadoran streets? The Mara Salvatrucha, also known as the MS-13, and the Eighteenth Street Gang, branded also as Barrio 18, are the two major youth gangs in El Salvador and Central America. According to different sources (Aguilar and Miranda 2006; USAID 2006), between 2002 and 2006, both gangs comprised more than 87 percent of gang membership in El Salvador. These gangs are known not only because of their control of Salvadoran neighborhoods and most of the prisons nowadays but also because they have evolved to become powerful criminal groups with the capacity of setting extensive extortion networks across the region. These organizations form a network of street gangs dwelling in every country of the North American hemisphere from Canada to Honduras. Yet the common answer to the question as to why MS-13 and the Eighteenth Street Gang are the major gangs in El Salvador and Central America is usually narrowed to the backward-and-forward migration of Salvadorans to the United States. The evidence points to a more intricate response.

Migration and deportation policies in the United States have indeed played an important role in boosting the phenomenon of street gangs in El Salvador, but it is an overstatement to say that the dominance of MS-13 and the Eighteenth Street Gang in Central America and their seemingly growing transnational character are essentially the result of the circular Salvadoran migration to the United States. Should we accept this argument alone, we would find it difficult to explain why the Eighteenth Street Gang, a gang originally formed by Chicanos and Mexican immigrants during the late 1960s, has not put down roots in Mexican soil as it has done in El Salvador, Guatemala, and Honduras or why the Belizean Crips and Bloods have not developed in the same way as the Salvadoran gangs.

Gangs are the outcome of different factors. Marginalization, migration, street cross-culturalization, and—what I shall call—the politics of violence being key to explaining the rise and predominance of the youth gangs in El Salvador, also locally known as *maras*. This chapter draws substantial theoretical insight from the work of Vigil (2002) on multiple marginalization, Hagedorn (2008) on gang institutionalization, and Decker on the dynamics of gang violence (Decker 1996; Decker, Bynum, and Weisel 1998; Decker and Van Winkle 1996) and is based on the research program on gangs developed by the University of Central America in San Salvador (Aguilar 2007; Carranza 2005; Cruz and Portillo Peña 1998; ERIC et al. 2001; Santacruz-Giralt and Ranum 2010; Santacruz and Concha-Eastman 2001). It argues that the main reason as to why Salvadoran gangs have ended being the powerful criminal organizations they were by the early 2010s is a direct yet unintended result of the *mano dura* (firm hand) policies that were developed in El Salvador—and in Central America in general—during 2003–6 as well as the violence generated by extralegal violent actors stemming from state institutions and civil society. The fundamental argument is that Salvadoran gangs transformed into more hierarchical and organized groups, capable of setting complex extortion rackets on the population, as a result of their need to face consequences of government crackdowns.

The chapter is divided into three sections. The first section quickly addresses the factors that lie behind the emergence of gangs as a major social issue in El Salvador, then the second reviews the path of gang strengthening, paying special attention to the unintended contribution of the *mano dura* policies in the transformation of street gangs in El Salvador and the internal processes through which they became street powerhouses not only in El Salvador but also in the region. Finally, the chapter explores the link between gangs and violence in a country considered one of the most violent nations in the western hemisphere (United Nations Office on Drugs and Crime 2007).

THE EMERGENCE OF SALVADORAN *MARAS*

Reports place the emergence of urban youth gangs in El Salvador in the 1960s following the processes of increasing urbanization and industrialization that the country began to experience in the 1950s (Savenije and van der Borgh 2006; Smutt and Miranda 1998). However, youth gangs started to draw some public notice in the late 1980s, in the middle of the twelve-year-long civil war that devastated the country. In March 1990, months after one of the most intense guerrilla offensives for the control of San Salvador, the capital of the nation, newspapers reported that youth gangs were collaborating with rebel forces in some outlying areas of the cities (see *La Prensa Gráfica* 1990). Those gangs, which were already known as *maras*,[1] essentially comprised young males coming from poor neighborhoods and dysfunctional families (Argueta et al. 1992).

In the late 1980s, myriad youth gangs populated not only San Salvador outskirts and peripheral areas of the big cities but also downtown and blue-collar neighborhoods that were experiencing a decline in city services as a result of the economic crisis and the ongoing civil war. Those gangs were characterized by turf-based groups or cliques who controlled specific, well-defined neighborhoods and streets. As Argueta et al. (1992) and Smutt and Miranda (1998) reported, these groups engaged in petty criminal activities and spent most of their time hanging out together and consuming soft drugs.

This pattern of many turf-based youth gangs started to change after the end of the civil war in 1992, when many Salvadoran refugees living in the United States started to go back to El Salvador, some of them voluntarily, but also many others through forced deportation. Although deportations were not a rare practice before the 1990s (see *San Francisco Chronicle* 1989), the bulk of forced returns took place after the United States passed the Illegal Immigration Reform and Immigrant Responsibility Act in 1995 (Thalé and Falkenburger 2006). This act would prove to have significant consequences for the later development of Salvadoran gangs.

The influx of young gang members back to El Salvador meant the diffusion of the cultural styles of the U.S. pattern of gang membership. These cultural styles comprised not only the names of gang organizations, such as MS-13 and the Eighteenth Street Gang, but also the use of tattoos, the utilization of hand signs to communicate, and, more importantly for the increase in violence and criminal behavior, norms, values, and knowledge about how to behave, about who is the enemy, and about who is a friend (Cruz 2007a; Santacruz and Concha-Eastman 2001). Those norms and cultural values were rapidly assimilated and transformed on Salvadoran streets, and they facilitated communication and mutual understanding between the local gangs and the newcomers who kept landing in El Salvador.[2]

The youth gangs, which at first comprised several small territorial groups, became two large groups of cliques, the MS-13 and the Eighteenth Street Gang. A survey conducted in 1996 with gang members in the metropolitan area of San Salvador, the country's capital, showed that 84 percent of gangs were affiliated with either MS-13 or the Eighteenth Street Gang; only 16 percent of gang members belonged to other gangs.

Yet it would be a mistake to ascribe the expansion of gang membership and the emergence of the "gang problem" in the 1990s to the constant influx of deportees and returnees of the postwar years. The majority of gang members joined the cliques and *barrios* on Salvadoran soil and had never been outside the country. The same study conducted in 1996 showed that only one in every ten gang members had joined the gang organization in the United States, predominantly in Los Angeles (Cruz and Portillo Peña 1998); all the rest had "jumped in" on Salvadoran streets. These percentages have barely changed since that study. In a similar study conducted by Santacruz and Concha-Eastman in 2001, only 12 percent of gang members said they had been in the United States; the most recent study available conducted only with imprisoned gang members revealed that only 7.3 percent had been in the United States (Aguilar 2007). So youth gangs in El Salvador were essentially formed by local teenagers who had never been in the United States. As noted by a former researcher of Salvadoran gangs, "the influence of U.S. urban and marginal cultures is not essential to the existence of Salvadoran gangs, but it affects and shapes those gangs" (Sisti 1996, 4).

Newcomers from the United States served as agents of cross-culturalization and social contact across borders; they were the brokers of the transnational forces that engulfed the countries of the Americas under the relentless push of globalization (Sassen 2007; Zilberg 2004), but the reasons why young people kept joining the gangs and why street organizations blew up into a major social issue were largely endogenous and related to the dynamics of violence, as we see later.

A society historically shattered by poverty, social inequality, and political violence, 1990s postwar El Salvador was far from solving the structural problems that contributed to driving it to civil war. By 1992, 65 percent of the population lived under the poverty line, and the poorest 20 percent received only 3.2 percent of the national income (PNUD 2003). In addition, the long civil war had left a fragmented and traumatized civil society, with tens of thousands internally displaced inhabitants making their way into the major cities and the flooding of the streets with weapons, which included assault rifles, grenades, and semiautomatic pistols (United Nations Office on Drugs and Crime 2007).

Youth gangs thrived in environments of economic marginalization, social exclusion, and violence. Every research project on gangs conducted since the early 1990s, whether carried out before the Immigration Act (Argueta et al. 1992), after it (Cruz and Portillo Peña 1998; Santacruz and Concha-Eastman 2001; Santacruz and Cruz 2001; Smutt and Miranda 1998; Carranza 2005), or after the *mano dura* law in the mid-2000s (Aguilar 2007; Aguilar and Miranda 2006; Demoscopía 2007), points to poverty, the existence of poor-quality formal education, the lack of career education, and the ubiquity of violence as the factors that remain behind the local emergence of youth gangs. On the issue of poverty, for example, some studies underscored the experience of being socially marginalized and economically stranded. More important than the lack of resources, these studies found that young people who had to drop out of school for economic reasons or who had to move to poorer neighborhoods tended to join the gangs in higher numbers than those who had been out of school or lived in extreme poverty all their lives (Cruz, Carranza, and Santacruz 2004; Smutt and Miranda 1998). Smutt and Miranda underlined the importance of the processes of rapid and unplanned urban growth, pointing out that such processes created hundreds of neighborhoods and slums lacking the most basic services. Youngsters found it easier to spend their time on the streets than at their own homes. In addition, many of these potential gang members came from families in which the use of violence against their own members was very common. Teens abandoned their homes not only because of the physical restraints that the household imposed but also as a result of the constant violence and threat that even the family represented to them (Cruz and Portillo Peña 1998; Santacruz and Cruz 2001; Savenije and van der Borgh 2006). As one Eighteenth Street Gang member once put it, "I have always lived with violence. At home, I suffered violence from my parents; the difference being on the streets is that I can pay it back" (Cruz and Portillo Peña 1998, 72).

All these conditions and processes point to what James Diego Vigil (1988, 2002) has called "multiple marginality." Salvadoran gangs emerged as a result of multilevel processes of marginalization. These mechanisms did not entail ethnic or racial discrimination, as ethnicity is not a major social issue in El Salvador; rather, they entailed socioeconomic discrimination that prompted other marginalization processes. In the 1990s, increasing numbers of young people found themselves living in the ecologically marginal areas of the city as a result of economic transformations and war displacements. In their communities, some youngsters were expelled from schools. Lacking adequate job training, they found no employment or suitable means to support their own lives. At home, dysfunctional and violent families, usually strained by shortages and deprivation, drove them to the streets. Facing several mechanisms of exclusion, many children and teenagers in postwar El Salvador found the response to their marginalization on the streets. Salvadoran barrios provided them with both pals and new sources of identity. Being a Salvatrucho or a Dieciocho (Eighteenth) would grant meaning to their lives, but more importantly, it would provide youths with ways to cope with marginality and exclusion because those imported identities have also been created as a result of marginalization in the megacities of Southern California (Vigil 2002).

THE TRANSFORMATION OF SALVADORAN *MARAS*

Young people joined gangs not because of the influx of U.S. deportees but because the local conditions in postwar El Salvador were ripe for the affiliation of hundreds of teenagers with these organizations. Furthermore, neither massive deportation nor marginalization alone explains why Salvadoran youth gangs have become so powerful in Central American streets. After all, massive deportation is not an exclusive feature of recent migration in El Salvador, and young people are also being relentlessly marginalized in "*maras*-free" countries such as Nicaragua (Rodgers 2006).

To understand how youth gangs have evolved over time in El Salvador, it is necessary to understand how they have become institutionalized, that is, how they have endured, grown stronger, and become a loose alliance of franchises across El Salvador and the hemisphere (Hagedorn 2008). It is necessary to pay attention to what I call the "politics of violence," namely, the collection of institutions, actors, and policies that boosted the extreme use of violence as a normal feature of Salvadoran youth gangs. This concept is fed by two different inputs. The first one is that gangs are strengthened in the long run by violence and the threat of violence coming from different social actors, not only other gangs. Conflicts and threats of violence lead to social cohesiveness among gang members, prompt the emergence of roles and structures within the gang, and reinforce the norms that justify the use of violence (Decker, Bynum, and Weisel 1998; Decker and Van Winkle 1996; Hagedorn 1988). The second idea comes from Charles Tilly (2003), who contends that when a phenomenon of large-scale collective violence occurs, as that of Salvadoran *maras,* state agents also play an important role in the overall violence. Putting these ideas together in the context of Salvadoran youth gangs, gangs transform to become protection rackets as a result, in part, of what the state and the actors associated with it have done to deal with gangs.

One of the characteristics of gangs in El Salvador is that they have been constantly transformed by the surrounding conditions. As Moore (1991) and others have argued regarding Los Angeles youth gangs, these types of organizations have never been allowed to evolve by themselves. Salvadoran gangs are no exception. They have developed from being turf-based, small gangs who spent most of their time hanging out together at the slums and city squares to being a confederation of cliques or networks who share a sort of brand franchise (MS-13 or Eighteenth Street), sometimes loosely, sometimes tightly; that control some of the prisons; and that have gotten involved in organized crime activities (Cruz 2007a).

Broadly put, it is possible to distinguish at least three different phases in the recent evolution of youth gangs in El Salvador up to 2010.[3] First, as we have seen in the section about the emergence of Salvadoran *maras,* youth gangs comprised a number of small, territory-based groups without any connection between them. Original *maras* were formed by young males and females, ages ranging from seven to thirty-five years old, with strong internal cohesiveness and a clearly defined leadership within the group (Argueta et al. 1992). These gangs usually engaged in minor violent conflicts for the control of some neighborhoods and public spaces and carried out different types of group activities, from partying together to planning criminal actions, such as robberies and street brawls. Some of these gangs served as neighborhood watchdogs and kept a close relationship with the community (Savenije and Andrade-Eekhoff 2003).

This configuration of gang phenomena changed after the end of the civil war. The return of young people who had witnessed gang culture in Southern California introduced identity patterns that yielded not only the reconfiguration of gangs in two larger franchises but also the transformation of gang warfare in El Salvador and, later, in northern Central America. As I have pointed out elsewhere (Cruz 2010), the adoption of U.S.-born gang identities facilitated the construction of two nationwide confederations of cliques that exacerbated the conflicts between gangs. Youth gangs not only fought over territory control, they also fought over identity. Southern California gang culture revolved around identities, and these identities prompted a different arrangement of the Salvadoran gang world. Instead of generating many other different *maras,* a sort of rainbow of gangs, as Vigil (2002) once put it in the case of Los Angeles, gang cross-culturalization straightened up existing gangs; it aligned all gangs with MS-13 or the Eighteenth Street Gang. Being a Salvatrucho or an Eighteenth became more important than controlling specific turf. By doing this, it redefined the meaning of gang warfare.

In El Salvador, where ethnic lines do not exist across the population, the difference between being a Dieciocho or a Salvatrucho is not one of racial or ethnic cleavages, as in other countries,[4] but rather an arbitrary one. Being all Salvadorans living in their own country, affiliation to MS-13 does not mean a particular citizenship trait; furthermore, Barrio 18 membership does not mean being less Salvadoran or rather a true Chicano.[5] Young people in El Salvador joined Mara Salvatrucha or the Eighteenth Street Gang because a certain clique happened to be in control of the neighborhood or community where the gang candidate roamed. Once a young man had jumped in, he was supposed to show his loyalty to the franchise by taking part in the warfare against the rival gang. Therefore young gang members and wannabes asserted their identity and their allegiance to the gang franchise by attacking and killing rival franchise gang members, even when the victims did not mean a direct threat to the clique neighborhood (Cruz 2007b). Escalation of violence was fueled by the availability of firearms but also by the absence of any significant program of gang prevention and control. In the mid-1990s, Salvadoran institutions were more concerned with applying the Washington Consensus guidelines than with strengthening public security and mitigating the devastating effects of structural adjustment (Cruz 2007b).

Gang warfare between Barrio 18 and MS-13 shaped the gang phenomenon in El Salvador during the 1990s. Cliques and neighborhood gangs—even the few that did not formally belonged to any of the franchises—were drawn into war, and this conflict dominated the dynamics of gang activities. Gang violence increased social cohesion among the cliques that happened to share the same franchise, even when their gang members barely knew between each other (Santacruz and Concha-Eastman 2001). It also provided wannabes who were seeking retaliation for the killing of friends and relatives with new reasons for being part of the gang (Santacruz and Cruz 2001). Violence among gangs redefined the struggle for urban spaces and the utilization of tattoos on their own bodies (Cruz 2007a). Instead of controlling specific turf, streets, and squares, gangs moved to claim collective identities. They spent more time tattooing their bodies to show their allegiance to the gang franchise than marking their territories through wall graffiti. Identity was more important than turf.

Two surveys conducted with nearly one thousand gang members each in 1996 and 2001 showed that the bulk of gang victimization was perpetrated by rival gangs (see Table 6.1). At this stage, although police officials were responsible for a significant share of violence against *maras,* youth gangs seemed to be more driven by seeking retaliation against rival groups than by confronting the police.

This second stage in Salvadoran gang development lasted until the early 2000s. In 2001, Santacruz and Concha-Eastman had already reported that gangs were slowly moving to more criminal-oriented behavior as a result, in part, of the introduction of hard drugs, such as cocaine and crack, onto the Salvadoran market.[6] However, the definitive push for the transformation of Salvadoran gangs came from the state. It came from the 2003 enactment of the Mano Dura Act. *Mano*

Table 6.1: Who has physically hurt you in the last six months? (%)

	Year of survey	
	1996	2001
Rival gang	55.8	48.5
Police	29.9	30.9
Private individuals	4.6	11.0
Same gang member	4.6	6.3
Others	3.5	2.0
Don't know	1.9	1.2

Sources: Cruz and Portillo Peña, 1998; Santacruz and Concha-Eastman, 2001

dura was a wide government effort to tackle gangs and to gain public support for the approaching elections of 2004 (Aguilar 2004). Accordingly, an anti-*mara* law was enacted in July 2003 under the administration of Francisco Flores. This act, known as Ley Antimaras, aimed to facilitate the detention and prosecution of suspected gang members based on the newly classified felony of "illicit association" *(asociación ilícita)* and gang membership (Thale and Falkenburger 2006). By mid-2004, this state initiative evolved to a superlative form called Super Mano Dura. These decrees gave complete authority to the police—and also to military personnel—to carry out arrests based on arbitrary decisions and thin evidence. Police could use the presence of tattoos, hand signals, some dress codes, and physical appearance as evidence of gang membership (Hume 2007). They also included a considerable media and public relations campaign aimed to depict gangs as shouldering the primary responsibility for violence and crime in El Salvador (Cruz 2011).

The *mano dura* policies put in motion a series of events that ended up transforming Salvadoran gangs. First, they unleashed massive police and military crackdowns on gangs. These operations allowed for the capture and mass incarceration of gang members, thus saturating and overpopulating the already inadequate prison system. For example, a 2005 report by the National Civilian Police details how, between July 23, 2003, and July 8, 2005, the police captured 30,934 alleged gang members. Although the majority of these indictments represented different captures of the same person (gang members were arrested, freed after forty-eight hours, and then arrested again), the figure reflects the volume of gang-related police activity that took place in a relatively short period of time. In addition, the massive indictment of gangs provided the latter with the opportunity to control several prisons across the country. By 2006, over 30 percent of the inmates in Salvadoran prisons were gang members (Aguilar and Miranda 2006). Four years later, by 2010, nearly 50 percent of the gang members identified by the Salvadoran police were under arrest (Martinez and Valencia 2011).

The second significant event related to the enactment of the *mano dura* policies was the reconstitution of gangs into organized networks. By overpopulating the prisons, the crackdowns provided the opportunity for gang organization and strengthening. Being in prisons, youth gangs began to organize themselves into hierarchical structures. Dozens of gang members who shared the same gang franchise but who came from different places in the country established contact, recognized other cliques, and refashioned gang organization. This was made possible, in part, by the decision of the authorities to separate gangs in detention centers according to their gang membership.[7] By allocating all youth gang members together, the *mano dura* policies nourished a sort of long-term national gang assembly and facilitated communication and connections among gang members both nationwide and internationally, insofar as deportees with contacts in the United States also served sentences inside the Salvadoran jails (Cruz 2010). The following statement from a fourteen-year-old Eighteenth Street Gang member highlights the role of Salvadoran prisons in the networking of gangs. Talking about his peers locked up in one single prison, he said that there are "like six-hundred who have the word, they are from different neighborhoods, but they are all in the same *barrio* (gang)... from *Campanera, Ciudad Delgado*... plenty of boys from different places, cities, all in there" (Cruz 2010, 391–92).

Third, the strike against gangs not only unleashed legitimate police operations against youth gangs but also opened the door to abuses and extralegal activities perpetrated by state agents and actors associated with them. Police abuses and the participation of police officers in extralegal cleansing operations increased under the *mano dura* laws. A couple of statements drawn from research conducted by Maria

Santacruz and Elin Ranum (2010, 245–46) with female gang members in Salvadoran prisons illustrate this point:

> Suddenly, they (the police) came, and they came at shooting at us. We had never crossed that line. It wasn't like it is now; now it's different because they set the tone.... They (the police) didn't use to mess with us (the gang).... they used to stop us to frisk us, but they'd let us go.... now, they mistreat us for everything.

Security institutions loosened their internal control and supervision systems, and gang persecution led to violation of the fundamental human rights of those arrested. Police officers started to abuse and mistreat gang members and suspects more frequently than before the *mano dura* plans. Again, statements collected by Santacruz and Ranum (2010, 246) provide a helpful view:

> Nowadays, they [the police] abuse us more.... It used to be, I used to go to jail ... but they didn't beat you, didn't mistreat you. Now they all take advantage.... [A cousin of mine] got arrested and they took him to the station and they put him in with rival gang members knowing he was their rival, and they started beating him up while the police watched it all. When he started having convulsions and the police were watching it all, they didn't say anything. They killed him inside.... It's big time corruption! They take advantage of people. That's why so many retaliate against the police. Now they are more abusive ... since the *mano dura,* they are more abusive.

In addition, the overall climate of the "war on gangs" made it possible for armed groups engaged in "social cleansing" to increase their activities against young people suspected of belonging to gangs (Cruz and Carranza 2006). A 2005 report by the Forensic Institute (Instituto de Medicina Legal) of El Salvador cited by Cruz, Fernández de Castro, and Santamaría (2012) stated that 59 percent of the more than thirty-eight hundred murders committed that year were by unknown assailants, many of them bearing the marks of summary executions. Highly regarded human rights organizations, such as the Archbishop Legal Aid Office in San Salvador, attributed many homicides of gang members in

Table 6.2: Opinion about who is responsible of murders against other gang members

Perpetrators	Percentage
Police and other government officials	43.0
Rival gang	21.2
Cleansing groups and vigilantes	11.4
Organized crime, drug traffickers	7.0
Same gang, same clique	3.8
Don't know	13.6

Source: Aguilar 2007

2006, 2007, and 2008 to social cleansing groups (Thale and Falkenburger 2006; Tutela Legal del Arzobispado 2007, 2008).

And finally, the *mano dura* policies allowed actors other than those linked to state apparatuses to participate in the war on gangs. This included involvement by businessmen from a variety of levels in financing illegal groups, the participation of civilians seeking retribution in the form of social cleansing, and the development of an economy of crime in which assassins were contracted to do away with enemies (Cruz, Fernández de Castro, and Santamaría 2012). Table 6.2 shows the opinions of more than three hundred imprisoned gang members in 2006 about who was responsible for killing their peers.

In response, gangs prepared for an all-out war against the state and its agents. As illustrated in one of the preceding statements, gang members sought opportunities to retaliate against the police and any group perceived as a threat to them. In doing this, they strengthened their own organization, established relations with other violent actors, and filled the ranks to be prepared for the all-out war. Again, the following statement by a female gang member reported by Santacruz and Ranum (2010, 246) highlights these dynamics:

Nowadays it's worse. They kill the gang members straightforwardly. I wish gangs didn't exist, but we know that it's not going to be that way.... They kill five but fifteen will jump in ... they are 11–12 year-old and they jump in. They put people in jail but there are 200 a year who go out to raise the cohorts. They knock some cohorts down, but there are other cohorts that they raise.

For the youth gang franchises, whether MS-13 or Barrio 18, this war did not have a political agenda, although some gang leaders have tried to articulate one (see Valencia 2009); rather, gang members prepared to face crackdowns by punishing those they suspected of collaborating with state agents or simply by incorporating more actively into the criminal networks that provided more resources to cope with the government strike (Cruz and Carranza 2006). As some gang scholars envisaged when analyzing the role of violence in U.S. gangs (Decker and Van Winkle 1996; Hagedorn 1988), Salvadoran *maras* responded to the *mano dura* law with more group cohesion, brand-new hierarchical organization, and resolved violence. The use of extralegal force by state actors expanded the spaces for the mediation of violence, and group confinement in jails provided them access to all sorts of criminal networks. Gangs also responded to state attacks by wielding extreme violence. Massive incarceration provided the strategic space, the resources, and the connections with other violent actors that allowed them to strengthen their own organizations.

In conclusion, the current situation of youth gangs in El Salvador is, in large part, the result of the politics of violence, which was essentially manifested in the *mano dura* policies. By raising the limits of legal violence and allowing frequent events of abuse and extralegal violence, state institutions set the conditions for the strengthening of Salvadoran gang networks. Gang identities and collective norms, facilitated by the influx of migration, were also instrumental to creating national cohesion among a really mixed bag of cliques and local groups. But the definite opportunity was created by state policy. The massive jailing of hundreds of gang members provided them with the opportunity to reorganize, elect leaders, and seek support from other violent groups and organizations. The increasing rapprochement of Salvadoran maras with big-league drug cartels is better understood under the light of this all-out war between state institutions and youth gangs (Aguilar and Carranza 2008). Unfortunately, the zero-tolerance crackdowns, which became very popular in Central America during the mid-2000s, set in motion a series of events that are still unfolding, even when the *mano dura* policies no longer exist.

THE VIOLENCE OF SALVADORAN *MARAS*

Young people, whether gang members or not, endure high levels of violence in El Salvador. A report from the same forensic institute mentioned previously reveals that 41 percent of murders in 2006 were perpetrated against young people aged ten to twenty-four years old.[8] Nevertheless, violent behavior takes a significant toll on gangs. A survey conducted with more than one thousand gang members in the metropolitan area of San Salvador showed that 70 percent of gang members in 1996 had lost at least one close friend or relative as a consequence of violence (Cruz and Portillo Peña 1998). The survey also revealed that nearly 52 percent of gang members had needed medical attention after being assaulted by other people. Santacruz and Concha-Eastman (2001) found that violent behavior usually brought with it high rates of victimization among gang members.

As gangs have institutionalized in El Salvador, the violence they have used has increased and turned more complex and organized. Before the transformation of gangs in the early 1990s, the *maras* criminal activities could be described as mugging, pickpocketing, shoplifting, brawling, and other rather low-level felonies. Occasionally, they would engage in deadly assaults, rapes, and robberies. Drug consumption was limited to marijuana, and early gangs used industrial glue as an inhalant to get high. Cocaine and other hard drugs were not mentioned in early studies (Argueta et al. 1992). Since the mid-1990s, gangs have become involved in more serious types of crimes. Research reports (Cruz and Portillo Peña 1998; Santacruz and Cruz 2001; Smutt and Miranda 1998) usually pointed out that gangs were involved in murders, rapes, assaults, and robberies; some of the cliques started collaborating with organized crime cartels in drug trafficking and began to consume hard drugs and use firearms more regularly. Santacruz and Concha-Eastman (2001), for example, reported that 40 percent of gang members in San Salvador were using drugs such as crack and cocaine; the same study revealed that youth gangs had easy access to firearms: 46.3 percent of male gang members had handguns, 21 percent had "homemade" guns, and 11.6 percent had grenades.

The *mano dura* blow seemed to have moved youth gangs toward a more organized type of violence, but criminalization of gang activities has led to even more difficulties in collecting data and researching gang life in El Salvador. Some recent research based on interviews carried out with gang members in prisons (Aguilar and Carranza 2008) or based on government intelligence (USAID 2006) points out that *maras* are increasingly engaging in racketeering and extortion activities against business owners and bus drivers in major cities. In fact, according to the police, 57 percent of the 1,427 arrests under the charge of extortion in 2006 were carried out against gang members; by 2009, that figure had climbed to 70 percent (Iraheta 2009). Gangs are also participating in hit-man activities and collaborating with cartels of organized crime and drug trafficking. According to the survey conducted among gang members in prisons in 2006, 27 percent of gang members who said that they had collaborated with organized crime cartels had also worked as hit men, 21 percent had smuggled arms into the country, and 17 percent had participated in carjacking (Aguilar and Carranza 2008).

Although government officials claim that youth gangs are taking over drug trafficking corridors in Central America and controlling organized crime cartels (USAID 2006), and there are some reports of contact between the Mexican cartels and the national gang leadership, the evidence is still rather weak and suggests that although some cliques might be fighting over the control of drug markets and collaborating with some drug-trafficking structures, others remain clearly separated from organized crime structures (Aguilar and Carranza 2008; Martinez and Valencia 2011). By 2010, there were even some indications that cliques are turning more autonomous from the franchise guidelines generated from the prisons, and they were going back to pursue their own particular economic interests in the neighborhood they control (M. Santacruz Giralt, pers. comm., April 13, 2009). In any case, these developments suggest that Salvadoran *maras* have a dynamic of their own, not necessarily following the patterns established by drug-trafficking organizations in the region.

In sum, violence is embedded in youth gang activities in El Salvador. The range and magnitude of violence and criminal activities have changed and have become more and more severe over time. Violence, whether perpetrated by the same gangs or perpetrated by the state, has transformed the *maras* and has contributed to their transformation in El Salvador and Central America.

CONCLUSION

Youth gangs in El Salvador are the result of complex mechanisms of marginalization and violence. Widespread poverty, inequality, and social exclusion provided the breeding ground for the emergence of groups of young men and women searching for identity and respect. They found them in the streets mingled with imported gang culture from Southern California. Such culture not only provided patterns of behavior, but also granted norms and values that reconfigured the gang phenomenon. In the 1990s, Mara Salvatrucha and the Salvadoran Eighteenth Street Gang took over the streets by assimilation, not by warfare. Nevertheless, since then, gang identity has been constructed through the use of violence, and local conditions, such as institutional weakness, availability of firearms, and relentless marginalization, have fueled the universal warfare between the two major gangs. The *mano dura* law only exacerbated gang violence. It institutionalized the state's use of violence against youths and provided the *maras* with the opportunity to organize, unite their cliques, and develop regional and national leaderships. In addition, the all-out war against gangs brought in new violent actors, more resources, and fresh motifs to the maelstrom of Salvadoran violence.

NOTES

1. There is a lot of misinformation regarding the origins of the term *maras* to label the Salvadoran youth gangs. For an explanation of the origins of the term, see Cruz (2010).

2. However, as early as 1996, some gang members in El Salvador, who had joined the gang in the United States, were complaining that Salvadoran gangs using not only the same name but also the same clique name would not follow the same norms as observed in Southern California. They described local gangs as *más locos* (crazier) and as more "on the loose" than they were in the United States (Cruz and Portillo Peña 1998; Santacruz and Cruz 2001).

3. For a comprehensive treatment of this topic, see Cruz (2007a).

4. See Hagedorn (2008) for a discussion about the importance of ethnicity in the United States, Brazil, and South Africa.

5. However, it is interesting to note that Mara Salvatrucha members usually claimed that Eighteenth Street gang members were traitors to their country because they swore allegiance to a "Mexican" gang (Cruz and Portillo Peña

1998). This charge, nonetheless, has to be understood as part of the gang warfare between Barrio 18 and MS-13. In any case, both gangs have also thrived among Guatemalans and Hondurans living in their own countries.

6. Rodgers (2008) found a similar pattern in Nicaraguan youth gangs.

7. In 2001, a prison policy was implemented that separated gang members by their gang identity to prevent outbreaks of violence inside the prisons. In practice, this has led to certain jails being known as Mara Salvatrucha prisons and others as Eighteenth Street jails; see Valencia (2009).

8. The report can be found at http://www.ocavi.com/docs_files/file_397.pdf.

REFERENCES

Aguilar, Jeannette. 2004. "La mano dura y las 'políticas' de seguridad." *Estudios Centroamericanos* 667:439–50.

———. 2007. *Pandillas juveniles transnacionales en Centroamérica, México y Estados Unidos.* San Salvador: Diagnóstico de El Salvador.

Aguilar, Jeannette, and Marlon Carranza. 2008. "Las maras y pandillas como actores ilegales de la región." In *Ponencia preparada para el Informe Estado de la Región 2008.* San José: Programa Estado de la Nación/Región.

Aguilar, Jeannette, and Lissette Miranda. 2006. "Entre la articulación y la competencia: las respuestas de la sociedad civil organizada a las pandillas en El Salvador." In *Maras y pandillas en Centroamerica. Las respuestas de la sociedad civil organizada,* edited by J. M. Cruz, 37–143. San Salvador: UCA.

Argueta, Sandra, Suyapa Caminos, Margarita Mancía, and María de los Angeles Salgado. 1992. "Diagnóstico de los grupos llamados 'maras' en San Salvador. Factores psicosociales en los jóvenes que los integran." *Revista de Psicología de El Salvador* 11, no. 43: 53–84.

Carranza, Marlon. 2005. "Detención o muerte: hacia dónde van los niños pandilleros en El Salvador." In *Ni guerra ni paz. Comparaciones internacionales de niños y jóvenes en violencia armada organizada,* edited by L. Dowdney, 187–205. Rio de Janeiro: Viveiros de Castro.

Cruz, José Miguel. 2007a. "El barrio transnacional: las maras centroamericanas como red." In *Redes transnacionales en la Cuenca de los Huracanes,* edited by F. Pisani, N. Saltalamacchia, A. B. Tickner, and N. Barnes, 357–81. Mexico, D.F.: Miguel Angel Porrúa.

———. 2007b. "Factors Associated with Juvenile Gangs in Central America." In *Street Gangs in Central America,* edited by J. M. Cruz, 13–65. San Salvador: UCA.

———. 2010. "Central American Maras: From Youth Gangs to Transnational Protection Rackets." *Global Crime* 11, no. 4: 379–98.

———. 2011. "Government Responses and the Dark Side of Suppression of Gangs in Central America." In *Maras Gang Violence and Security in Central America,* edited by T. C. Bruneau, L. Dammert, and E. Skinner, 137–57. Austin: University of Texas Press.

Cruz, José Miguel, and Marlon Carranza. 2006. "Pandillas y políticas públicas. El caso de El Salvador." In *Juventudes, violencia y exclusión: Desafíos para las políticas públicas,* edited by J. Moro, 133–76. Guatemala City: MagnaTerra.

Cruz, José Miguel, Marlon Carranza, and María Santacruz. 2004. "El Salvador: Espacios públicos, confianza interpersonal y pandillas." In *Maras y pandillas en Centroamérica: Pandillas y capital social,* edited by ERIC, IDESO, IDIES, and IUDOP, 81–114. San Salvador: UCA.

Cruz, José Miguel, Rafael Fernández de Castro, and Gema Santamaría. 2012. "Political Transition, Social Violence, and Gangs: Cases in Central America and Mexico." In *In the Wake of War: Democratization and Internal Armed Conflict in Latin America,* edited by C. Arnson, 317–49. Washington, D.C.: Woodrow Wilson Center Press and Stanford University Press.

Cruz, José Miguel, and Nelson Portillo Peña. 1998. *Solidaridad y violencia en las pandillas del gran San Salvador. Más allá de la vida loca.* San Salvador: UCA.

Decker, Scott H. 1996. "Collective and Normative Features of Gang Violence." *Justice Quarterly* 13, no. 2: 243–64.

Decker, Scott H., Tim Bynum, and Deborah Weisel. 1998. "A Tale of Two Cities: Gangs as Organized Crime Groups." *Justice Quarterly* 15, no. 3: 395–425.

Decker, Scott H., and Barrik Van Winkle. 1996. *Life in the Gang: Family, Friends, and Violence.* Cambridge: Cambridge University Press.

Demoscopía. 2007. *Maras y pandillas. Comunidad y policía en Centroamérica. Hallazgos de un estudio integral.* Guatemala City: Agencia Sueca de Cooperación Internacional para el Desarrollo.

ERIC, IDESO, IDIES, and IUDOP. 2001. *Maras y pandillas en Centroamerica.* Managua: UCA.

Hagedorn, John. 1988. *People and Folks: Gangs, Crime, and the Underclass in a Rustbelt City.* Chicago: Lake View Press.

———. 2008. *A World of Gangs: Armed Young Men and Gangsta Culture.* Minneapolis: University of Minnesota Press.

Hume, Mo. 2007. "Mano Dura: El Salvador Responds to Gangs." *Development in Practice* 17, no. 6: 739–51.

Iraheta, Oscar. 2009. "El setenta por ciento de las extorsiones son cometidas por maras." *El Diario de Hoy,* August 19.

La Prensa Gráfica. 1990. "Denuncian el grave daño causado por 'mara gallo.'" March 2.

Martinez, Carlos, and Roberto Valencia. 2011. "Hay pandilleros que hasta dan tumbes de droga en altamar a narcotraficantes locales." *El Faro,* April 24.

Moore, Joan W. 1991. *Going Down to the Barrio: Homeboys and Homegirls in Change.* Philadelphia: Temple University Press.

PNUD. 2003. *Informe sobre Desarrollo Humano, El Salvador 2003. Desafíos y opciones en tiempos de globalización*. San Salvador: Programa de las Naciones Unidas para el Desarrollo.

Rodgers, Dennis. 2006. "Living in the Shadow of Death: Gangs, Violence, and Social Order in Nicaragua, 1996–2002." *Journal of Latin American Studies* 38:267–92.

———. 2008. "A Symptom Called Managua." *New Left Review* 49:103–20.

San Francisco Chronicle. 1989. "U.S. Ousting More Gang Members." April 12.

Santacruz, María, and Alberto Concha-Eastman. 2001. *Barrio adentro. La solidaridad violenta de las pandillas*. San Salvador: IUDOP-UCA/OPS-OMS.

Santacruz, María, and José Miguel Cruz. 2001. "Las maras en El Salvador." In *Maras y pandillas en Centroamérica*, edited by ERIC, IDIES, and IUDOP, 17–107. Managua: UCA.

Santacruz-Giralt, Maria, and Elin Ranum. 2010. *"Seconds in the Air:" Woman Gang Members and Their Prisons*. San Salvador: UCA.

Sassen, Saskia. 2007. "The Global City: One Setting for New Types of Gang Work and Political Culture." In *Gangs in the Global City: Alternatives to Traditional Criminology*, edited by J. Hagedorn, 97–119. Urbana: University of Illinois Press.

Savenije, Wim, and Katherine Andrade-Eekhoff. 2003. *Conviviendo en la orilla. Violencia y exclusión social en el Area Metropolitana de San Salvador*. San Salvador: FLACSO Programa El Salvador.

Savenije, Wim, and Chris van der Borgh. 2006. "Youth Gangs, Social Exclusion, and the Transformation of Violence in El Salvador." In *Armed Actors: Organised Violence and State Failure in Latin America*, edited by K. Koonings and D. Kruijt, 155–71. New York: Zed Books.

Sisti, Elvio. 1996. *Violencia juvenil en El Salvador: una perspectiva psicosocial*. Unpublished manuscript. San Salvador.

Smutt, Marcela, and Lissette Miranda. 1998. *El fenómeno de las pandillas en El Salvador*. San Salvador: UNICEF/FLACSO Programa El Salvador.

Thale, Geoff, and Elsa Falkenburger. 2006. *Youth Gangs in Central America: Issues on Human Rights, Effective Policing, and Prevention*. Washington, D.C.: Washington Office on Latin America.

Tilly, Charles. 2003. *The Politics of Collective Violence*. Cambridge: Cambridge University Press.

Tutela Legal del Arzobispado. 2007. *La violencia homicida y otros patrones de grave afectación a los derechos humanos en El Salvador 2006*. San Salvador: Comisión Arquidiocesana de Justicia y Paz.

———. 2008. *La violencia homicida y otros patrones de grave afectación a los derechos humanos en El Salvador 2007*. San Salvador: Comisión Arquidiocesana de Justicia y Paz.

United Nations Office on Drugs and Crime. 2007. *Crime and Development in Central America: Caught in the Crossfire*. New York: United Nations Publications.

USAID. 2006. *Central America and Mexico Gang Assessment.* Washington, D.C.: USAID.

Valencia, Daniel. 2009. "Los alegatos de Frankenstein." *El Faro,* April 13.

Vigil, James Diego. 1988. *Barrio Gangs: Street Life and Identity in Southern California.* Austin: University of Texas Press.

———. 2002. *A Rainbow of Gangs: Street Culture in the Mega-City.* Austin: University of Texas Press.

Zilberg, Elana. 2004. "Fools Banished from the Kingdom: Remapping Geographies of Violence between the Americas (Los Angeles and San Salvador)." *American Quarterly* 56:759–79.

PART II. PROBLEMATIZING GANGS

7

Youth Gangs and Otherwise in Indonesia

LOREN RYTER

In December 2008, Japto Soerjosoemarno, until today the unchallenged leader of Pemuda Pancasila, or Pancasila Youth,[1] by all accounts the most powerful youth gang in Indonesia during the last decades of Su-harto's rule, denied that his youth gang had ever existed (pers. comm., December 23, 2008).[2] The reason for his denial, and the outright mendacity of it, says much about the nature of youth gangs in Indonesia. It illustrates the degree to which youth gangs learned to thrive as long as they sought formality and recognition and transformed themselves—or, more precisely, insisted on perpetual efforts to transform themselves—from amalgamations of toughs into innocuous associations of noble purpose, usually but not always nationalist.

The Siliwangi Boys Club (SBC), the 1960s "gang" whose existence Japto denied, was *not* Pancasila Youth but rather one of its precursors. I'll return to the SBC shortly, but first I must introduce Pancasila Youth, the "gang" for which he was most famous. Though popularly understood as a gang, Pancasila Youth was officially not a gang at all but rather a state-recognized youth group, one among dozens of members of the Indonesian National Youth Council. Japto, born in 1949, assumed the national leadership of Pancasila Youth in 1981 at the age of thirty-one. To allow Japto to retain the top post well into his fifties, sometime after the resignation of Suharto in 1998, the youth group altered its legal status to become a social organization, thereby bypassing Pancasila Youth's leadership age cap of fifty-five. I raise this to underscore that any definition of youth gangs that caps membership at twenty-five is not applicable in Indonesia, and with that restriction, there would be no "youth gangs" at all. The category of "youth" *(pemuda)* in fact is understood in Indonesia in terms other than demographic, which I also discuss further later.

From the 1980s through the 1990s, Pancasila Youth became the most prominent of several state-sanctioned youth groups who enjoyed virtual impunity from prosecution for running gambling, prostitution, drug distribution, and protection rackets; for extortion (primarily of wealthy ethnic Chinese); and for general thuggery in exchange for service as militant supporters of the Suharto regime and as personal bodyguards of Suharto's family and political and business cronies. Crudely put, they served as the regime's "brown shirts." During election campaigns and on patriotic holidays, they were mobilized by the tens of thousands for rallies and parades. At such rallies, they wore orange and black camouflage uniforms, which were meant both to announce an affinity with the army and visibly index the bravado of wild game hunting (Figure 7.1).[3] Nominally acting spontaneously out of a perfected sense of national allegiance, they intimidated regime critics, such as nongovernmental organization activists and students; accused them of treason; broke up protests; and occasionally abducted and tortured them.

Like mafias elsewhere, they were frequently employed by industrialists as strike-breakers against labor agitation, with the added value that as loyalists of the anti-Communist regime, they could also accuse labor organizers of Communism and thus treason. Therefore, the threat that they brought to bear was not only of physical violence but of the full force of law of an authoritarian state. Employed also by politically connected property developers, its local leaders made out like bandits by evicting residents who resisted the displacement required for the transformation of urban centers such as Jakarta into modern metropolises. Like those against labor organizers, threats against recalcitrant residents and squatters also carried the ring of treason, insofar as to obstruct so-called development, the regime's raison d'être, was trumpeted as tantamount to betraying the nation. They thus developed a concrete interest in the "concrete," with large numbers of local leaders founding local contracting companies and turning to their members for labor supply.[4] National membership estimates from the late 1990s ranged from four to ten million members, which would have put its

Figure 7.1. Pemuda Pancasila members at a Jakarta demonstration, 1998. Photograph by the author.

membership at nearly 4 percent of the total Indonesian population.[5] While most of the rank and file were youngsters under twenty-five and mostly without means, leaders at all levels were considerably older, and given the lucrative potential of the rackets, they generally desired to hold on to top positions as long as possible. For the most part, leaders rose through the ranks, making Pancasila Youth an effective vehicle of upward mobility for the poor and unconnected.

The "gang" Japto denied existing was something closer to what we might think of as a real gang, a group of army brats who called themselves the SBC, after the Siliwangi Army Division officer's barracks where most of them resided. The SBC was from the late 1950s into the 1970s arguably the most feared of the youth gangs of Jakarta. Japto's father was a general, while most of the other members of SBC were sons of middle-ranking officers. Its members had a reputation for packing pistols borrowed from their fathers, unlike members of other gangs, whose access to firearms was more limited or entirely lacking. Japto himself earned a reputation for violence with impunity after facing no charges for the murder of a rival in 1963, when he was but an adolescent. Although it was actually one of his buddies who shot the boy, Japto earned the street cred (U. Lumbanradja, pers. comm., May 27, 1998).[6]

SBC members were HAM radio enthusiasts and communicated with each other on military shortwave radio. Its members all smoked unfiltered and thus macho Ji Sam Soe clove cigarettes. *Ji sam soe* is Chinese for "2–3–4," so the club was also known as 234-SC, the 234 Siliwangi Club. Even as Pancasila Youth expanded into a national organization with millions of members later, 234-SC was retained as a designation of Japto's inner circle, the SC becoming glossed as Soerjosoemarno Clan rather than Siliwangi Club. A 234-SC window decal affixed to one's car or home window became a feared, protective amulet in much the same way as a Special Forces decal was.

SBC's chief rival, the Berenlan (Bearland) Boys, was housed in a former Dutch colonial army barracks for noncommissioned officers and enlisted men located across town. Other rival gangs of the era in Jakarta included the Selendang (Shawl) Boys, Marabunta, Tarantula, and LEGOS, an acronym for Lelaki Goyang Senggol, which can loosely be translated as "Don't You Dare Bump Into Us Guys." While these other gangs were not based around army barracks, it was common for their leaders to be either sons of officers or bureaucrats. Those who were not were eventually drawn into associations of senior army or intelligence officers.[7] Members of these gangs took to the streets as auxiliaries to student activists (if they were not also students themselves) in the demonstrations that ousted Sukarno, purged the Indonesian Communist Party (PKI), and brought Soeharto to power after 1965. In the freewheeling years that followed, these gang members, now older, hung out at a number of new nightclubs and steam baths established in several districts of town, often graduating from simply drinking and whoring for free (owing to their imposing reputations and obnoxious behavior) to gaining employment in club security, and sometimes later securing an ownership stake in the clubs themselves.[8]

According to Japto, in 2008, however, there was never such a thing as the SBC. What there was, he said, was the Indonesian Siliwangi Youngsters Association. "It was just local to the barracks. We played sports, soccer, volleyball, and badminton. We held birthday parties," he told me. The acronym he used—IPPSI (Ikatan Pemuda-Pemudi Siliwangi Indonesia)—is counterfactually gender inclusive, turns the group into a formal association rather than a gang, and appends the de rigueur national modifier to this highly localized group. Japto was only anachronistically formalizing his fraternal association in the manner that all had become accustomed to do after the formalization of street gangs into youth groups beginning in the 1980s. It seemed to matter little how unbelievable the claim actually was.

What is even more striking about his denial is the fact that, earlier in the same year that he issued this denial, he and two of his sons formerly resurrected 234-SC, now calling it the 234 Solidarity Community. According to its founding statement posted on multiple web forums in 2008,[9]

> History recounts that in the beginning 234SC was a special community, an abbreviation of the 234 SILIWANGI CLUB, and an abbreviation of the 234 SOERJOESOEMARNO CLAN with membership limited to the family and close associates of the HONORABLE FATHER UNCLE NOBLE JAPTO S.S. [It has now been expanded] by the sons of the HONORABLE FATHER UNCLE NOBLE JAPTO S.S., that is the HONORABLE NOBLE ABI SHALOM S.S. and the HONORABLE NOBLE YEDIDIAH S.S.
>
> 234SC possesses wide wings and is well-known/regarded [which] gave rise to an interest among many people to join.... Upon this basis, the high leaders of 234SC have opened it up to the public, [and have changed its abbreviation to] the 234 SOLIDARITY COMMUNITY. 234SC aims to unite all youth ... to make them feel a part of the family and possess a high level of solidarity.
>
> The Chief instructs: "IF ONE OF OUR FRIENDS IS PINCHED, WE ALL FEEL PINCHED AND WE MUST RETALIATE AGAINST ANYONE WHO HAS PINCHED OUR FRIEND. WE CAN'T DISTURB OR TROUBLE OTHER PEOPLE. IF THEY'RE SELLING, WE NEGOTIATE IN GOOD FAITH. IF THEY PUSH FOR TOO MUCH, WE TAKE IT ALL."
>
> At its core, the activities of 234SC involve doing good things, guarding smooth relations *(silaturahmi)* & tightening the unity of the youngsters of the Indonesian nation. VIVA 234SC!

This mission statement describes characteristics we would associate with a gang or mafia: the kinship of an extended family, a code of honor, a community founded on mutual protection, an assertion of bravado expressed in the final right of seizure. But this is no secret society; it is a formal mission statement of a public organization with an imagined national scope. And although it refers to youngsters, anecdotal evidence of its gatherings and public relations suggests that the ages of its members vary widely. Indeed, their public gatherings resemble, more than anything else, auto enthusiasts' rallies. According to one of Japto's chauffeurs, they meet in Jakarta's Senayan Stadium parking lot, where thousands of members turn up to show off their sporty, souped-up cars.[10] On the Web, members are moderators of the leading Indonesian auto modification enthusiast websites. One gets the impression that the membership of 234-SC comprises both established wheelers-and-dealers in or beyond middle age, many nostalgic about their own youth days in the 1950s and 1960s, and their children, attracted by the tales of bravado of their fathers.

The younger generation seems to be attracted to this revitalized 234-SC out of a sense that there is something they missed out on. More than ten years after the fall of Soeharto (1998), Pancasila Youth and the other youth groups that supported the regime but fought among themselves for turf no longer enjoy the untouchable status that they had previously. With growing competition from new organizations, often based on religion and ethnicity, and in many cases with their former membership dispersed among these newcomers, they no longer command the streets. Furthermore, many of their leaders have since turned to the formal political system, running for and winning seats in now more assertive national, provincial, and municipal parliaments or else seeking executive office in local administrations. Japto himself founded the Patriot Party, which, despite efforts to compel Pancasila Youth members to support it, failed to cross a 2 percent electoral threshold in 2009 and therefore to gain a single seat in the national parliament. (Pancasila Youth leaders, however, did exceptionally well in 2004 and 2009 as candidates for the major parties.)

Why the need for this quasi-gang at all? The reformation of 234-SC can be seen in this context as a way for Japto to build support for his political party, and hence as yet another example of the tendency to mobilize gangs in politics. From another perspective, however, this reawakening indexes a profound dissatisfaction with the politicization of gangs and heralds a desire for a return of the days when gangs were gangs, or at least seemed to be. To explain how Indonesian gangs arrived at this point, we now turn to a narrative of the vicissitudes of criminality and authority from the late Dutch colonial era to the present.

COLONIALISM THROUGH REVOLUTION

As European manpower in the Netherlands East Indies was never suf-
ficient for direct rule, the late colonial administration relied on local
authorities to keep the natives in line (Onghokham 1978, 1984). In each
administrative region, a Dutch resident supervised a native regent, who
in turn subcontracted coercion to a network of local strong men, known
as *jago,* or literally, "cocks."[11] Legality was barely an afterthought in this
arrangement, as the *jago* was allowed to skim off the top of extraction
and frequently engage in banditry, rustling, and the like, usually as long
as he limited his plunders to neighboring villages. Some such *jagos* were
inducted into the ranks of the native police force belatedly introduced at
the turn of the twentieth century. By the 1920s, as the first stirrings of a
nationalist movement were beginning to be felt, the Dutch, through the
regents, relied on the *jagos* as spies and informants. However, their loyalties fell into doubt, as many harbored sympathies or even joined forces
with nationalist groups. The Dutch turned to Eurasians, their bastard
offspring whose privileged status was threatened by assertive natives, as
thugs to intimidate and assault the nationalists. These squads constitute
an early example of toughs organized for extralegal violence who adopted harrowing names meant to advertise their capacity to menace.[12] That
is to say, they were the first of what we would now recognize as gangs.

During its wartime occupation, Japan organized a number of paramilitary units comprising young men to help fend off the anticipated
Allied counterassault. At this time, the idea of "youth," or *pemuda,*
as a politically conscious social force crystallized (Anderson 1972).
Because these *pemuda* fought the returning Dutch, they later became
lionized as the heroes of the revolution in the nationalist imaginary.
The category of "youth" thus came to be understood, and primarily defined, in terms of a martial or revolutionary spirit. Those who had been
pemuda in 1945 remained so until old age; those who later proclaimed
an uncompromising nationalist affinity, regardless of their age, would
be recognized as *pemuda.*

Meanwhile, the revolution also cemented a certain marriage between
national heroism and personal opportunism. The formal Republican
Army comprised former Royal Dutch Army officers and some units of
the Japanese-formed paramilitary youth groups. Alongside the Republican Army, spontaneously organized militias that would collectively

become known as *lasykars* routinely engaged the Dutch throughout Indonesia. In most cases, these *lasykars* were organized by *jago* figures who recognized both the changing tide and new opportunities. In addition, some of the youths who had received Japanese paramilitary training joined *lasykar* bands rather than the formal army. The *lasykars* were known for their daring and became experts in raiding and expropriating Dutch stocks of munitions and supplies and in confiscating property and assets. Generally the *lasykars* were responsible for raising funds to support their subsistence, which meant, of course, extortion and looting (Cribb 1991; Stoler 1988).

After national independence was secured in 1949, rationalizing the army presented a considerable challenge to officers. Many *lasykar* leaders understandably expected to be regularized rather than demobilized (Horikoshi 1975). Some of those who could not be retained, lacking in other opportunities, turned to professions in accordance with their experience: smuggling and robbery. Lieutenant Colonel Imam Syafe'i, for example, became the boss of a gang of pickpockets at the Senen market in Jakarta, before being appointed as special minister of security by Sukarno in 1966. Army officers maintained sympathetic relations with such figures, seeing them as erstwhile revolutionary comrades and also as potentially useful contacts. As one army colonel lamented in his memoirs (Surbakti 1997, 216–17),

Theoretically . . . a new nation which wants to be modern needs a . . . professional army. But people shouldn't forget that for the Indonesian Republic born of revolution, the armed *pemuda* fronts were the blood and bones that defended the [republic], not consisting only of clever, educated, well-built, and athletic people . . . but of those from "all kinds" of backgrounds. . . . The consequences of rationalization for the armed forces . . . produced restlessness. A large number of honorably "discharged" fighters became bands of robbers. . . . They caused disturbances because . . . they had been used and discarded. . . . We'll never know what the cost of "wiping them out" was, but it's certainly large.

GANGS ON THE MARGINS IN SUKARNO'S INDONESIA: 1949–1966

Youth groups that we would recognize as gangs began to form in the 1950s in many urban locations in Indonesia.[13] In Medan, Indonesia's second largest city, the emergence of gangs was linked to the dynamics of demobilization described previously, but in the wake of a failed regional rebellion. One of the sources of conflict between the outer-island military commanders and Jakarta during the 1950s was that the former insisted on compensating for shortages in Jakarta's support by operating smuggling networks, thus withholding trade revenues from Jakarta. In an effort to retain the loyalty of his "restive officers" by distributing ever larger sums of money to them, Colonel Simbolon, the commander of the First Territorial Command based in Medan, expanded his barter trade in rubber between North Sumatra and Singapore until it led to open rebellion, which the central government put down in 1956 (Kahin and Kahin 1995, 54–61; Lev 1964, 20).

The aftermath of Colonel Simbolon's defiance marks an important shift for *pemuda* in Medan because it signaled the end of direct military mobilization, but not the end of mobile *pemuda*. Around this time, a new use of an older term became popular to describe these young men who inhabited a liminal space between the martial and the civil and between the criminal and the legal. Gradually, the term *preman*, today understood as "gangster," began to displace the term *pemuda*, as the latter became increasingly an historical category and as the structures of legality and authority became progressively established in the consolidating state. Luckman Sinar, a prominent historian of Medan, explained (pers. comm., October 14, 1998),

> *Preman* came to Medan in the 1950s with the backing of military commanders who were also largely Bataks. In 1956, Simbolon had recruited and armed them all. They were badly trained, and were soon finished off by Republican forces. . . . For a while, Medan was devoid of *preman*. But by the end of the 50s, they were back in force. They squatted Malay land. In the city they hung out at *warung* [roadside stalls] and became scalpers at the movie theaters. They frequently fought each other. . . . By the end of the 1950s, each alley had its *preman*.

Luckman's explanation does not precisely locate the emergence of *preman*. *Preman* are at once synonymous with the *pemuda* loyalists Simbolon brought with him in his retreat and with the migrants who followed his forces back into Medan after the failed campaign. Moving out of Medan, then, they were simultaneously *pemuda* and *preman*, but moving into Medan after Jakarta's assertion of authority, they were only *preman*.

The semantic vicissitudes of the term *preman*, its derivation from the Dutch term *vrijman* or "free man," and the particular subjectivity it consequently implies are crucial to an understanding of the ambiguity between criminality and the state. First, *preman* refers to an official, usually a soldier, who is off-duty or in his civvies. This highlights the ambiguity between civilians and soldiers for the postrevolutionary *pemuda* discussed earlier, as if neither is a stable category but distinguished merely by a state of attire. Second, *preman* establishes a notion of freedom that is always bound to authority—the term *preman* can be said to refer to youths who don't want to be bound to any dependencies, including a job or a contract. Yet this perceived independence is illusory insofar as *preman* must exist within a wider field of power. Third, as a result of this semi-officialdom and bounded freedom, *preman* stood at and for the margins of the law and therefore also on the edge of criminality.

By the end of the 1950s, *preman* carved out turf around town. Lacking capital—one might say other than their labor power—they established themselves as brokers between suppliers and buyers, relying on their commanding statures to monopolize these positions in particular areas even when they added little value to exchange. They also began to congregate around the movie theaters, performing a similar service in brokerage between the box office and moviegoers, acquiring tickets and selling them at marked-up rates, as is further elaborated later. Municipal authorities saw these activities as a criminal problem.[14]

Groups of *preman* were not at the time referred to as gangs, even though the term was available in Dutch in a more immediate way than in English. Modern Dutch still uses the word *gang* to mean an alley or street, as it did in archaic English, and Indonesian continues to use the word *gang* to refer to a narrow alley. But the term used for gangsters at the time, *crossboys* (in English), still refers to street corners and the boys who hung out at them. However odd the term may be, the fact that English terms like *boys* are used says much about the character of the gangs at the time. They self-consciously looked toward American culture, especially rock 'n' roll and cowboy and adventure films, for their styles and identities. Members tended to be admirers of James Dean, Errol Flynn, Clarke Gable, Elvis Presley, and, later, the Beatles. Medan's youth gangs of the era included the Warlocks, the Attila Boys, the Mongol Boys, and the Apache Boys. Members of these gangs were relatively quaint by today's standards, sporting leather jackets and slicked-back hair, straight out of *West Side Story* or *Blackboard Jungle.* Such youth gangs were often also called *pemuda roman,* or "romantic youth."

Their attraction to American film, in combination with the choice of occupation that was a natural outgrowth it, namely, scalping tickets, was highly significant to political and ideological developments from the late 1950s through the 1960s and ultimately to their being drawn back into the orbit of the army and coming to resemble their later shape. As Sukarno turned leftward, he promoted a cultural campaign against neocolonial culture, lambasting rock 'n' roll as unintelligible noise threatening the cultural identity of the young generation.[15] In 1964, he declared a ban on the distribution of American films. This ban offended the sense of liberty of gangs in Medan and cut into their livelihood, as theater attendance dropped dramatically.

Meanwhile, Sukarno's 1959 proclamation of Guided Democracy, which emasculated the parliament, meant that the political parties could no longer survive through electoralism but required mass mobilization. For bodies, the parties turned to gang leaders who commanded followings on the street. The North Sumatra branch of an army party (IPKI), led nationally by General Nasution, the CIA's then-favored potential coup-maker against Sukarno, turned to the *preman* who controlled the movie theaters for mass support. The leader of this group, Effendi Nasution (no relation to the general), had since 1958 succeeded in unifying most of the gangs mentioned previously into the Medan City Youth Association (P2KM), which conducted night patrols in ethnic Chinese neighborhoods and thus operated as a protection racket. IPKI's North Sumatra headquarters was located directly across the street from the Medan Theater, and the local party chairman offered Effendi and his boys in P2KM the use of IPKI's office facilities. In 1962, Effendi's inauguration as the head of the Medan branch of Pemuda Pancasila, IPKI's youth wing, was attended by a representative from the governor's office and an army major representing the Sumatra military command (Nasution n.d., 195).[16]

Meanwhile, the Communists recruited a gang of the sons of Javanese railway workers into their youth wing, the People's Youth. This gang of Effendi's rivals had already made failed forays into ticket-scalping turf, so at the time Sukarno issued the ban on Western films, they enthusiastically took to the streets in support of the ban as a way to snub their dominant rivals. Ultimately this portended their demise. For when Soeharto assumed emergency powers after the so-called failed Communist coup of 1965, Effendi Nasution and his Pancasila Youth retaliated with a vengeance, becoming some of the most willing executioners in the purge against suspected Communists in North Sumatra.

Because of the viciousness of these purges (by many estimates, one million people were killed throughout Indonesia), these developments left Pemuda Pancasila and other youth groups who supported Soeharto and the army against Sukarno in a dominant position in Medan after 1966, with a great ability to take over all manner of rackets. In Jakarta, where Communists were more often jailed or had their assets expropriated rather than murdered, the various gangs who took to the streets for Soeharto felt equally entitled but were more disorganized. Most often they returned to their original gangs, confident that Soeharto's pro-Western alignment would mean an end to the sorts of cultural assaults of previous years. It would not be until the 1980s, after a period of experimentation in criminality on the part of the new regime, that the coalescence of youth gangs into official youth organizations would finally occur, with Pemuda Pancasila becoming a formidable national force for the first time, under the leadership of Japto S.S.

EXPERIMENTS IN CRIMINALITY AND YOUTH: 1966–1983

As with the *jagos* in the *lasykar* militias after the revolution, the demobilization of the youth of the 1965 Generation presented certain challenges to the new regime.[17] The task became to separate the new-style *pemuda* from the lingering rabble-rousing student demonstrators of 1965–66, which in turn would set the stage both for the institutionalization of youth and for the various and varyingly successful efforts to integrate gangs into the state apparatus, which culminated in the Mysterious

Killings of criminals (1982–83) and thereafter in the rise of Pemuda Pancasila. The so-called resolution of student opposition to Soeharto's wife Tien's fantasy park project "Beautiful Indonesia"-in-Miniature at the end of 1971 represented a significant turning point in authorizing politically compliant "youth" (gangs) and criminalizing troublesome youth (students). Some youth and student groups continued to press for change into the 1970s, failing to realize that with Soeharto's assumption of power, their mission was already considered accomplished. Their criticism of the land evictions required for the construction of the Mini Park and of wasteful extravagance only made Tien Soeharto "all the more perfect in tackling the issue."[18]

Tien's "perfection" in tackling the problem found expression in the assault on demonstrators by members of the Berenlan gang. In December 1971, a group of long-haired boys confronted a number of youth demonstrators at the Miniature Project secretariat, which shared offices with Tien's Our Hope Foundation. When challenged, one said, "*Wah, here's a crossboy wants to make trouble, nih,*" pulling out a machete. Two demonstrators were stabbed, and one was shot in the thigh. The Berenlan Boys later claimed in court that they mistook the demonstrators for rivals from other gangs, including Siliwangi.[19] Thus army brats who happened to be gangsters passed as long-haired rowdy youths picking fights with "crossboys," who turned out to be demonstrators yet resembled rivals from another barracks. In this confused failure of recognition, the transformation of gangsters into youths and youths into delinquents was effected.

The "clash" between these "rival youths" precipitated efforts to regularize and authorize youths, refiguring opposition as wild elements and subordinating gangsters (already informally linked to the army through their parents or other patrons) to the intelligence apparatus by "dissolving them." In January 1972, KOPKAMTIB[20] General Soemitro issued an instruction dissolving and outlawing "groups and gangs of teen-youths" with the following considerations (*Bappenkar Jatim* 1972):

1. Recently especially in the large cities there have emerged groups of teen-youths calling themselves, *inter alia*, BERENLAAN GANG, GANG IC STRAAT, GANG SARTANA and so forth whose activities tend toward criminal acts, *inter alia*, fighting/battery/murder/

rape/extortion/illegal Narcotic Drug use and robbery, and im-
proper behavior.

2. Other than that it has been proven ... that these GANGS were used
   by the Anti-"Beautiful Indonesia"-in-Miniature Movements to
   incite riots, which resulted in many people wounded in inter-
   GANG fighting and then these victims were used as martyrs by
   the Anti-"Beautiful Indonesia"-in-Miniature Movements to stir
   up emotions and mass movements.

3. With this in mind, the growth and development of the lives of
   our teen-youths must be saved.

Although Tien had mobilized the Berenlan gang to attack opponents,[21] the instruction faults the demonstrators for organizing their own
attack with the intent of making themselves into martyrs, enunciating
a procedure later to become standard: speak of your own infiltrators
as your target's agitators. "Dissolution" of the gangs proceeded apace
with the formation of various units to tackle the newly defined youth
problem. The approach tended to focus on turning youths, on one hand,
into teens and, on the other, into political resources. Not to be outshone
by KOPKAMTIB, BAKIN[22] expanded a body established to control
smuggling, creating a subunit known as the Executive Body to Tackle
Narcotics and Child–Teen Delinquency.[23] In 1972, a solemn ceremony
took place at the Jakarta Provincial Council, where some two thousand
pemuda surrendered their "gang logos" and other parts of their "gang
outfits" to the district police chief and were given a chance to speak their
minds. A representative of one gang blamed gang members' parents:
"We are like newborn babies and are hurting because our parents don't
give us milk." Another "demanded" that they be given jobs. The BAKIN
subteam obliged, assembling the "former" heads of gangs for industrial
training as mechanics, establishing a pattern of access to *preman* followed by other army commanders.[24]

During the following decade, intelligence officials undertook a variety of efforts to institutionalize these former gangs and turn them into
patriotic, loyalist youths, some of them more successful than others.
In 1973, General Ali Moertopo of BAKIN promoted the establishment
of the Indonesian National Youth Council (KNPI). The intent of KNPI
was to detach political party youth wings from their parent parties and
thus depoliticize them. At the same time, he encouraged the formation

of a number of local "young generation" groups tied to army divisions, mostly throughout Java.[25] However, it seems to have been recognized that this juvenilization had its limits. So by the early 1980s, gangs of "recidivists" were being formally sponsored by senior officers and encouraged to run extortion rackets under formal banners. The most prominent of these was literally called "Prems," initially an acronym for "Aware *Preman*" that was later changed to the Project for Material and Spiritual Rehabilitation. Prems had office spaces in several cities and offered services in private security. During the 1982 elections, Moertopo mobilized Prems and the local army-attached "young generation" groups in various black ops to guarantee an overwhelming victory for the state party, Golkar.[26]

After the 1982 elections, the gangsters Moertopo had mobilized grew ever bolder. Bloated with a sense of importance, they openly boasted of their connections and demanded higher protection fees. Soeharto apparently not only considered that this situation had grown out of hand but also suspected Moertopo himself of intending to use his network of gangsters as a personal power base in a potential bid to challenge him. Therefore, in early 1983, the so-called Mysterious Killings campaign commenced, during which thousands of suspected criminals were shot by death squads, their mostly tattooed bodies left in the streets as an example. Most of the targets were the gangsters who had formed part of Moertopo's network, though the campaign was publicly about tackling "inhuman" criminality. Soeharto entrusted his new KOPKAMTIB chief, General Benny Moerdani, to organize these massacres, and Moertopo himself was pushed aside, soon passing away (Bourchier 1990; van der Kroef 1985).

THE RISE OF THE YOUTH SOCIAL ORGANIZATIONS: 1983–1998

Under Moertopo, the pattern of organization of the surviving gangsters into formal youth organizations became consolidated and would remain intact up through and beyond the end of the Soeharto regime in 1998. Up until the Mysterious Killings, the KNPI remained feckless, its constituent youth groups mostly the remnants of the youth wings of old parties that had been forced to consolidate. With the survivors of the Mysterious Killings fleeing to army-affiliated groups, KNPI grew to become a dominant and influential umbrella. In 1985, the youth groups were officially designated as Youth Social Organizations (OKP) in a further effort to disconnect them from any party affiliation and further depoliticize them. Under the new social organization law, they were all required to adopt Pancasila as their ideological foundation, which further disempowered religious, socialist, and nationalist youth groups. The "young generation" groups that Ali Moertopo (FKPPI) had organized joined either the Sons and Daughters of the Indonesian Armed Forces or the Indonesian Renewal Young Generation (AMPI), the official youth wing of Golkar. Later, Pemuda Panca Marga, or Veterans' Youth, would come to share dominance in KNPI with the others mentioned, including Pemuda Pancasila.

Pemuda Pancasila itself had begun its own revival in the years preceding the Mysterious Killings, with Japto Soerjosoemarno being invited in 1980 to resurrect the group by the old Pemuda Pancasila seniors from Medan. They saw in Japto a notorious street figure from the Siliwangi gang, the son of a general and related distantly to Soeharto's wife, Tien. Japto recruited a half-Chinese gambling boss and crocodile hunter from Papua named Yorrys Raweyai, and together they established Pemuda Pancasila branches throughout Indonesia. Jakarta police were initially suspicious of Japto, and they tried to arrest him on gun charges in 1981, when he was about to take over leadership. This illustrates that the process of formalizing gangsters into youth organizations of national scope did not occur merely at the initiative of the army. Leaders of the gangs took the initiative to gain recognition. It was not until 1985 that the group achieved a meeting of minds with the senior army command. Through his family relations, Japto continued to make overtures to the Soehartos, until the group became entrusted as the personal bodyguards of Soeharto's sons, who themselves eventually joined the organization.

After the Mysterious Killings through to the end of the New Order in 1998, these OKP all enjoyed *carte blanche* by virtue of their vociferous support of Soeharto and Golkar, while being left to compete with each other for turf. Throughout the 1980s, they had all established national organizations with hierarchical branches right down to the village level. Members proudly owned group attributes, such as camouflage uniforms, achievement badges, and group logos, and would carry around a group's bylaw book as if it were a Bible.[27] In many cities, every street was marked with a formal signpost for one organization or the other. From time to time, they would clash violently over this turf, tearing down signposts and killing each other off.[28] Revenues from controlling turf ranged from collecting parking fees to extorting protection money from proprietors to rights to employment in factories and entertainment spots as security. Entertainment districts were particularly lucrative, with local branch posts of the OKP plainly visible in the vicinities of them. Controlling security at the discos by the 1990s also meant monopolies in controlling prostitution and the distribution of drugs such as ecstasy, whose national distribution franchise was widely rumored to be held by Soeharto's own grandson. Yorrys eventually owned Stadium, one of the biggest discos in Jakarta, outright.

THE REALIGNMENTS OF REFORMATION: 1998 AND BEYOND

In the years since 1998, the influence of these OKP on the streets has waned but has by no means disappeared. Senior local leaders have taken the opportunity provided by the new parliamentary democracy to get involved in party politics again, and thousands of OKP leaders now hold elected office at all levels of parliament (Ryter 2009). They have had to contend with a host of new rivals on the streets, mostly adopting Islamic, ethnic, or new party youth wing banners, but essentially operating in the same manner (see Lindsey 2001). The Islamic Defenders Front is notorious for raiding vice operations, such as discos and brothels, in the name of Islam but actually intending to move in on the protection racket business. Such new groups have absorbed many of the old OKP members. The scores of new political parties since 1998 have found themselves in a position similar to that of the parties under Sukarno's Guided Democracy, with the need to recruit rank-and-file OKP members into their own party youth wings and to run their leaders as candidates.[29]

Pemuda Pancasila leaders, by the organization's own design, distributed themselves throughout the party system. At its 1999 Special Congress, Pemuda Pancasila declared itself "independent" and freed its members to support any political party they wished. One senior Pemuda Pancasila leader established himself a close associate of current president Susilo Bambang Yudhoyono, serving him as an "anticorruption" official from 2004 to 2009 and as a parliamentarian from the president's party since 2009. Yorrys Raweyai leads Golkar's new youth wing and again holds a parliamentary seat (after being removed as a Soeharto crony in 1998). Japto founded his own political party, called the Patriot Party, which, though it has yet to live up to Japto's overly grandiose expectations given Pemuda Pancasila's membership in the millions, has still managed to pick up a few parliamentary seats in local and national elections. By hedging its bets throughout the political system, Pemuda Pancasila has thus effectively adapted to the new competitive electoral regime.[30]

At local levels, the old OKP have hardly vanished from the streets. In Medan, North Sumatra, where *Pemuda Pancasila* has enjoyed its longest history, the group is now more dominant than ever and nearly as visible, because its chief OKP rival, the Youth Works and Deeds Association (IPK), was quickly sidelined after 1998. IPK had, since the mid-1980s, been run almost entirely within North Sumatra by the late gambling kingpin Olo Panggabean, who maintained tight relations with the provincial army command through the end of the Suharto years and somewhat beyond. Olo was rumored to have supplied logistical support for army counterinsurgency operations in Aceh and to provide free R&R "facilities" in the form of girls, booze, and drugs to army personnel stationed in Medan. Prominent discos and brothels surrounded by uniformed IPK members were common features of the landscape in certain quarters of Medan until sometime after 1998. Unlike Japto, Olo never made any efforts to cultivate a politically savvy leadership, preferring to keep decision making within a tight circle. Thus IPK was ill-prepared to weather the changes after 1998.[31]

Pemuda Pancasila leaders were delighted for the police to hand them the head of their chief rival. During and after the police crackdown on gambling, many of them oriented their political careers around public opposition to gambling and narcotics. During this time, Pemuda Pancasila and other OKP leaders outside of IPK founded antinarcotics organizations, even as their members continued to depend on narcotics and other trades in vice. As with the Islamic Defenders Front's raids on Jakarta's dens of iniquity, their move was likely intended as a protection racket aiming to gain a greater share of drug trade revenues and may have also provided a rather bold cover for direct engagement in the drug trade itself.[32] OKP leaders with large followings have discovered new kinds of protection racket schemes in the environment of political "reformation" since 1998. They can organize raucous demonstrations of any sort, either for hire (as against a politician's opponent) or on their own initiative (in which case, there is a price for them to call off their dogs).[33]

CONCLUSION: NOSTALGIA FOR THE PURE GANG

The connections between politics and gangs in Indonesia should be quite clear. What is striking in the Indonesian case is that the formalization of gangsters into recognized organizations has settled into relative stability for over a quarter century, with the consequence that nothing like a pure youth gang with a continuous institutional history has existed since the 1970s. The OKP since the early 1980s, and then a number of new organizations, such as the Islamic Defender's Front and the political parties themselves since 1998, have taken their place. What is even more remarkable is that, despite the stability of this pattern of institutionalization, or perhaps because of it, many established and wannabe *preman*, to use the most inclusive sense of the term, feel a profound dissatisfaction with the arrangement, as if something were missing. Many look back on the romantic era of the *crossboys*, and even the brash days of the SBC, with palpable nostalgia. In 1998, the Ex-Menteng Teenagers (XRM) Club sponsored a self-consciously nostalgic reunion for the erstwhile "street youth and lovely maidens of Menteng," which was in the 1950s and 1960s the elite neighborhood of Jakarta. Japto was on the invitation list, along with a host of generals, ministers, and businessmen who had grown up in the district. Those were the days when they kept it real, when brashness and bravado proved a strength of character unencumbered by crutches of pretense. There was no need to seek legitimacy in grandiose articulations like nationalism or Pancasila, or in moral crusading, such as in campaigning against drugs and vice. There was no need to seek cover in formal, national organizations when one's small clique, or gang, as it were, provided all the solidarity one needed. One's subsequent success and perhaps disturbingly too easy comfort seemed to prove that this was true. As such, the nostalgia for the return of something *more like* a pure gang has become palpable. Out of this sentiment, the popular attraction within certain quarters of a group like the 234 Solidarity Community, which at once references and extends Japto's 234 Siliwangi Club gang of the 1960s, whose very existence he was compelled to deny, can be more fully appreciated. The 234 Solidarity Community returns to basic black, stripping off the orange and black camouflage paramilitary uniform of Pemuda Pancasila to reveal something closer to the heart.

NOTES

1. *Pancasila* (pancha-see-lah), Sanskrit for "five principles," is the official Indonesian national ideology and basis of the state, formulated by Indonesia's first president, Sukarno. The principles are Belief in One God, Just and Civilized Humanity, Indonesian Unity, Democracy Guided by Wisdom of Representatives and Deliberation, and Social Justice (see http://en.wikipedia.org/wiki/Pancasila_(politics)). Under Suharto, the principles themselves were stripped of content, and *Pancasila* became little more than a mark of unquestioned allegiance to the state, with charges of being anti-*Pancasila* becoming a cudgel to beat opponents and critics, much like charges of anti-Americanism were used during the McCarthy era in the United States.

2. The spelling of Japto used here conforms to the older Dutch orthography, the way he would have spelled it until the national spelling standardization sometime in the 1970s, after which time he accordingly began spelling it Yapto. "Japto" more clearly shows his heritage, as his Dutch Jewish mother appended the common Javanese suffix for names, -to, to a common Dutch name, Jap.

3. Japto is an avid international wild game hunter, and numerous animal trophies adorn his massive home in South Jakarta. Excess trophies form a large basis of his friend and co-*Pancasila* Youth leader Rachmat Syah's Wildlife Museum in North Sumatra.

4. Indeed, Japto elaborated the notion of the "concrete" as an ideology of pragmatism in various publications aimed at his membership.

5. These estimates have been claimed in a variety of press statements by PP leaders themselves and are probably greatly exaggerated. The lowest end of the range seems more plausible.

6. Ucok's brother was the real killer. Some sixteen members of the Siliwangi Boys spent several months under house arrest at Japto's house after the incident, but none faced jail time.

7. In the 1970s, leading LEGOS members, such as Leo Tomasoa and Freddy Latumania, were recruited as operatives by National Intelligence Board (BAKIN) chief Ali Moertopo, and they carried out his experiments with creating a new national youth politics. Through the Special Operations ("Opsus") wing of BAKIN, they formed the core of the Group of 10, whose chief purpose was to cut off any university students who continued to be critical of government policies.

Later they would be involved in the establishment of the National Youth Council, or KNPI, another Opsus project.

8. Business rivalries among the clubs' owners themselves sometimes came to a head with the violent involvement of gang members. The manager of the Latin Quarter, a popular nightclub near the National Monument, was beaten with a motorcycle chain by a Siliwangi Club gangster (Santoso 1975).

9. http://www.facebook.com/group.php?gid=43347358736. The word *noble* is a gloss of the title *mas*, a conventional Javanese term of respect for an older brother that traditionally was reserved for the aristocracy but has been adopted into wider usage. Through his father, Japto, and consequently his sons, are descendants of the Mangkunegaran Sultanate in Solo. As mentioned previously, Japto's mother is a Dutch Jew, which explains Abi Shalom, and also "Jap" (a Dutch name).

10. Japto's residence in South Jakarta has a covered tent garage that houses dozens of vehicles. The Senayan Stadium, also known as the Brother Sukarno Stadium, was first built to host the 1962 Asian Games.

11. *Jago* also referred to the fighting cocks of cockfights.

12. Evidence for this comes from a historical novel, which is based on newspaper reports that unfortunately no longer exist (Pramoedya Ananta Toer 1992). In the novel, the main such gang was known as *De Knijpers* or "the Knives." In 1998, Pramoedya insisted this was the actual name of the gang according to the news reports (pers. comm., circa 1998).

13. Some of this section is adapted from Ryter (2002).

14. A 1959 city publication characterizes contemporary trends in this way: "With a shortage of school rooms to accommodate new students and limited job opportunities, unemployment multiplied, resulting in a rise in security disruptions and juvenile crime" (Djawatan Penerangan Kota Besar Medan 1959, 146). As this quotation suggests, *preman,* like *pemuda,* referred to a wide range of ages, encompassing those from school age to significantly older men most prominent in the market areas, as if it was the ambiguity of employment that came to define these categories.

15. Sukarno coined the onomatopoetic phrase "*ngak ngik ngok*" to refer to the nonsense sound of rock 'n' roll. Disapproving parents widely adopted the president's humorous disparagement starting in the 1950s.

16. A pretext for the mobilization of youth groups around that time was Soekarno's December 19, 1961, announcement of the TRIKORA campaign to liberate West Irian from the Dutch. The TRIKORA instruction (Tri Komando Rakyat, or People's Triple Commando) called for crushing the Dutch puppet state of Papua, raising the Indonesian flag in West Irian, and preparing for popular mobilization of volunteers to be sent to Irian. On January 23, 1962, Effendi Nasution, in the name of Pemuda Pancasila, signed a document proclaiming the group's preparedness to be sent to the front lines in Irian Jaya. The news was published in Ibrahim Sinik's IPKI organ, Harian Tjahaya (American Consulate in Medan 1961–75). Some time before joining forces with Pemuda Pancasila, presumably

near the end of 1961, P2KM had also declared its preparedness to liberate West Irian, announcing the formation of the West Irian Suicide Mission Force (Pasu-kan Djibaku Irian Barat) (Asmara et al. 1996, 20–21). Many other youth groups throughout Indonesia produced similar declarations of volunteerism, but none to my knowledge was ever actually sent.

17. Some of this section is adapted from Ryter (2001).

18. Tien Suharto, quoted in *Kompas,* December 16, 1971. On Taman Mini "Indonesia Indah," see Pemberton (1994, 152–61).

19. See *Tempo,* January 1, 1972; *Kompas,* December 24, 1971 to January 5, 1972; and *Kompas,* May 9, 1972. I am also grateful to Asmara Nababan for a conversation on the subject on July 28, 1998.

20. KOPKAMTIB, or Command for the Restoration of Security an Order, was an intelligence body with extraordinary powers established in 1966 by Soeharto, who led it until around the time he became president.

21. Several sources confirm that Tien Suharto ordered the attack.

22. BAKIN, the National Intelligence Board, became KOPKAMTIB's rival. It was led by General Ali Moertopo during these years.

23. BAPPENKAR, or Badan Pelaksana Penanggulangan Narkotika & Ke-nakalan Anak-Anak Remaja. Its first publication (Bappenkar Jatim 1972) was titled "Total War against Narcotics for the Salvation of Our Teen Generation as the Hope and Dream of Our Nation" and was, in addition to being an outline of the juvenile delinquency problem, a frame for the dissemination of Soemitro's instruction.

24. See *Tempo,* January 15, 1972, February 17, 1973, July 14, 1973, and January 26, 1972.

25. I refer here to groups like Anak Muda Siliwangi (different than the Sili-wangi Boys) and Anak Muda Diponegoro (AMD).

26. The most famous such black op involved Prems members dressing up as Golkar's opposition party members and setting fire to a stage at a rally for Golkar, with the intent of discrediting the opposition party, PPP.

27. One thinks of Chairman Mao's "red book."

28. In Medan, one can visit graves that identify the dead by their organiza-tions and the dates of their fatal clashes. New or contested turf was often marked by painted graffiti, until formal signposts could be put up and new permanent posts established.

29. Rank-and-file OKP members were desirable to the parties because they were ready and willing to be mobilized for election rallies and consequently vis-ibly demonstrated a party's quotidian mass support. Local OKP leaders, to whom members owed their allegiance, have been valuable vote-getters for the parties, and they also brought with them both the political experience and street smarts necessary to run a successful campaign in a newly competitive electoral system.

30. During interviews I conducted in 2006, local and national leaders hold-ing parliamentary seats concurred that relations among erstwhile OKP leaders

tended to drive agenda setting and deal making more than party affiliations.

31. Disregarding the rise of the parties, Olo made no serious effort to field IPK associates in elections. More fatal still, Olo failed to anticipate that the police, which he had long derided as a junior partner to the army and routinely flouted, would sharpen its teeth after its formal separation from the armed forces. In 1999, police mobile brigades shot at Olo's private residential compound, which was widely believed to conceal a high-stakes casino. General Sutanto, the Indonesian national police chief (2005–8), marshaled an all-out war against "gambling" whose main target was Olo, shutting down most of his operations. Sutanto had harbored a grudge against Olo since the late 1990s, when, as North Sumatra's chief of police, he proved feckless against Olo, who routinely made clear who was boss. With most of his operations eradicated or driven underground, Olo retired to Singapore, where he passed away in 2009 (see *Kompas,* December 29, 1999; *Tempo* [English edition], September 4, 2006).

32. Though this claim remains speculative, there is evidence to support the general pattern. In February 2010, antidrug activists in Medan were arrested with hundreds of ecstasy tablets. I have not yet been able to confirm whether those arrested had OKP ties, but the likelihood is high (see *Jakarta Post,* February 8, 2010).

33. Yorrys Raweyai encouraged Papuan secessionists to press their claims against Jakarta, yet many suspected his real target was a payoff from the mining transnational Freeport-McMoRan, which operated in the disputed territory.

REFERENCES

American Consulate in Medan. 1961–75. "Medan Press Summary." Medan: USIS.

Anderson, Benedict R. O. 1972. *Java in a Time of Revolution: Occupation and Resistance, 1944–1946.* Ithaca, N.Y.: Cornell University Press.

Asmara, Drs. Sakhyan, et al., eds. 1996. *Pemuda Pancasila: Sejarah dan Tokoh Utama—Menelusuri perjalanan organisasi dan dialektika tokoh Pemuda Pancasila Sumatera Utara.* Medan: DPW PP Sumut and the Development Anthropology Research Center of FISIP USU.

Bappenkar Jatim. 1972. *Perang total melawan narkotika demi keselamatan generasi remaja kita sebagai harapan cita-cita bangsa: instruksi PANGKOPKAMTIB tanggal 15-1-1972, nomor INS-001/KOPKAM/I/72.* Surabaya, East Java.

Bourchier, David. 1990. "Crime, Law, and State Authority in Indonesia." In *State and Civil Society in Indonesia,* edited by A. Budiman, 177–212. Victoria, Australia: Monash Asia Institute.

Cribb, Robert. 1991. *Gangsters and Revolutionaries: The Jakarta People's Militia and the Indonesian Revolution 1945–1949.* Honolulu: University of Hawaii Press.

Djawatan Penerangan Kota Besar Medan. 1959. *50 tahun Kotapradja Medan.* Medan.

Horikoshi, Hiroko. 1975. "The Dar ul-Islam Movement in West Java (1942–62): An Experience in the Historical Process." *Indonesia* 20:58–86.

Kahin, Audrey R., and George M. Kahin. 1995. *Subversion as Foreign Policy: The Secret Eisenhower and Dulles Debacle in Indonesia.* New York: New Press.

Lev, Daniel S. 1964. "The Transition to Guided Democracy in Indonesia: 1957–1959." PhD diss., Cornell University.

Lindsey, Tim. 2001. "The Criminal State: Premanisme and the New Indonesia." In *Indonesia Today: Challenges of History,* edited by G. J. Lloyd and S. L. Smith, 283–97. Singapore: Institute of Southeast Asian Studies.

Nasution, Effendi. n.d. Autobiographical manuscript, mimeo.

Onghokham. 1978. "The Inscrutable and the Paranoid: An Investigation into the Sources of the Brotodiningrat Affair." In *Southeast Asian Transitions: Approaches through Social History,* edited by R. McVey and A. Suddard, 112–57. New Haven, Conn.: Yale University Press.

———. 1984. "The Jago in Colonial Java, Ambivalent Champion of the People." In *History and Peasant Consciousness in South East Asia,* edited by A. Turton and S. Tanabe, 327–43. Osaka, Japan: National Museum of Ethnology.

Pemberton, John. 1994. *On the Subject of "Java."* Ithaca, N.Y.: Cornell University Press.

Pramoedya Ananta Toer. 1992. *House of Glass.* Translated by M. Lane. New York: Penguin Books.

Ryter, Loren. 2001. "Pemuda Pancasila: The Last Loyalist Free Men of Suharto's Order?" In *Violence and the State in Suharto's Indonesia,* edited by B. Anderson, 124–55. Ithaca, N.Y.: Cornell Southeast Asia Program Publications.

———. 2002. "Youth, Gangs, and the State in Indonesia." PhD diss., University of Washington, Seattle.

———. 2009. "Their Moment in the Sun: Indonesia's New Parliamentarians from the Old OKP." In *The State of Authority in Indonesia,* edited by G. V. Klinken and J. Barker, 181–218. Ithaca, N.Y.: Cornell Southeast Asia Publications.

Santoso, Djoko. 1975. "Masalah Kegiatan Gang Anak dan Pemuda di Jakarta (Khusus dari Kalangan Keluarga ABRI)." Bachelor's thesis, Penguruan Tinggi Ilmu Kepolisian, Jakarta.

Stoler, Ann Laura. 1988. "Working the Revolution: Plantation Laborers and the People's Militia in North Sumatra." *Journal of Asian Studies* 47, no. 2: 227–47.

Surbakti, Colonel A. R. 1997. *Catatan Perjalan Hidup Seorang Prajurit '45.* Jakarta: Anak/Menantu and Cucu.

van der Kroef, Justus M. 1985. "'PETRUS': Patterns of Prophylactic Murder in Indonesia." *Asian Survey* 25, no. 7: 745–59.

8

"Playing the Game": Gang–Militia Logics in War-Torn Sierra Leone

MATS UTAS

So when we were in the camp we just wanted to listen to [Tupac] Shakur music. So we went singing "West Side" and go on "ah-ah-ah-ah" [like the background fill-in in many rap songs]. So all the other soldiers they made the name famous. So we began to plait our hair and behave like American boys. If you go to some towns in the interior you will still see West Side Niggaz written on the walls. It was only when the government put charges against us that they started to call us West Side Boys. We called ourselves West Side Niggaz, yes [he says the last words slowly, as if tasting it with full satisfaction].
> —interview with a mid-level West Side Boys
> commander, 2005

When I recently read Sudhir Venkatesh's (2008) *Gang Leader for a Day*, I was struck by the feeling of total familiarity. I felt that I knew the setting and the actors to the extent that I could almost guess what would happen on the next page. In particular, the similarities were striking between the lives of the Black Kings, the Chicago Southside gang Venkatesh studied, and the ex-combatant street corner youths with whom I worked in postwar Freetown, Sierra Leone. These similarities, on one hand, likely originated from a shared interest in comparable research questions. Venkatesh (2006, xi), for example, states,

> I was interested in one small part of this history—namely, how the organization came to develop and manage its lucrative drug-trafficking enterprise. I hoped to understand why young people chose this risky path (compared with other, mainstream avenues that might have been available); how they invested, saved, and spent the money they earned; and how a gang dealt with all the conflicts and problems that arose while running a business that was entirely illegal.

My own interests were arguably much the same, but instead of drug trafficking, I was interested in what might be termed the "war enterprise." My research focused on young men (and some women) who had actively participated in the Sierra Leone civil war (1991–2002), and I wanted to understand how and why they had done so.

On the other hand, as Venkatesh (2000, 282) argues in another book, "all local worlds have their own intrinsic historicity, an internal dialectic of structure and practice that shapes, reproduces, and transforms the character of everyday life within them"; he goes on to suggest that "it is the interaction of these local worlds with the structures, agents, and ideologies of the larger world that produces observable social patterns." Seen from this perspective, it can be argued that there is much more to the observation that similarities exist between the gang studied by Venkatesh in Chicago and the ex-combatant youths whom I study in Freetown than a simple coincidence of research interests. In particular, drawing on studies of U.S. ganglands by Venkatesh (2008), Wacquant (2008), Bourgois (1995), and Hagedorn (2008), in this chapter I suggest that these similarities allow us to understand the logics of youth in post-war Sierra Leone in a much more nuanced way than more conventional approaches to studying war combatants.

The chapter is structured as follows. I begin by considering the relationship between youth and politics in Sierra Leone. I then provide a brief overview of the country's tormented history of violence and war and trace the origins of a youth group known as the West Side Boys (WSB), a splinter militia group that emerged as key players in the conflict around 1999–2000 and who were one of a range of actors that emerged during the Sierra Leone civil war. Most Western media accounts suggest that the WSB were nothing more than renegade, anarchistic bandits, devoid of any long-term goals. In actual fact, the WSB were a cohesive and well-organized militia that played an important role in the conflict; military commanders and politicians employed them as part of their larger military and political strategies (Utas and Jörgel 2008). Most importantly, perhaps, the WSB adopted the global rebel and gang icon Tupac Shakur as a primary reference point for their social being, as the epigraph to this chapter reflects well. The relationship between Tupac, youth militias, and warfare in Sierra Leone is then explored, and I highlight how the emergence of militias such as the WSB is related to a broader form of youth struggle against "the system." The relationship between youth and politics in postwar Sierra Leone is then explored through the U.S. gang literature, as it applies to the lives of a group of ex-combatant youth who hung out on a Freetown street corner called the "Pentagon."

YOUTHS AND POLITICS IN SIERRA LEONE

Youths in Sierra Leone are often referred to by scholars, such as Ibrahim Abdullah, Ismael Rashid, and Patrick Muana, as "lumpens," or the "lumpenprolitariat" of Sierra Leone (Abdullah 1997a, 197b; Abdullah et al. 1997; Abdullah and Muana 1998; Abdullah and Rashid 2004; Rashid 1997, 2004). The archetypal figure epitomizing this condition has traditionally been the *rarray boy,* who is visible hanging out with peers on street corners. The rarray boy does not just idle about, as popular perception would have it;[1] rather, he actively participates in the socio-spatial organization of the street and of his neighborhood, catering for local security arrangements and engaging in casual labor and petty trade. Although such groups of rarray boys tend to display loyalties that are too fluid for them to be considered gangs, many of their functions are typically ganglike, as they are deeply involved in the illegal street economy and frequently employ violence as an instrumental means of attaining their commercial goals.

At the same time, Michael Banton ([1957] 1969, 7ff.) has described how emerging youth street culture in postcolonial Freetown blended art, economics, and politics in interesting and unusual ways. In particular, youths played key roles in emerging forms of urban secret societies, social clubs, and masquerade societies that, far from just performing colorful street carnivals, actively catered for their members in all sorts of socioeconomic ways, including, for example, by providing informal forms of social security (see, e.g., Banton [1957] 1969, 168ff.; see also Nunley 1987). Banton terms these "latent functions," which can be said to imbue these societies with the character of a "solidarity network" (Chabal 2009, 167) or "voluntary association" (Meagher 2010, 105ff.). Another latent function was political, however. Many leaders of urban secret societies were either politicians or their close affiliates, and they acted as powerful brokers in patron–client relations and also functioned as sociopolitical switchboards between socioeconomic elites and youths—in particular, connecting youths and politics through violence.[2]

Certainly politics and violence are intimately related in Sierra Leone, with elections typically being times of heightened and sometimes violent tension, both historically and in the recent past (Banton [1957] 1969, 176–78; Nunley 1987, 209–15; Rosen 2005, 76–82; Christensen and Utas 2008). Urban youths have, since independence, been key players in this violence. As Ibrahim Abdullah (2002, 24–25) has pointed out, the 1967 election saw youths' "involvement in large numbers as thugs for the ruling party" because "the violent aspect of *rarray boy* culture made them an electioneering asset for politicians." David Rosen (2005, 77) equally identified the 1967 election as a critical moment in the involvement of marginalized youths in political action when the "SLPP [Sierra Leone People's Party] made use of 'action groups,' bands of teenage males dressed in white bandanas and vests bearing the palm-tree symbols of the SLPP, to intimidate voters." Later, the rival All People's Congress (APC) also engaged with marginalized youths in this way, institutionalizing youth violence to create "an atmosphere of anarchy and terror" in support of a one-party state (Rosen 2005, 77). APC youths "set people on fire, burned down their houses, shot children, paraded citizens and beat them, brought opponents before youth-run kangaroo courts, and hacked men and women to death with machetes" (Rosen 2005, 78).[3]

THE "SYSTEM" AND THE "GAME"

At the same time, however, youths are not just pawns in a political game but are also very much active "social navigators" (Christiansen, Utas, and Vigh 2006; Vigh 2006), and although they sometimes conform to the logic of political leaders, at times they also confront it, simultaneously making room for individualized trajectories. The way that Sierra Leonean youths express this ambiguity today is in terms of a conceptual contrast between the "system" and the "game." "Na de system de morna we" (The system is troubling us) is a popular song by the Sierra Leonean musicians Jungle Leaders. The expression can roughly be related to the sociological notion of "structure," akin to the sense developed by Loïc Wacquant (2008) in his work on advanced marginality in the inner-city ghettos of Chicago and suburban *banlieues* of Paris, where it is a form of violence from above (or "structural/systematic" violence; cf. Galtung 1969; Žižek 2008).[4] At the opposite spectrum of the "system" is the "game," a term originating from hip-hop and rap (see, e.g., Freddy Will, "Focus Your Mind," on the 2009 album *While I'm Still Young—The Talking Drums*: "Yo I peep *the game* closely and I never choke / From the east coast chose me now I've got the toast / I was born in the west but I represent the east / Brookfields, Freetown, from where came the beast / I learn the game from the homies that'll never put the heat down"). This can be seen as equivalent to the "social art of the hustler" that Wacquant (1998) discusses in his more ethnographic writing. In its broadest sense, the game can be seen as a kind of social navigation fitting neatly with Bourdieu's (2000) notion of *illusio,* routinized forms of social interaction where individuals are aware of their bets.

As Ibrahim Abdullah (2002, 33) has pointed out, "playing the game" against "the system" has always been a major occupation of Sierra Leonean youths. From the 1960s onward, Freetown university students often qualified themselves as "revolutionaries," explicitly claiming that they were against the system, "playing the game" of ideological proselytizing in Freetown *potes,* or ghettos, for example (Abdullah 2002, 33; see also Utas 2003). Although the vast majority of these university students were extremely distant from "the street," and visited Freetown ghettos mainly to smoke joints, their actions can perhaps be seen as having laid the seeds for revolutionary inspiration to blossom as a result of broader developments in the Sierra Leonean environment. More specifically, the outbreak of civil war in 1991 led to a profound upheaval in youth culture as armed conflict became a primary symbol of resistance to "the system" and the means to seek retribution and economic redistribution (Richards 1996; Abdullah et al. 1997; Rashid 1997; Abdullah and Rashid 2004; Utas 2007, 2008a, 2008b, 2009).[5] As such, the war can be said to have led to the emergence of new ways of playing the game.

WARSCAPE SIERRA LEONE

Sierra Leone's postcolonial history since independence in 1961 has been dominated by two political parties: the SLPP and the APC. The SLPP ruled between 1961 and 1967 and again between 1996 and 2007. The APC ruled between 1968 and 1992 and returned to power in 2007. Political transitions between the two parties have never been easy, and three military governments have also held sway in Sierra Leone, in 1967–68, 1992–96, and 1997–98. During the 1990s, however, political tensions gave way to a full-fledged civil war. Siaka Stevens, the APC leader and the country's president between 1968 and 1985, turned Sierra Leone into a one-party state and reigned in typical cold war style with internationally "accepted" institutionalized forms of state violence and mismanagement of government funds. The APC's abuse of power paved the way for revolt first by the rural-based Revolutionary United Front (RUF) rebel group from 1991 onward and later by two "urban" military governments, the National Provisional Ruling Council (1992–96) and the Armed Forces Revolutionary Council (1997–98).

This factionalism very much reflected the country's divided political allegiances, although these were clearly very fluid. The National Provisional Ruling Council (NPRC) government (1992–96), for example, was formed by junior army officers originating from the Daru and Kenema barracks, who professed loyalty to the SLPP, then in opposition. Yet the Armed Forces Revolutionary Council (AFRC) coup that toppled the SLPP government headed by Ahmad Tejan Kabbah on May 25, 1997, was led by junior officers, predominantly from Freetown, many of whom had actually served as personal bodyguards to ministers in the previous NPRC government.[6] At the same time, although not directly loyal to or directed by the APC, the AFRC was clearly politically sympathetic to the APC.

The AFRC coup marked a break in Sierra Leonean history, insofar as, contrary to previous regimes, upon taking power, it invited the opposition, in this case the RUF, to join in a coalition government, in a bid to end the war. The AFRC–RUF junta ruled for eight months before being deposed by a mix of West African peacekeepers (the Economic Community of Western African States Monitoring Group, or ECO-MOG), urban militia, and rural civil defense forces who were called in by the deposed SLPP government. The AFRC and RUF were forcefully expelled from Freetown and retreated into the interior of the country, mainly to Kailahun, Kono, and Koinadugu districts, where the pact of convenience disintegrated between the AFRC and RUF forces. The toppled AFRC leader Johnny Paul Koroma fled to Kailahun but was subsequently taken prisoner by the RUF, who then handed him over to Liberia. The AFRC military began to fall apart, and this led to the emergence of numerous splinter groups. It was from some of the AFRC units in Kono that the WSB emerged.

THE WEST SIDE BOYS, TUPAC, AND WARFARE

Many of the WSB were youths who were sons of AFRC soldiers and had grown up in military barracks or the surrounding neighborhoods in western Freetown. This background could plausibly have contributed to the name "West Side Boys," but the principal reason for the name was the music of the American gangsta rapper Tupac Shakur. The group originally called themselves "West Side Niggaz," a name taken from the intro of Tupac's 1996 track "Hit 'em up" ("So I ain't got no friendz / West Side bad boys Killaz / You know who the realist is, Niggaz"). The commander of the D Company, or the Dark Angel Battalion of the AFRC troops, called Junior Lion, was fond of Tupac's music, and his musical interest spread.

The influence of Tupac Shakur is by no means surprising; he has been an inspiration for other youth militias around the world. Around the time the Sierra Leone WSB emerged, there was a Tupac Outlaws/West Side Outlaws militia group in Guadalcanal (Wehrfritz 1999), while in both eastern DRC and Côte d'Ivoire, rebel groups were, a few years later, reportedly using Tupac T-shirts as their uniforms (Figure 8.1) (Ferreira 2002; Sengupta 2003). Even within Sierra Leone, the Tupac

Figure 8.1. Tupac on the West Side from western Freetown. Photograph by Danny Hoffman.

imagery was not restricted to the WSB but was also a major reference for youthful members of the RUF as well. As Jeremy Prestholdt (2009, 198) discusses in relation to the latter, they "sought broader meaning for their experiences, justification for their actions, and psychological solace from the chaos they were unleashing" in the lyrics of Tupac. Borrowing from Appadurai, he points out how "Tupac appeals to diverse self-images in ways that constitute and reflect a disjointed *community of sentiment* across differing, even political landscapes."

Certainly the lyrics of his songs can be said to be "steeped in the rhetoric of resilience, of overcoming unjust conditions. . . . Tupac's perceived invincibility offered psychological solace for young people who experienced violence as part of their everyday life" (Prestholdt 2009, 201). There likely existed little difference in the socio-ideological backgrounds of the Tupac-inspired RUF youth and the WSB, and certainly psychologically, they probably both found meaning and solace within the same community of sentiment, something that explains the forthrightness with which ex-combatants have subsequently mingled in the postwar situation, combining efforts rather than fighting each other. At the same time, however, Prestholdt (2009, 206) also suggests that the invocation of Tupac indicated a broader youth discontent—with clientelism and corruption, exclusion, poverty, and inequality (Richards 1996; Utas 2003; Peters 2011).

Indeed, WSB followers often tended to see joining their outfit as part of their "game." To many, it was not very different from the prewar kinds of mobilization that had previously taken place around the masquerade societies whose networks were in fact amply used to recruit youths. Indeed, leaders of societies with stakes in the war would often gather numbers of young men from their groups or areas that were already socioeconomically loyal to them. As Danny Hoffman (2007a, 402) has pointed out, West African cities, or spaces in cities, can in many ways be conceived as barracks concentrating "bodies (particularly male bodies) and subjects into formations that can be deployed quickly and efficiently to any corner of the empire." The Freetown ghetto during the civil war was such a space par excellence, "organiz[ing] male sociality itself around the exercise of violence and circulat[ing] that violence within an exchange economy" (Hoffman 2007a, 402). The logic of war thus became the militarization of already existing social networks and social logics—or a "web" of social relations (see Hoffman 2007b). Certainly the WSB clearly mobilized through existing social networks.[7] When they were placed in new, more powerful roles, however, commandeered by trained militaries and armed with military equipment, logically their new practices, particularly of violence, became part of a new way of playing the game against a system perceived as oppressive. What happened after the war, however, was another matter altogether.

GANGLAND SIERRA LEONE

Between 2004 and 2006, I spent almost every day hanging out on a street corner called the "Pentagon," located in one of Freetown's back streets. Most of what I know about the city, Sierra Leone, and the country's civil war I learned at this very location, informed by encounters and discussions with hundreds of individuals who resided or passed through this area, but most of all, I learned from the Pentagon guys, a group of approximately fifteen youths who spent their days and nights on the street corner, making their living mainly by washing cars but also from selling marijuana, fencing stolen items, and engaging in various forms of petty theft (Figure 8.2). Most of them had fought in the civil war, some on the RUF side, but the core as part of the WSB. There were no obvious tensions between those who had fought with these different groups. Rather, the fight for survival, the search for a feasible future, being able to fend for children, girlfriends, and obtaining social respect were the common denominators of the marginal lives of this loosely structured group of young people.[8]

The Sierra Leonean state was not a positive presence in their lives, and they had limited contacts with kin, although they did have relatively strong ties to socially influential persons—popularly referred to as "Big Men." Most of the Pentagon guys were living rough and slept in parked taxis or simply under a tarpaulin roof on the street corner itself, although the more fortunate who could afford to pay for housing or lived with relatives or friends resided in a nearby area called "Jamaica." This was a typical urban slum area with makeshift shelters of corrugated iron. Many youths residing in Jamaica also frequented "Convention," an area where predominantly young men would gather to smoke marijuana, drink *atai*[9] or *poyo*,[10] meet up with friends, and jointly make sense of the latest news from near and far, including their positions in the world.

Areas such as Pentagon, Jamaica, and Convention are crucial areas of gangland Sierra Leone, yet a specific feature of Freetown is that its social geography is considerably mixed, with the city's poor and rich often living side by side. Rather than a small, wealthy elite generating citywide "white dots" of social inclusion on a black canvas of social exclusion and poverty—large uncontrolled spaces, or "black holes of social exclusion" (Castells 1998, 164)—Freetown emerges as a space of interaction, to the extent that it makes limited sense to talk about a "Tin Roof Boundary Line" (Neuwirth 2005, 1). Although on the surface, the Pentagon guys or the youths meeting at Pentagon or Convention may have seemed like a crowd just killing time on street corners (Ralph 2008), their gatherings were also spaces where youths made themselves available for work—legal as well as illegal.

As one of the Pentagon guys put it, "the street is my office, my living room, and my bedroom." On the same street corner, he finds his daily bread, he strategizes, he socializes with his friends and, in a few cases, kin, and he sleeps—in an abandoned vehicle, in a parked taxi, or under the tarpaulin roof that makes the physical location of Pentagon. Environments such as the Pentagon corner are the primary social contexts for tens of thousands of young people, predominantly male,

Figure 8.2. Sisqo washing a car in front of Pentagon. The street name "Sisqo" is taken from a popular American hip-hop artist. Prior to this name, he went by the name "Slim Shady," an Eminem alias. Sisqo always wears a T-shirt or a baseball cap with an American flag or logo on it. Photograph by the author.

in Freetown. Similar to American ghetto experiences, it is thus to the point to describe "the street as key domain of lived experience" (Ralph 2006, 62). Certainly Philippe Bourgois (1995, 8), in his seminal book on Puerto Rican drug dealers in New York, *In Search of Respect,* talks about Harlem inner-city street culture as "a complex and conflicting web of beliefs, symbols, modes of interaction, values, and ideologies that have emerged in opposition to mainstream society" and "offers an alternative forum for autonomous personal dignity." Among the social practices that emerge are (Bourgois 1995, 34)

> regular displays of violence . . . essential for preventing rip-offs by colleagues, customers, and professional holdup artists. Indeed, upward mobility in the underground economy of the street-dealing world requires a systematic and effective use of violence against one's colleagues, one's neighbors, and, to a certain extent, against oneself. Behavior that appears irrationally violent, "barbaric," and

ultimately self-destructive to the outsider, can be reinterpreted according to the logic of the underground economy as judicious public relations and long-term investment in one's "human capital development."

Similarly to Puerto Rican crack dealers in inner-city New York, violence is both a central power marker of the socially "powerless" and a key feature in their social navigation in their aim to climb the social ladder in Freetonian street life. The capacity to use violence is central to the relative success of individuals but has become heightened in the post–civil war context, as many of those vying for power through violence are ex-combatants. Seen from this perspective, it can be argued that the logic of street violence in contemporary Sierra Leone is a continuation of the logic of military violence.

In his article "'Flirt[ing] with Death' but 'Still Alive,'" Michael Ralph (2006, 64, 62, 68) states that life in ghetto–gangland USA "holds very little for [black] men at present," as death is seen as "a constant force," with life a "war of survival." Ghetto dwellers are "imperiled because they are 'trapped in the streets' with few—if any—alternatives." Ralph (2006, 68–73) invokes the lyrics of American hip-hop music to describe how black, male ghetto inhabitants perceive of themselves as born into a violent environment—a negative socioeconomic turf to which they are subjected, rather than the opposite. In particular, he points out the songs of artists such as Nas, B.I.G., and Styles, highlighting how these suggest that "it is almost as if their lives are over before they even get started. And the streets immediately emerge, in these rap narratives, as a force to be reckoned with. Nas is famous for saying he 'shot [his] way out [of] his mom['s]' womb" (Ralph 2006, 68–69).

Survival, according to Ralph (2006, 69), is in fact so perilous that it "robs black men of their childhood, drawing them into the game at ages younger and younger so the next generation is doomed to walk the same path." He emphasizes this quoting his favorite hip-hop poet, Nas: "Life is like a jungle, black, it's like the habitat of Tarzan / Matter of fact, it's badder than most can imagine" (Ralph 2006, 69).

There are obvious correspondences between gangland Southside Chicago and post–civil war Freetown with respect to the violence and insecurity of life, so it is hardly coincidental that young people in Freetown find clear points of reference in lyrics coming out of the former setting. As Jeremy Prestholdt (2009, 201) put it, hip-hop lyrics that "reso-nated with urban America ... transcended ... specific circumstances." When Bone, a pimp from the Convention ghetto, was cut up badly and subsequently bled to death on top of a car right next to Pentagon, the very next day, Mohammed took over his job, quoting Nas: "a thug dies, another steps in his shoes." In terms of the Sierra Leonean youth notion of playing the game against the system, there existed, however, a significant ambiguity, as the next section details.

ECONOMIC AND WOOING GAMES

In his study of gold digging in Colombia, Michael Taussig (2004, 11) famously talks about "that vibrant, daredevil youth economy bursting to the surface, fists full of gold destined for liquor, women, and weapons." At first glance, such a description also appears to fit young people's economic behavior in poor places such as Sierra Leone. Previously working with ex-combatants in Liberia, I was fascinated by a story narrated by a young soldier of how he and a comrade washed their car in beer after successfully looting a store (Utas 2003). This story is only one of a substantial bank of stories about a wartime looting economy. In both Liberia and Sierra Leone, young people being part of this economy of loot would suggest that this type of money must be spent quickly because it is "blood money." The same ideas can be found both in the Sierra Leone diamond economy and in the urban illegal economy, where consumption is fetishized the same way as in gangland USA: "The tendency to overspend income windfalls conspicuously is universal in an economy that fetishizes material goods and services. Crack dealers are merely a caricaturally visible version of this otherwise very North American phenomenon of rapidly over-consuming easily earned money" (Bourgois 1995, 91) (Figure 8.3).

Conspicuous consumption and flamboyant use of money remain the symbols of the few who have been successfully fighting their way up the ladder. As such, it can clearly be interpreted as an expression of the game against the system. Yet, for most street youths in urban Freetown, the illegal economy is not "fists full of gold" but bare survival. In their book *Freakonomics,* Steven Levitt and Stephen Dubner (2005) devote a section to the work of Venkatesh. They ask with reference to drug

Figure 8.3. Freetown musician Aik exposing his "bling." An irony of the blingifica-
tion of Sierra Leone youth culture is that many of the youths digging diamonds
in the rich fields of rural Sierra Leone have little idea that the diamonds they dig
are the very bling fetishized in the hip-hop videos they watch. They often have
very diffuse ideas of how diamonds are used. Some suggest they are for window
glass, others something in airplanes. Photograph by the author.

dealing, "So if crack dealing is the most dangerous job in America, and
if the salary was only $3.30 an hour, why on earth would anyone take
such a job?" before then proposing that "an editorial assistant earning $22,000 at a Manhattan publishing house, an unpaid high-school
quarterback, and a teenage crack dealer earning $3.30 an hour are all
playing the same game, a game that is best viewed as a tournament" (94,
96). To the crack pusher in Chicago's Southside ghettos or the youth
surviving in the streets of Freetown, the earnings clearly do not add up
to the risks of the game that they play. But a youth has a slim chance of
moving up the ladder if he plays the game wisely, and if "God agrees,"
as a Sierra Leonean would certainly add. Legal alternatives are few and
far between, and generally promise much less in the way of rewards,
making future prospects bleak or nonexistent.[11]

But there is also a street logic that has escaped Levitt, Dubner, and

Venkatesh, as their economic calculations hinge on the individual person and her income. Informal income systems, such as drug dealing or the Pentagon guys' wheeling and dealing, are not individually centered but rather rest on group loyalty—thus the individual drug dealer in the street, or the Pentagon guy, is part of a broader network of sharing where his real income is not just what he gets in his pocket. As part of the network, he gets additional yet irregular sums of money and, more important, access to the resources and services provided informally by the Big Men. This fact must be accounted for to fully understand street livelihoods and also underpins a paradox relative to the notion of playing the game against the system, which was that, in many ways, the game that youths such as the Pentagon guys played aimed at gaining access to the system that they putatively opposed.

This is something that is particularly clear when considering the issue of access to and control over women. Certainly this is a major element of the conspicuous consumption scheme, both in Chicago and in Freetown. Women are widely viewed in both locations as icons of success, and once again, U.S. music is a common link between the two contexts. As Tricia Rose (as cited in Ralph 2006, 72) states, "black rappers speak to men's fears and the realities of the struggle for power in teenage [but not only teenage] heterosexual courtship in a sexist society." In the American ghetto, and certainly among Sierra Leonean youths, "the possession of women" is seen "as evidence of male power" (66). At the same time, however, for poor youths on the Freetonian streets, a girlfriend was something of a rare gem. Moreover, if the Pentagon guys had girlfriends, these were more often than not simultaneously working as prostitutes.

Street youths frequently express pain at having to bear the fact that their girlfriends are involved in commercial sex with other men.[12] This was linked to the fear that many Freetonian men of different walks of life share with American hip hoppers: "that a woman will sleep with your friends and enemies" (Ralph 2006, 72). In 1998 in Monrovia, the capital of neighboring Liberia, the song "Anything Can Happen" (*The Carnival,* 1997) by Wyclef Jean was tremendously popular, especially the line "Sleeping with the bride, even though I ain't the groom." Anything could happen, and a local tune that was played in bars went "somebody's girlfriend is somebody's *hopo-jo* [prostitute]—somebody's girlfriend is somebody's handkerchief" (i.e., used to clean off the customer's sperm after sex). There existed a widespread nervousness about Freetonian youths that someone might come and take over, or sexually use, a girlfriend. The taxi driver would take her from the car washer, a sugar daddy would borrow a poor man's wife, and so forth. This insecurity appears to fit well even with rap stars coming out of the uncertainties of the ghetto: "for every rich and famous rapper there is someone even larger" (Ralph 2006, 73). But for the poor car washer in Pentagon, the axiom of Dogg Pound is ringing his ears: "It ain't no fun, if the homies can't have none" (Ralph 2006, 77). To this extent, much of the game that the youths played can in many ways be said to have aimed at becoming part of the system—Big Men—that promised not just wealth but also sociosexual security.

CONCLUSION

In this chapter, I have discussed the logic and dynamics of youth in war-ridden Sierra Leone as seen through the lens of U.S. gangs. There are clear similarities between the two contexts as well as in the ways in which particular practices are enacted and understood. Yet the differing politicoeconomic structures of the United States and Sierra Leone do allow for different responses. In the United States, in settings where the state wears thin (whether structured or not), it allows for gang-related wars over street turf and hinges on the illegal drug economy, but in Sierra Leone, it allows for direct military upheavals. In Sierra Leone, partly because of a nationwide lack of state control over violence, the logic of ganglike groups lends itself to direct militant forms and thus the creation of military movements instead. Historically, this involved the creation of military structures running parallel to the national army, such as the WSB. Both pro-government and antigovernment groups drew support from such youth militia (see, e.g., Richards 1996; Keen 2005; Hoffman 2007a, 2007b, 2011; Peters 2011). The twists and turns of civil war, however, led to a widespread feeling of disillusion among Sierra Leonean youths, who, rather than organizing themselves for or against the state, have turned increasingly toward other imagined communities, ones that might be termed the "rarray boy nation."

Lyrics from U.S. hip-hop have been the basis for such communities of sentiment. Being "ready to die"—also the title of Notorious B.I.G.'s first album—is, according to Ralph (2006, 75), of central significance for "hip hop's utopian, nationalist project," and this is a sense that has emerged very strongly from the experience of civil war that many youths have undergone. To this extent, the rarray boy nation can perhaps be said to have seen death become a fetish during the civil war—and the deadly poetry of American hip-hop become a meaningful template through which to interpret such experiences positively. In the face of never-ending marginality, uncertainty, suffering, and conspicuous consumption linked to deep structural injustices, the proto-hip-hop nation has on the local scene merged with rarray boy life into a proto–rarray boy nation. In equal part, they can be seen as a source of social resistance as well as young street entrepreneurs of violence who make their lives in relation to national politics and the logic of socioeconomic Big Men. The logic of this gangland Sierra Leone morphed during the war into the logic of warscape Sierra Leone, with loose gang structures turning into somewhat (but far from entirely) more cohesive militia and rebel structures, which, by the end of the conflict, yet again became the loose structures of new urban ganglands. Street skills were turned into skills of combat and then again into street skills—the methods changed, but the logics have, to a large extent, remained.

In the case of the Pentagon guys, many were, during the war, more or less formally organized in the militia WSB. During the war, loose networks of street youths were organized, or mobilized, into much stricter military groups, informal security forces, criminal gangs, and the like. However, they transformed just as easily into looser informal networks after the war. Instead of arguing that this is a typical feature of a Sierra Leone gangland, I would rather suggest, along with John Hagedorn (2008, xxiv), that "gangs are not a unique form but one of many kinds of armed groups that occupy the uncontrolled spaces of a 'world of slums'" and that "today's youth gang might become a drug posse tomorrow, even transform into an ethnic militia or a vigilante group the next day"—or vice versa.

NOTES

This chapter is based on research conducted in Freetown during two years of fieldwork between 2004 and 2006, with follow-up trips in 2007, 2008, and 2009. The text is dedicated to Koisi and Abu: R.I.P.

1. International journalists, INGO workers, and so on, often carry this idea. See, for example, the much-discussed works of Robert Kaplan (1994, 1997).

2. See also Hoffman (2011) for poignant cases from rural Sierra Leone.

3. To this extent, one could argue that "the template for the contemporary child soldier in Sierra Leone was forged under the APC regime" (Rosen 2005, 79). Youth were socialized into violent party-related practices and taught how such practices offered a path of upward mobility in a strongly hierarchical social system.

4. Wacquant might, however, contest my interpretation of his work, because, following Habermas, he proposes that the materialization of structure, the "hyper-ghetto," relates to the "life-world" and not the "system."

5. See also Hoffman (2011) and his use of Deleuze and Guattari's concept of the "war machines."

6. The Sierra Leone Army's rampant culture of making political and economic deals with rebel groups was widely recognized in the fact that soldiers were often said to actually be "sobels"—"soldiers by day, rebels by night" (Richards 1996; Gberie 2005; Keen 2005).

7. One day I joined a group of former senior and mid-level commanders of the WSB for a drinking spree on the beach. After some beers, they started to use sentences and sing songs in Yoruba stemming from an urban secret society. They were all members of a particular secret society, and they pointed out the importance of their secret camaraderie for organizing their military unit during the war and how it was still a central point of organization in the postwar era.

8. See Utas (2006, 2008b) for more details. See also http://www.nai.uu.se/events/multimedia/pentagon/.

9. A West African version of tea made from gun powder tea leaves (see Ralph 2008). Sometimes *kumbayjara,* a wild narcotic leaf (a type of hemlock/conium/*Datura stramonium*) is also added to the tea to get high.

10. Palm wine.

11. For a similar point, see also Jensen (2008).

12. In some cases, the "traditional" gender balance in such a relationship is turned upside down. The Pentagon guy Justice, for instance, had a girlfriend who would frequently beat him up, come and go as she wished, and all too seldom share her money with him. This imbalance stemmed in part from the fact that women in the street economy can sometimes have an easier time making money than men, at least in terms of the range of opportunities open to them (Ralph 2006).

REFERENCES

Abdullah, Ibrahim. 1997a. "Bush Path to Destruction: The Origin and Character of the Revolutionary United Front (RUF/SL)." *Africa Development* 22, nos. 3–4: 45–76.

———. 1997b. "Introduction. Special Issue on Lumpen Culture and Political Violence: The Sierra Leone Civil War." *Africa Development* 22, nos. 3–4: 5–18.

———. 2002. "Youth Culture and Rebellion: Understanding Sierra Leone's Wasted Decade." *Critical Arts* 162:19–37.

———, ed. 2004. *Between Democracy and Terror: The Sierra Leone Civil War.* Dakar: CODESRIA.

———. 2005. "'I Am a Rebel': Youth, Culture, and Violence in Sierra Leone." In *Makers and Breakers: Children and Youth in Postcolonial Africa,* edited by Alcinda Honwana and Filip de Boeck, 172–87. Oxford: James Currey.

Abdullah, Ibrahim, Yusuf Bangura, Cecil Blake, Lansana Gberie, L. Johnson, K. Kallon, S. Kemokai, Patrick K. Muana, I. Rashid, and Alfred Zack-Williams. 1997. "Lumpen Youth Culture and Political Violence: Sierra Leoneans Debate the RUF and the Civil War." *Africa Development* 22, nos. 3–4: 171–216.

Abdullah, Ibrahim, and Patrick Muana. 1998. "The Revolutionary United Front of Sierra Leone." In *African Guerrillas,* edited by Christopher Clapham, 172–93. Oxford: James Currey.

Abdullah, Ibrahim, and Ishmail Rashid. 2004. "'Smallest Victims: Youngest Killers'—Juvenile Combatants in Sierra Leone's Civil War." In *Between Democracy and Terror: The Sierra Leone Civil War,* edited by Ibrahim Abdullah, 238–53. Dakar: CODESRIA.

Banton, Michael P. (1957) 1969. *West African City: A Study of Tribal Life in Freetown.* London: Oxford University Press.

Bourdieu, Pierre. 2000. *Pascalian Meditations.* Cambridge: Polity Press.

Bourgois, Philippe. 1995. *In Search of Respect: Selling Crack in El Barrio.* Cambridge: Cambridge University Press.

Castells, Manuel. 1998. *The End of the Millennium: The Information Age—Economy, Society, and Culture.* Malden, Mass.: Blackwell.

Chabal, Patrick. 2009. *Africa: The Politics of Suffering and Smiling.* London: Zed.

Christensen, Maya, and Mats Utas. 2008. "Mercenaries of Democracy: The 'Politricks' of Remobilized Combatants in the 2007 General Elections, Sierra Leone." *African Affairs* 107, no. 429: 515–39.

Christiansen, Catrine, Mats Utas, and Henrik Vigh. 2006. "Youth(e)scapes: Introduction." In *Navigating Youth—Generating Adulthood: Social Becoming in an African Context,* edited by Catrine Christiansen, Mats Utas, and Henrik Vigh, 9–28. Uppsala, Sweden: Nordic Africa Institute.

Ferreira, E. 2002. "Strife-Torn Ivory Coast Bans Camouflage as Fashion Statement." *Agence France Presse,* November 13.

Galtung, Johan. 1969. "Violence, Peace, and Peace Research." *Journal of Peace Research* 6:167–91.

Gberie, Lansana. 2005. *A Dirty War in West Africa: The RUF and the Destruction of Sierra Leone*. Bloomington: Indiana University Press.

Hagedorn, John M. 2008. *A World of Gangs: Armed Young Men and Gangsta Culture*. Minneapolis: University of Minnesota Press.

Hoffman, Danny. 2007a. "The City as Barracks: Freetown, Monrovia, and the Organization of Violence in Postcolonial African Cities." *Cultural Anthropology* 22, no. 3: 400–28.

———. 2007b. "The Meaning of a Militia: Understanding the Civil Defence Forces of Sierra Leone." *African Affairs* 106, no. 425: 639–62.

———. 2011. *The War Machines: Young Men and Violence in Sierra Leone and Liberia*. Durham, N.C.: Duke University Press.

Jensen, Steffen. 2008. *Gangs, Politics, and Dignity in Cape Town*. Chicago: University of Chicago Press.

Kaplan, Robert D. 1994. "The Coming Anarchy." *Atlantic Monthly*, February, 44–76.

———. 1997. *The Ends of the Earth: A Journey to the Frontiers of Anarchy*. New York: Vintage Departures.

Keen, David. 2005. *Conflict and Collusion in Sierra Leone*. Oxford: J. Currey.

Levitt, Steven D., and Stephen J. Dubner. 2005. *Freakonomics: A Rogue Economist Explores the Hidden Side of Everything*. New York: William Morrow.

Meagher, Kate. 2010. *Identity Economics: Social Networks and the Informal Economy in Nigeria*. Rochester, N.Y.: James Currey.

Neuwirth, Robert. 2005. *Shadow Cities: A Billion Squatters, a New Urban World*. New York: Routledge.

Nunley, John W. 1987. *Moving with the Face of the Devil: Art and Politics in Urban West Africa*. Urbana: University of Illinois Press.

Peters, K. 2011. *War and the Crisis of Youth in Sierra Leone*. Cambridge: Cambridge University Press.

Prestholdt, Jeremy. 2009. "The Afterlives of 2Pac: Imagery and Alienation in Sierra Leone." *Journal of African Cultural Studies* 21, no. 2: 197–218.

Ralph, Michael. 2006. "'Flirt[ing] with Death' but 'Still Alive': The Sexual Dimension of Surplus Time in Hip Hop Fantasy." *Cultural Dynamics* 18, no. 1: 61–88.

———. 2008. "Killing Time." *Social Text* 26, no. 4: 1–29.

Rashid, Ishmail. 1997. "Subaltern Reactions: Lumpens, Students, and the Left." *Africa Development* 22, nos. 3–4: 19–44.

———. 2004. "Student Radicals, Lumpen Youth, and the Origins of Revolutionary Groups in Sierra Leone, 1977–1996." In *Between Democracy and Terror: The Sierra Leone Civil War*, edited by Ibrahim Abdullah, 66–89. Dakar: CODESRIA.

Richards, Paul. 1996. *Fighting for the Rain Forest: War, Youth, and Resources in Sierra Leone*. Oxford: James Currey.

Rosen, David M. 2005. *Armies of the Young: Child Soldiers in War and Terrorism.* New Brunswick, N.J.: Rutgers University Press.

Sengupta, Somini. 2003. "Motral Combat Rages, but 'Mortal Kombat' Rules." *New York Times,* June 10.

Taussig, Michael. 2004. *My Cocaine Museum.* Chicago: University of Chicago Press.

Utas, Mats. 2003. "Sweet Battlefields: Youth and the Liberian Civil War." PhD diss., Uppsala University.

———. 2006. "Der Staat als Feind." *Der Überblick* 42, no. 3: 6–9.

———. 2007. "Fighting (in) the Badlands of Modernity: Youth Combatants in the Liberian Civil War." *Journal of Social Sciences and Management* 1, no. 1: 37–43.

———. 2008a. "Abject Heroes: Marginalised Youth, Modernity, and Violent Pathways of the Liberian Civil War." In *Years of Conflict: Adolescence, Political Violence, and Displacement,* edited by J. Hart, 111–38. Oxford: Berghahn Books.

———. 2008b. "When the State Is a Threat." In *Africa on the Global Agenda: Nordic Africa Institute Annual Report 2007,* 20–24. Uppsala, Sweden: Nordic Africa Institute.

———. 2009. "Malignant Organisms: Continuities of State-Run Violence in Rural Liberia." In *Crisis of the State: War and Social Upheaval,* edited by B. Kapferer and B. E. Bertelsen, 265–91. Oxford: Berghahn Books.

Utas, Mats, and Magnus Jörgel. 2008. "The West Side Boys: Military Navigation in the Sierra Leone Civil War." *Journal of Modern African Studies* 46, no. 3: 487–511.

Venkatesh, Sudhir Alladi. 2000. *American Project: The Rise and Fall of a Modern Ghetto.* Cambridge, Mass.: Harvard University Press.

———. 2006. *Off the Books: The Underground Economy of the Urban Poor.* Cambridge, Mass.: Harvard University Press.

———. 2008. *Gang Leader for a Day: A Rogue Sociologist Takes to the Streets.* New York: Penguin Press.

Vigh, Henrik. 2006. *Navigating Terrains of War: Youth and Soldiering in Guinea-Bissau.* New York: Berghahn Books.

Wacquant, Loïc. 1998. "Inside the Zone: The Social Art of the Hustler in the Black American Ghetto." *Theory, Culture, and Society* 15, no. 2: 1–36.

———. 2008. *Urban Outcasts: A Comparative Sociology of Advanced Marginality.* Cambridge: Polity.

Wehrfritz, George. 1999. "Rebels of the Pacific." *Newsweek,* August 16, 20–23.

Žižek, Slavoj. 2008. *Violence: Six Sideways Reflections.* New York: Picador.

9

"For Your Safety": Child Vigilante Squads and Neo-Gangsterism in Urban India

ATREYEE SEN

In December 2003, riots broke out between Hindus and Muslims in the northern quarters of Hyderabad, a communally (religiously) sensitive city in southern India. Arshed, a ten-year-old boy from a slum area that was particularly affected by the rising interreligious tensions, was sent off for safekeeping to his uncle's house in another part of the city. His brother, a six-year-old, remained behind as his parents were sure that a small child could be hidden in a box or a barrel if communal antagonisms escalated into violence. Arshed returned to the slums after a few weeks and found his mother sitting at the doorstep of their small family shack; she had a glazed look and held her head in her hands. His father sat on a creaky bed, swaying from side to side and whispering, "He is gone, he is gone." Their neighbor walked up to Arshed, put his hand on his shoulder, and said, "Come and say good-bye to your brother." He walked with Arshed to the cemetery and explained how his brother had been struck on the head while trapped between rioters on the streets and had succumbed to his injuries after two days. The neighbor pointed toward a freshly covered grave. When Arshed bent over and touched the earth, his hand caught the stringed net of flowers resting over the grave. "My small brother was tugging at my arm," he told me. Later, Arshed's uncle said to him, "You are all that your parents have right now, you will grow up and be their crutch," to which Arshed replied, "Let me grow up first." That evening, Arshed was summoned by the local vigilante group made up of other riot-affected slum boys, who expressed their concern about the survival of younger children in similar social and familial circumstances. One of the older boys in the group gave Arshed a crude sword, "for your self-protection" (tere suraksha ke liye). Arshed realized that "there was no looking back" and that he was now officially a member of the local child patrol. He insisted, however, that he did not belong to a gang but had rather volunteered to join "soldiers" battling in the midst of an "urban war."

Certainly it has to be said that urban gangs in India are rarely at the heart of contemporary scholarly debate about violence and conflict. The study of criminal tribes, criminal gangs, and *dacoits* (bandits), especially in the northern belts of India, has long been of interest to historians and anthropologists (Nigam 1990; Major 1999; Radhakrishna 2001), but the role of widespread city-based gangs has been largely marginalized by academics in analyzing the nature and culture of organized violence. Most academic research on urban violence, "antisocial elements," and youth cultures in the region focus on the despairs of poverty and un-employment, the allure of terrorism and militant organizations, the significance of caste, communal and communist politics, the crisis of masculinity and unfettered consumerism, violence as sport, and the vulnerabilities generated by migration and dislocation (e.g., Bonner 2004; Jeffrey 2008; Hansen 2001; Verkaaik 2004). Yet the search for both brutality and humanity within gang cultures, the romance of powerful yet ethical gang lords, and the intrigues of international crime syndicates operating out of cities remain vibrantly alive in blockbuster films, scattered police records, comics and crime fiction, journalistic and editorial pieces, criminological discourses, political reflections on urban societies, and personal confessions of celebrities and ordinary citizens threatened and attacked by land sharks and extortionists.[1]

Scholars and public intellectuals often attribute this discrepancy to the fuzzy boundaries (in terms of rhetoric and practice) between the religious, political, police, and crime mafia in urban centers of India.[2] In this chapter, I explore how these porous and permeable borders between crime, communalism, and conflict impact the internal dynam-ics of young people acting as violent collective units on the ground. I use an ethnographic lens to comprehend how and why groups of "armed and dangerous" urban slum boys openly embrace a number of ganglike behaviors and yet emphatically refrain from labeling their mobilization strategies and violent actions as being gang related. My research site is Sultanpur, a communally fraught Muslim-dominated ghetto in the northern quarters of Hyderabad, where large sections of impoverished boys aged between nine and fourteen years have formed local child squads and violently attempt to claim and control peripheral, public spaces, for the safety and mobility of riot-affected children. The coordinated actions of these child squads point to Sultanpur being a complex urban turf that has spawned and sustained a particular culture of collective belligerence. The boys use words such as "soldiers" *(sepahi)* instead of "gangs" and "war" *(ladai/yudh)* instead of "vigilantism," and they employ these categories to position themselves in (their impression of) an urban "warscape"—for them, the city is "war" (yeh sheher ek jung hain).

VICTIMS TURNED AGGRESSORS: SULTANPUR AND THE BIRTH OF CHILD VIOLENCE

Throughout its history, from an independent Islamic city state under Nizami rule to being violently incorporated into a Hindu majoritarian postcolonial Indian state, Hyderabad has witnessed and survived the ebbing and flowing of communal tensions between Hindus and Muslims. Since the annexation of Hyderabad by the Indian army in 1948—an event also known as the "Police Action"—communal polarization has become acute, with pan-Indian Hindu nationalist organizations infiltrating Muslim-dominated residential areas in the city.[3] Rumor-mongering (Kakar 2005) and religious electioneering (Engineer 1991) have subsequently polarized social and political practices in Hyderabad, while Naidu's (1990) study of inflammatory communal relations in the old city suggests that post-Partition influx of Hindu refugee families coupled with rural–urban migration from surrounding Hindu-dominated areas also significantly affected intercommunity associations. Between 1978 and 1984, Hyderabad saw an increasing number of communal riots, sparked off by issues ranging from a Muslim woman being raped in a police station to conflict over the immersion of idols during Hindu festivals.

In 1992, when Hindu nationalist groups made their first attempt to tear down the Babri Masjid mosque in the temple town of Ayodhya in north India (claiming that the mosque was built on the historical site of the birth of a Hindu god, Ram), Hyderabad witnessed more than a fortnight of crippling riots that left more than a hundred people dead and many more critically injured. These clashes marked a new trend in mob violence when rioters specifically attacked male children; boys were maimed or killed with swords, spears, and stones and were hung from doorways. Even though police reports at the time did not divulge information about the community backgrounds of these children, according to my informants, mainly poor Muslim boys were attacked, and this trend to kill off male heirs and obliterate a minority community has continued over the next two decades. Partly as a result of these brutalities, Hyderabad's slums have become increasingly reorganized along communal lines and turned into "hyperghettos" (Wacquant 2007), with clear demarcations between Hindu and Muslim neighborhoods. Moreover, some of the public areas, especially the bazaars, once breathing spaces for inclusivity and sociality, came to be known as the Indo-Pakistan Line of Control. Flueckiger's (2006) ethnography of the life of a healer in Hyderabad shows how sections of urban Muslims retained nostalgia for the days before the Police Action, when knowledge of other cultures was welcomed within most communities. Certainly Aroma, the chief protagonist in Flueckiger's account, remains worried that children growing up in segregated colonies encounter tensions and vulnerability, yet they do not experience the interfaith camaraderie that once characterized times of peace.

In 2005–6, I conducted anthropological research in a Muslim-dominated slum in the northern quarters of Hyderabad, which I call Sultanpur. According to its inhabitants, this ghetto, located close to the Charminar mosque, one of the city's chief tourist attractions, housed approximately ten thousand Urdu-speaking, Muslim families.[4] The area was organized into a neatly structured mosaic of enclaves and shanties and relatively well-maintained lanes and by-lanes. For many generations in Sultanpur, this locality was the primary home and hub of craftsmen and traders who operated out of the nearby bangle, fabric, and pearl bazaars. Despite the definite lack of affluence in their everyday lives, the residents prided themselves as "experts," urban professionals, and a rooted community, which made them distinct from rural, un-skilled migrants in other ghettoes. Some parts of Sultanpur, however, were notorious for harboring a range of illegal industries, such as arms and land dealing, the flesh trade, and profiteering. "We have day jobs

and they have night jobs," said Mahmud, a bazaar trader, while pointing to prostitutes and dope dealers squatting under the pillars of the
Charminar at night. Thus legal and illegal trades coexisted and were
even codependent—several known gangsters were celebrated as gener-
ous money lenders and charitable donors to the two prominent local
mosques. The police, tax authorities, and corporation members were
bribed well by gangs and traders alike, however, and the state machinery
did little to interfere with the moral and fiscal economy of Sultanpur.

Historically, Sultanpur has witnessed a number of sporadic communal clashes between local Muslim inhabitants and middle- and
lower-class Hindus usually living around the Charminar area. These
discords were described to me as having been more often than not
sparked off by basic issues, such as slum dwellers siphoning off water
from Hindu-dominated housing estates, and were generally speedily
resolved by negotiations among community leaders. With the rise of an
aggressive Hindu nationalism in the 1990s, these quotidian clashes became more violent expressions of religious discontent and involved the
burning of homes, looting of shops, and physical attacks against people,
eventually driving a deeper wedge into local Hindu–Muslim relations.
Sultanpur suffered bouts of rioting in 1992, and again in 2003, when
local Hindus tried to restrict Muslim residents from publicly marking
the tenth anniversary of the destruction of the Babri mosque. In 2007,
a pipe bomb blast near the local Mecca Masjid, followed by serial blasts
near the Charminar, killed a number of residents of Sultanpur, including children, and the ensuing blame game between members of local
Hindu and Muslim political parties brought communal tensions in the
area into the media limelight. Even as recently as March 2010, a dispute
over the placement of religious flags in public places led to large-scale
communal rioting in Hyderabad. According to media sources, there
were several dead, more than a hundred people were critically injured,
almost two hundred people were arrested for rioting and destroying
property, twenty police stations imposed a curfew in their areas, and
paramilitary forces were deployed to control the rioting, especially in
the Charminar constituency.

The local residents of Sultanpur, and the employees of various concerned nongovernmental organizations (NGOs) active in this area,
repeatedly suggested to me that "child soldiering"—*fauji bacche/sepahi
bacche,* as the children chose to call themselves—was a consequence

of escalating communal antagonisms. According to some local social workers, since the 2003 riots, a number of riot-affected male children had established surveillance teams in the area, and their numbers had grown rapidly over a period of two years. At first, community leaders—mainly elderly male traders—had overlooked this phenomenon, since having children parade around in groups to protect themselves was perceived as "normal" fallout of communal conflict. Over time, however, the number of boy squads mushroomed: the children involved had developed strategies for recruitment, acquired arms, and exercised direct violence on people and property even within the slum. These activities brought issues of acceptance or outrage over child violence to the forefront of community debates in Sultanpur.

The apprehensions concerning vigilantism particularly revolved around the dissonance between contemporary behavior patterns among young boys and the reminiscence of an idealized notion of (male) childhood. There was widespread nostalgia among Sultanpur inhabitants that "children used to be children" (bacche to bacche the); although boys spent time with their mates, they had previously balanced their lives between work and studies, maintained a certain standard of hygiene and religiosity, and, most importantly, had respected elders. Furthermore, boys had previously been admiring and afraid of their fathers, affectionate toward their mothers, and playful with their older and younger siblings. "Who were the worst child offenders? The boys who smoked a *bidi* [cigarette] and we could pull their ears if we caught them," said Aiyaz, one of the slum dwellers I met in Sultanpur. This idyllic, gentle childhood was commonly believed to have been lost to communal violence, despite that by the time I began my research in Sultanpur, public memories about who had initiated this kind of group activity had become rather vague.

Most adults blamed children from "other" families as having "sown the seed of violence" in the minds of their own vulnerable children. For their part, none of the boys clearly remembered "the first guys" who came out on the streets as child patrols (they were not forthcoming about offering glory to one squad over another), but they usually recollected being incited by a friend, a brother, or an acquaintance to join the gangs. However, "for your own safety" was a key phrase used by all the children. The children began to feel safer in groups, showed plenty of internal bonhomie, and used persuasive tactics of enrollment on other children; these strategies eventually attracted more child "troops" into everyday vigilantism. Even though local families disapproved of child armies inhabiting street corners, very few inhabitants of Sultanpur openly questioned the children's contribution toward enhancing safety measures within the neighborhood, and even community leaders were unwilling to take on the wrath of "angry, unpredictable *fauji bacche*." Along the course of this chapter, I show how the ambivalence toward the child armies (by parents, NGO workers, the police, etc.) gave the boys free rein to imagine and develop discourses and dictates around urban child violence.

PATROLLING, POLICING, AND PERSECUTION: CHILDREN CLAIMING PUBLIC SPACES

While conducting research in Sultanpur, I attempted to design an intimate history of child soldiering through the voices of children themselves. While chatting with the boys about forming child squads, I discovered that their initial decisions to join were often related to being faced with their own mortality—"after seeing the face of death" (maut ke mooh dekhne ke baad), as they put it. Some of these choices centered on the direct experiences of riots (mobs targeting male children, children seeing the funerals of their friends and families, "touching fresh graves and imagining what it felt to lie under it," hearing about the death of children in past riots, etc.). Most of the children also suffered forms of displacement (children being sent back to the villages for safekeeping, taken out of school, having their mobility restricted, etc.). Most children were touched by violence even if they did not see rioting masses or were not subjected to physical assaults. This constant state of fear and flux, especially while negotiating communally tense public places, also made the boys acutely aware of diminishing numbers of male children in the slums. Several children decided to "take matters into their own hands," and a few of them initiated a system of night-and-day neighborhood patrolling.

Most of the boys involved in my study attended local educational institutions around the Sultanpur slums.[5] These formal and informal schools were usually run by faith-based organizations, various NGO schemes, philanthropists, and city corporations; there were no networks of madrasas (Islamic schools) active in this area. Male children helped their real or adoptive parents and relatives in their work, and those from families with businesses in handicrafts were encouraged to learn the trade. Almost all the boys were involved in petty crime, such as pickpocketing, ferrying illegal goods, and selling soft drugs, activities that were normalized within Sultanpur's semilegal economy (although often justified by the wider community as "boys will be boys"). A significant number of boys did day or night shifts as laborers, seeking out employment in the informal labor market for an additional income.

During my stay in the slum, I documented the activities of fifteen local child "armies" with memberships of ten to twelve children. The members of a particular squad usually lived on the same lane. The boundaries of these groups were flexible, as boys often moved between the squads, depending on new friendships and love for common sporting activities ranging from cricket to football to flying kites. Each child squad in Sultanpur took on the task of "guarding all things precious in their territory." As part of their everyday activities, the child squads concentrated on patrolling and protecting the streets, abusing or pelting stones at "suspicious" Hindu neighbors, watching over local mosques, chasing away people from other faiths visiting tombs of local saints,[6] making threatening gestures in crowded areas, swiftly drawing out their crude weapons to scare away unknown passersby, and so on. "These are the same streets where we were abused as dirty kids from the slum, now people step aside to let us pass," eleven-year-old Alam told me.

In their study of the impact of the 1992–93 riots on Dharavi, a large slum in Bombay, Chatterji and Mehta (2007) contend that sustained communal clashes often lead to people's withdrawal from public places. They show how Muslim families lost their sense of familiarity and mobility on the streets of Dharavi and encouraged their children to negotiate urban spaces through fear, distrust, and a constant state of alertness. In Clifford's (1997, 54) approach to mapping city spaces, "an urban neighborhood may be laid out physically according to a street plan, but it is not a space until it is practiced by people's active occupation, their movements through and around it." Chatterji and Mehta (2007, 24) argue that by the same reasoning, such spaces can also lead to "extraordinary closures." The taut sociopolitical atmosphere in Sultanpur was closing off the streets to poor children. But most slum boys were desperate to negotiate the public space for labor, fast cash, school, play, and childhood friendships. The ethnography mapped earlier highlights the collective attempts made by Muslim boys not only to overcome their fear of communally tense public places but also to chart and affirm the movement of children within them. The boys' status as urban warriors dissuaded local people from indulging in everyday physical and symbolic violence against them, which in turn allowed some poor Muslim children to temporarily enjoy a relatively independent childhood in poverty without being haunted by the fear of assaults and death.

The children's squads in Sultanpur tried to simultaneously control and correct some of the internal "weaknesses" of community existence within a volatile neighborhood. In this respect, most of the boys felt that the fragility of urban slum life had been brought about by the loose morals of local women. Eleven-year-old Abdul Rahman said to me, "It's not just during the riots that men from other communities come into in our slums; outsiders come and go as they please, and at all times. The local women open their doors to them, invite them inside, you know what I mean. If you dig holes into the walls of your own house, bad winds will blow in, isn't it?" The child squads set up surveillance teams and regularly exchanged information on "deviant" community members. The street corners and playing grounds became informal courts where the children took collective decisions on the form of retributive justice. The boys harassed women to wear veils (not as a religious dictate but because women were softer targets for children) and, at times, brutalized their own mothers and sisters for disobedience of directives enforced by the child groups.

Mumtaz, a widow, for example, was dragged out of her house and beaten by a group of child soldiers, including her ten-year-old son, for allegedly flirting with a Hindu salesman. Displaying her bruises to me, she said, almost sympathetically, "The children don't want to be victims anymore, and they have started to victimize their own people to manage their hurt." When I asked the children involved about the significance of this act, they eventually admitted that they had strategically chosen Mumtaz, as she did not live with male family members who could rescue her. She also did not receive enough support from the community because of her "bad reputation as a flirtatious widow." The children carried out the beating in the afternoon, when all the strong male slum dwellers were either away at work or taking a nap. So the children were aware (and afraid) of the fact that their actions might receive adult resistance and that their army could be publicly vanquished by a group of outraged men. Even though the children went after a frail target, they chose a public beating over an attack at home because their primary aim was to exhibit their capacity for direct violence on the streets. "We did not use any arms on Mumtaz, because our intention was not to kill her but to send out a warning to the community," concluded Abdul Rahman.

The boys' intracommunity vigilante activities also involved trashing Muslim shops where the owner had established business links with other communities, and this theatricality of armed children parading the streets affected trade relations between Hindus and Muslims. Muslim traders, who would normally shoo away children loitering around the market, felt compelled to treat local boys as distinguished guests. Most shop owners selling fragile, combustible goods became secretive about their transactions to avoid blatantly challenging the child armies. Sadid, a bangle seller, said,

> I keep offering tea and biscuits to the child patrols. Many Hindu women come to my shop, I have to be charming to them, often touch their wrists to help them put on bangles. I am terrified. Every item I sell is made of glass, and if the children smash my shop, I will not be able to repair the damage. So I am trying to avoid having Hindu customers in my shop, even at a loss.

Over the years of communal tension, Muslim children had lost family members, had seen women getting raped and killed, and some of the boys had been maimed for life. Even though they have endured a status as victims in riot situations, the child armies in Sultanpur were eager to reinvent themselves as empowered aggressors and at times refused to risk their public lives for peace or profit in the adult world.

Although the children openly occupied the streets of Sultanpur, they also built small hideouts in the slums, primarily to store their weapons. Partially sheltered from public view, these hideouts would simultaneously act as arms workshops and as gathering grounds for the local boys. While hammering carved wooden handles onto large kitchen knives (to make crude swords), the boys would share food, smokes, and conversation or just sit in companionable silence. Many of the children I interviewed claimed that such moments of quietude were forms of meaningful exchange, much more so than "empty" speeches about violence. A few boys would simply enjoy a nap and escape the afternoon sun. Most of the children toyed with knives and guns,[7] showed off new arms, discussed the value of user-friendly weapons, complained about a shortage in the supply of bullets, and exchanged information "off the streets." Squatting for hours, the boys would try to stitch additional pockets onto their shirts and trousers, mainly to carry small arms. There was generally a clear sense of comradeship, visible in the intense look in their eyes, the gentle smiles of admiration, and the constant slapping of shoulders. But most importantly, these hideouts acted as a safe haven for children tired of patrolling the streets.

"NOT GANGS SURELY": CONFUSED PUBLIC OPINION AND COMMUNITY SUPPORT FOR CHILD SQUADS

Plenty of children in Sultanpur did not take part in the squads. However, their body language and friendly gestures displayed a clear sense of solidarity with the child soldiers. Many boys played football and board games with the child militants or just idled time away in vigilante hideouts. Some of them eventually succumbed to the pressure of recruitment, whereas others volunteered for softer tasks such as ferrying weapons and messages. It was clear, however, that direct violence drew more attention and status. Twelve-year-old Shakeel, a "respected" soldier, told me that the children who did not fight could be easily identified from hesitations in their speech and movements. "Those boys try to skulk past us, have their eyes cast down, give us furtive smiles, look embarrassed," he said. The fact that the "passive" children felt inferior to the violent boys, and offered the latter envious admiration, propped up the superior status of Sultanpur's child soldiers. Several nonviolent children explained to me that they had not yet actualized plans to "combat" but were thinking of joining soon; most of them claimed that they would eventually compensate for their current shortcomings by being aggressively violent men in the future.

Despite their overt claims of discontent, slum dwellers in Sultanpur generally had an uncertain stance on child soldiering. On one hand, I met families who were proud of their children having a prominent public role in a locality faced with occasional threats from "outsiders"; some parents argued that the presence of child patrols made the streets safer. Older women, in particular, were pleased that young girls were not eloping with Hindu men in fear of vigilante disciplinary action. Yet, on the other hand, there was significant ambivalence about the futures of these violent boys. Alisha, the mother of a twelve-year-old child vigilante, was explicitly hopeful that that her son would eventually mature out of his "fascination with patrolling" and get a job. During one conversation, she also said to me, "Don't say 'gang' in your research, it will ruin their future." Alisha implied that gang membership entailed following a prolonged path of violence, but child soldiering involved a temporary engagement with violent collective units, which would dissolve with age, mobility, and resolution of conflict. Her plea for dissociating child vigilantism from gangsterism indicated that, despite the power, presence, and popularity of adult gangsters in the locality, "gang" was a pejorative concept, and most members of the community retained a faint hope that maturing out and away from child soldiering would allow the local boys in Sultanpur to return to and engage with mainstream social and economic life.

Parents continued to view boy squad members as small in size, still playing games, and abstaining from strategic financial engagement with religious or political leaders for personal gains. Even beaten-up women did not imagine their sons as "gang" members. The boys themselves were also careful to distance themselves from what they understood to be "gangsterism." It is interesting to note in this respect that many studies on rising urban gang behavior around the world have emphasized the importance of territorialization in gang activities—the idea of dividing and ruling the city—and how this is fundamental to notions of self-identification among gang members (e.g., Alexander 2000; Bourgois 1996; Rodgers 2006; Venkatesh 2009). Although the child squads were territorial in their spatial practices, their identity was less bound up in notions of protecting or extending territory and more invested in protecting and controlling the community. Similarly, the absence of initiation rites and the flexibility in group pecking orders, hierarchies, and leadership roles are also major differences between typical gangs and child vigilantism in Sultanpur. Perhaps the biggest difference was that the children claimed that their group endeavors had little to do with burglaries, drug dealing, or supporting family incomes by illegal means, which have often been depicted as major motivations of gang activity in economically precarious neighborhoods (Padilla 1992; Jankowski 1991).

This concern to distinguish the child squads from gangs was partly fostered by an ambiguity among local authorities in relation to the vigilantes. Although, as Nancy Scheper-Hughes (1984, 1987) has documented in the context of Brazil, state and religious organizations often perpetrate atrocities against poor children who engage in symbolic and direct violence, especially through indifference to the routinization of child death on the streets, in Hyderabad, the local-level state machinery and the dominant mosques had discriminatory policies *in favor* of child squads. The officer-in-charge of the Sultanpur police station, for example, dismissed my concerns about them and argued that "they are protecting their own community, nothing else," explicitly suggesting that child soldiering to save a vulnerable community and escape the threat of street deaths was not the same as gang patrolling to fight a territorial war. As a result, the local police stations rarely treated child soldiers as delinquents and ignored the complaints of violated women and disgruntled shopkeepers. At the same time, some of the boys acted as local informants for the police, secretly offering information about slum activities in exchange for unrestricted mobility on the streets. Ultimately, the rapid rise and small successes of child squads in urban slums did not pose a challenge to the complex police–criminal–politician nexus in Indian cities.

Similarly, local mosques did not forbid the practice of child soldiering. Instead of criticizing the children as early gang members, religious spokespersons justified their actions as a way of countering Hindu supremacy. Scholars studying Muslim youth in the expanding ribbon of working-class neighborhoods across the world usually propose a strong link between collective violence and nationalism (cf. Din and Cullingford 2006; Ewing 2008; Hart 2002). Among them, Hart's (2008) study of adolescent Muslim men in a Palestinian refugee camp in Jordan particularly highlights how controlling women and engagements with debates about Islam marked the transition to social adulthood in marginalized sociopolitical spaces. Even though the boys in Sultanpur displayed aggression toward unveiled women or Hindu traders accused of predatory behavior, and this could be construed (especially to heads of mosques) as an attempt to revive an idealized Islamic past, in their everyday actions, the children had an unguided engagement with issues concerning Islam, gender, or religious practice in the slums, along with an uninformed understanding of media images of the war on terror.

Certainly all the boys I encountered were fairly inattentive and restless during discussions about contentious social and political subjects at the mosques or during meetings among community leaders. The activities of the child squads were oriented more toward reminding the inhabitants of Sultanpur, local Hindus and Muslims, of the power and presence of male children than toward displaying genuine concern about the purity of Islam. In many ways, their daily lives etched in relief against a violent sociopolitical landscape had more than anything else made the boys inclined to distance themselves from religious–nationalist tags, to the extent that when the boys met on the street corners, they openly discussed their apathy for various religious labels.[8] To this extent, lenient police practices and supportive religious sermons glorifying the child squads allowed "boy soldiers" to perceive their conduct as worthy of a greater cause. Anxious families in Sultanpur were dissuaded from seeking help from the mosques as well, because these institutions were unconcerned about the suppression of child militancy. This also reinforced the boys' overt rejection of grand nationalist and religious ideologies in favor of "boys' army" identities, the latter being created and collated among the slum children through peer group debates, decisions, and deeds.

Over the period of my research, the children involved in the Sultanpur child squads offered several reasons for preferring an exalted status as "soldiers." Some boys explicitly feared a police backlash if children became marked as gang members involved in tough, illegal transactions, whereas others felt too fragile to compete with the economic and political mafia well established in the area. At the same time, "soldiering" involved "glorious" violence to save others in what was perceived as a legitimate social role. Although many scholars have argued that sexuality is possibly the most important social domain for the construction of aggressive masculinities in South Asia (Alter 1994; Chakraborty 2010; Hansen 1996; Srivastava 2004), the child discourses around violence could not be linked to male sexual practices. Smaller children in the squads did not display an overt interest in capturing women through seduction or force. As many vigilantes had not reached puberty, the boys did not see girl children as direct objects of desire. As nine-year-old Arif claimed, "this was not about girls." Even the older boys were at pains to emphasize that their actions were not designed to satisfy pubescent sexual desires. To offer a brief comparative perspective, the vigilante boys I studied in the slums of Bombay (see Sen 2007) indulged in building bodies to imitate well-muscled movie stars and attract girls, which was an integral aspect of slum life; despite similarities in the collective actions of these two groups, sexual media images were not integrated (as yet) into the practice of child vigilantism in Sultanpur.[9]

Both the internal dynamics of the child squads, their logic and objectives, and the way in which they embedded themselves within the broader social, religious, and political landscape meant that there was a definite space for social acceptability around child squads in Sultanpur, which reinforced rather than distorted violent child identities. At the same time, the practice of child soldiering did dislocate given and accepted meanings of masculinities, childhoods, familial relations, gangsterism, and even notions of community, thereby subverting the very sociopolitical unity that the child squads sought to promote. In addition, child soldiering also created status anxieties among poor children because all the boys in Sultanpur did not display the courage to take on the challenge of public violence. These rifts also fragmented the male child world, which the boy squads aspired to unify and protect. To this extent, far from being vectors for the constitution of strong and shielded local communities, the clustering of child squads and their display of dominance over their localities merely reinforced the seditious effects of urban terror that reportedly fragment so many of the world's cities (Vigil 2002; Jensen 2008).

CONCLUSION

A substantial amount of academic research on gangs has reinforced and responded to representations and realities of gang formation across the world. Anthropologists have played a key role in challenging the supposed pathologies of gangs and gang leaders and have offered emic perspectives on the social logics of investment in gang cultures and identities, drawing out the paradoxes and putative pleasures of being a gang member in working-class, marginalized neighborhoods (Decker and Weerman 2005; Gore and Pratten 2003). While evaluating the brutality and human losses involved in gang conflicts, scholars have tried to map the connections between local gang concerns and larger capitalistic social structures and urban renewals (Rodgers 2009), and the ways in which the latter create and sustain a shared grammar of violence and territoriality in "ganglands" on the ground (Beall 2002; Matusitz and Repass 2009). Shifting away from a focus on gangs, this chapter has examined the social histories, complex subjectivities, and multiple layers of children's practices of collective violence in a communally tense urban neighborhood in India. In particular, I have highlighted the ways in which young boys negotiate notions of respectability, dignity, and morality and attempt to create a "soldiering" culture that could be said to fall somewhere between gangsterism and vigilantism. This has allowed Muslim slum boys to operate as violent collective units without being negatively branded as gangs or *jihadis*.

Most studies of violent children in urban settings remain focused on legal studies, delinquency, child crime, and street children. Violent and armed male children are found more extensively in the chronicles of rural war zones, especially in South Asia. For example, the analysis of child soldiering in Sri Lanka (in the Liberation Tigers of the Tamil Eelam), Burma (in the National Army), and Nepal (in the Maoist movement) highlights the loss of psychosocial and sexual innocence among male children and their initiation into hypermasculine discourses (de Silva, Hobbs, and Hanks 2001; Kanagaratnam, Raundalen, and Asbjørnsen 2005; Kohrt et al. 2008). In this chapter, I have sought to open an ethnographic window into the lives of a cluster of urban, self-styled child squads whose members were *neither* street children *nor* (forcibly or voluntarily) recruited into state-sponsored or antistate political movements. This localized form of urban child violence shows how the terminology as well as the imagination of ethical "soldiering" allowed the children to move between victimologies of social injustice and discourses of retributive violence, neither of which were associated with profit making or illegal gang behavior as understood by the state, religious institutions, NGO workers, or local community members. By using the trope of child soldiering, I also raise and recast questions about unconventional violent clique formations in urban India.

At the same time, the material presented in this chapter highlights how a riot-torn slum can become a spatial template for the enactment of volatile social and symbolic communication, sustaining a rhetoric of blame and suspicion and creating a particular environment that gives rise to unique yet conflicted social relations. Life in constant negotiation with this environment creates a "poor child's world" that is continuously crafted, not always by play or wonder, but by learning the skills to build life anew within a landscape of death and destruction in the city. When out on an evening patrol with Arshed, he once asked me rhetorically, "Shall we exist in the city, endure it, or shall we erase it?" Without waiting for my reaction, he then vanished behind a maze of reassembled, fragile shanties to find his group and enquire about further "duties," leaving me to wonder, rather sadly, how the decrepit, communally fragmented space of the city can generate a peculiar culture of violence around children's concerns about survival.

NOTES

The fieldwork for the research discussed in this chapter was funded by the British Academy's Small Research Grants scheme.

1. For example, films such as *Sathya* (Truth; directed by Ram Gopal Varma, 1998) and *Company* (directed by Ram Gopal Varma, 2002), as well as antihero comic books such as *Doga* (Raj Comics), reveal the inner workings of Mumbai's murky underworld.

2. See *The Indian Police Journal* (2010) for recent analyses offered by anticrime task force chiefs as well as criminologists on terrorism, extremism, and youth violence in urban India.

3. For detailed studies of communal relations in Hyderabad under Nizami sovereignty, see Copland (1988) and Kooiman (2002); for citizenship battles among Hyderabadi Muslims, see Sherman (2010).

4. Surveys by nongovernmental organizations, housing figures, and census operations by the local municipal corporation estimate the number to be closer to thirty thousand.

5. In Sultanpur, girls usually had limited mobility, took on more domestic responsibilities than their male siblings, and were discouraged from attending school.

6. The children often chased away unfamiliar Muslims who did not sport visible signs and symbols of Islam.

7. It was striking that children's gangs in Sultanpur seemed to have easy access to and frequently carried small arms in addition to sticks and swords, in contrast to other Indian urban centers (Sen 2007). One reason for this, as Alam explained, was that "smaller children felt relieved to be able to shoot from a distance without having to physically overpower larger opponents." Even though I did not see the children discharge their weapons directly on people, I was still curious to know how the boys equipped themselves with guns without a steady income. After several weeks of prodding and probing, the children took me on a "get-a-gun" tour. Several children worked in shops and factories and saved a part of their income to buy a gun from a local dealer. Some children actually worked in illegal weapons warehouses and were rewarded with a gun. Yet other boys did drug drops for adult gangs and were given a gun for self-protection. Local

traders, moreover, acquired illegal guns to protect their shops, homes, women, and inflammable goods during the riots. Many residents of Sultanpur justified these acquisitions on the grounds that there was a distinction between the work ethics of an armed gangster and the everyday practicality of a fearful, poor Muslim keeping a gun under his pillow. These guns were often stolen by local children. One day, a young vigilante called Abdullah pointed to the local police station as the source of his guns. He said, "I mop floors at the station and simply steal the guns from unlocked weapons vaults. No one ever cares or counts."

8. This can be related to the way that certain labels have come to justify the targeting of particular groups in India within the local context of anti-Muslim-antiminority passions and the broader global context of the war on terror. For example, there were large-scale arrests of poor Muslims following the cell phone-triggered Mecca Masjid blasts in Hyderabad (May 18, 2007); according to my informants, these arrests were justified by state officials on the grounds that Muslims were "all *jihadis.*"

9. For a detailed study of child masculinities in Sultanpur, see Sen (2011).

REFERENCES

Alexander, Claire. 2000. *The Asian Gang: Ethnicity, Identity, Masculinity.* New York: Berg.

Alter, Joseph S. 1994. "Celibacy, Sexuality, and the Transformation of Gender into Nationalism in North India." *Journal of Asian Studies* 53, no. 1: 45–66.

Beall, Jo. 2002. "Globalization and Social Exclusion in Cities: Framing the Debate with Lessons from Africa and Asia." *Environment and Urbanization* 14, no. 1: 41–51.

Bonner, Philip L. 2004. "Migration, Urbanization, and Urban Social Movements in Twentieth Century India and South Africa." *Studies in History* 20, no. 2: 215–36.

Bourgois, Philippe. 1996. "In Search of Masculinity: Violence, Respect, and Sexuality among Puerto Rican Crack Dealers in East Harlem." *British Journal of Criminology* 36:412–27.

Chakraborty, Kabita. 2010. "Unmarried Muslim Youth and Sex Education in the Bustees of Kolkata." *South Asian History and Culture* 1, no. 2: 268–81.

Chatterji, Roma, and Deepak Mehta. 2007. *Living with Violence: An Anthropology of Events and Everyday Life.* New Delhi: Routledge.

Clifford, James. 1997. *Routes: Travel and Translation in the Late Twentieth Century.* Cambridge, Mass.: Harvard University Press.

Copland, Ian. 1988. "'Communalism' in Princely India: The Case of Hyderabad, 1930–1940." *Modern Asian Studies* 22, no. 4: 783–814.

de Silva, H., H. C. Hobbs, and H. Hanks. 2001. "Conscription of Children in Armed Conflict: A Form of Child Abuse: A Study of 19 Former Child Soldiers." *Child Abuse Review* 10, no. 2: 125–34.

Decker, Scott H., and Frank M. Weerman. 2005. *European Street Gangs and Troublesome Youth Groups.* Lanham, Md.: AltaMira.

Din, Ikhlaq, and Cedric Cullingford. 2006. "Pakistani Gangs in Bradford." *Police Journal* 3, no. 79: 258–78.

Engineer, Asghar Ali. 1991. "Hyderabad Riots: An Analytical Report." In *Communal Riots in Post-independence India,* edited by Asghar Ali Engineer, 288–98. New Delhi: Orient Blackswan.

Ewing, Katherine Pratt. 2008. *Stolen Honor: Stigmatizing Muslim Men in Berlin.* Stanford, Calif.: Stanford University Press.

Flueckiger, Joyce Burkhalter. 2006. *In Amma's Healing Room: Gender and Vernacular Islam in South India.* Bloomington: Indiana University Press.

Gore, Charles, and David Pratten. 2003. "The Politics of Plunder: The Rhetorics of Order and Disorder in Southern Nigeria." *African Affairs* 102, no. 407: 211–40.

Hansen, Thomas Blom. 2001. *Wages of Violence: Naming and Identity in Postcolonial Bombay.* Princeton, N.J.: Princeton University Press.

Hansen, Thomas Blom. 1996. "Recuperating Masculinity: Hindu Nationalism, Violence, and the Exorcism of the Muslim 'Other.'" *Critique of Anthropology* 16, no. 2: 137–72.

Hart, Jason. 2002. "Children and Nationalism in a Palestinian Refugee Camp in Jordan." *Childhood* 9, no. 1: 35–47.

———. 2008. "Dislocated Masculinity: Adolescence and the Palestinian Nation-in-Exile." *Journal of Refugee Studies* 21, no. 1: 64–81.

Jankowski, Martín Sánchez. 1991. *Islands in the Street: Gangs and American Urban Society.* Berkeley: University of California Press.

Jensen, Steffen. 2008. *Gangs, Politics, and Dignity in Cape Town.* Johannesburg: Wits University Press.

Jeffrey, Craig. 2008. "'Generation Nowhere': Rethinking Youth through the Lens of Unemployed Young Men." *Progress in Human Geography* 32, no. 6: 739–58.

Kakar, Sudhir. 2005. "Rumours and Religious Riots." In *Rumor Mills: The Social Impact of Rumor and Legend,* edited by Gary Alan Fine, Véronique Campion-Vincent, and Chip Heath, 53–60. Piscataway, N.J.: Aldine Transaction.

Kanagaratnam, Pushpa, Magne Raundalen, and Arve E. Asbjørnsen. 2005. "Ideological Commitment and Posttraumatic Stress in Former Tamil Child Soldiers." *Scandinavian Journal of Psychology* 46, no. 6: 511–20.

Kohrt, Brandon A., Mark J. D. Jordans, Wietse A. Tol, Rebecca A. Speckman, Sujen M. Maharjan, Carol M. Worthman, and Ivan H. Komproe. 2008. "Comparison of Mental Health between Former Child Soldiers and Children Never Conscripted by Armed Groups in Nepal." *Journal of the American Medical Association* 300, no. 6: 691–702.

Kooiman, Dick. 2002. *Communalism and Indian Princely States: Travancore, Baroda, and Hyderabad in the 1930s.* Delhi: Manohar.

Major, Andrew J. 1999. "State and Criminal Tribes in Colonial Punjab: Surveillance, Control and Reclamation of the 'Dangerous Classes.'" *Modern Asian Studies* 33: 657–88.

Matusitz, Jonathan, and Michael Repass. 2009. "Gangs in Nigeria: An Updated Examination." *Crime, Law, and Social Change* 52, no. 5: 495–511.

Naidu, Ratna. 1990. *Old Cities, New Predicaments: A Study of Hyderabad.* New Delhi: Sage.

Nigam, S. 1990. "Disciplining and Policing the 'Criminals by Birth,' Part 1: The Making of a Colonial Stereotype—The Criminal Tribes and Castes of North India." *Indian Economic Social History Review* 27, no. 2: 131–64.

Padilla, Felix M. 1992. *The Gang as an American Enterprise.* Washington, D.C.: Library of Congress.

Radhakrishna, Meena. 2001. *Dishonoured by History: "Criminal Tribes" and British Colonial Policy.* Hyderabad: Orient Longman.

Rodgers, Dennis. 2006. "Living in the Shadow of Death: Gangs, Violence, and Social Order in Urban Nicaragua, 1996–2002." *Journal of Latin American Studies* 38, no. 2: 267–92.

———. 2009. "Slum Wars of the 21st Century: Gangs, *Mano Dura,* and the New Urban Geography of Conflict in Central America." *Development and Change* 40, no. 5: 949–76.

Scheper-Hughes, Nancy. 1984. "Infant Mortality and Infant Care: Cultural and Economic Constraints on Nurturing in Northeast Brazil." *Social Science and Medicine* 19, no. 5: 535–46.

———, ed. 1987. *Child Survival: Anthropological Perspectives on the Treatment and Maltreatment of Children.* Dordrecht, Netherlands: D. Reidel.

Sen, Atreyee. 2007. *Shiv Sena Women: Violence and Communalism in a Bombay Slum.* Bloomington: Indiana University Press.

———. 2011. "Surviving Violence, Contesting Victimhood: Communal Politics and the Creation of Child-Men in an Urban Indian Slum." *South Asia: Journal of South Asian Studies* 34, no. 2: 276–97.

Sherman, Taylor C. 2010. "Moral Economies of Violence in Hyderabad State, 1948." *Deccan Studies* 8, no. 2: 65–90.

Srivastava, S. 2004. *Sexual Sites, Seminal Attitudes: Sexualities, Masculinities, and Culture in South Asia.* New Delhi: Sage.

Venkatesh, S. A. 2009. *Gang Leader for a Day: A Rogue Sociologist Crosses the Line.* London: Penguin.

Verkaaik, Oskar. 2004. *Migrants and Militants: Fun and Urban Violence in Pakistan.* Princeton, N.J.: Princeton University Press.

Vigil, James Diego. 2002. *A Rainbow of Gangs: Street Cultures in the Mega-City.* Austin: University of Texas Press.

Wacquant, Loïc. 2007. *Urban Outcasts: A Comparative Sociology of Advanced Marginality.* Cambridge: Polity Press.

10

"We Are the True Blood of the Mau Mau": The Mungiki Movement in Kenya

JACOB RASMUSSEN

During the past decade, the Mungiki movement in Kenya has gained a reputation as one of East Africa's most dangerous criminal organizations. For example, following a visit to Nairobi as part of his global tour investigating the world's "worst gangs," the British actor turned popular journalist Ross Kemp (2008, 167) described Mungiki as having a reputation for "cutting off people's heads, arms and other parts of the anatomy" and for being involved in "protection rackets, extortion and extremely violent murder—the stock-in-trade of gangs around the world." Similarly, the report produced by the Official Commission of Inquiry into Post-election Violence about the riots and brutality surrounding the 2008 elections discussed Mungiki in the section on "Organized Gangs" (Waki Report 2008, 258). Members of the Mungiki movement whom I interviewed during the course of anthropological research in Nairobi between 2008 and 2010, however, unambiguously reject the "gang" label and categorize themselves simply by stating, "We are Mungiki!" In Kikuyu language, the word *mungiki* means "masses" or "people" (see Wamue 2001, 454; Gecaga 2007, 68), and the name is thus arguably an index of Mungiki's ambition to be a popular movement rather than a ganglike organization. Indeed, the notion of representing "the people" and their needs and wishes is in fact central to the Mungiki's narrative about itself and to its relation to wider Kenyan society. To its members, "Mungiki" is more than a name; it symbolizes the movement's internal unity and represents a collective ambition for the future.

In this chapter, I consider the profound disjuncture between official and Mungiki discourse concerning the movement, focusing in particular on Mungiki narratives to highlight how the members perceive, place, and legitimize the movement in relation to the rest of Kenyan society. Writing on the relation between narrative and reality, the cognitive psychologist Jerome Bruner (1991, 13) argues that narratives construe rather than refer to reality. This basic understanding of the character of narratives informs the analysis offered here of Mungiki's narrative.[1] While the narrative is central to the construction and presentation of a collective identity for the narrators, it is also a reflection of the surrounding society's reaction to them (Jensen 2006). Analyzing both Mungiki's narrative and wider Kenyan society's reaction to it, I trace both the construction of Mungiki's collective identity and the movement's institutionalization. I begin with a brief overview of Mungiki's origins and its remarkable transformative capacities before proceeding with a deeper consideration of Mungiki's historical relationship with the Kenyan Mau Mau liberation movement. This is followed by an analysis of the institutionalization of the movement in Kenyan society. A final section concludes by elaborating on the relational aspects of Mungiki's narrative and the societal position from which they claim to speak, approached through Michel Foucault's (2001) concept of the "truth-teller."

THE CHAMELEON AND THE MUGUMO TREE: MUNGIKI ORIGINS AND TRANSFORMATIONS

In his work comparing gangs through space and time, the social scientist John Hagedorn (2008, 30) argues that while many gangs have transformed from juvenile delinquents to organized criminals, others have developed interests in local politics or else have displayed the potential to change into more overtly political social forms such as militias or social movements. Rejecting restrictive gang typologies, he therefore argues that the "only constant in today's world of gangs is that they are changing" (31) and contends that we must adopt broad and dynamic conceptions of gangs to truly understand them, so as not to reduce them to mere criminals, and to highlight the complex set of intertwined and changing interests and activities that underpin them. Seen from this perspective, Mungiki is clearly conceivable, if not as a gang, certainly as a ganglike organization.[2] At the same time, however, it is less the question of whether Mungiki is a gang that provides us with an understanding of the movement than the focus on the transformations and the internal and external factors motivating these transformations. It is arguably these that in the final analysis make Mungiki ganglike, and to this extent, this chapter will seek to understand Mungiki and their activities, whether criminal, violent, political, or religious, in a broad-brush manner.

Having said this, it is important to note that Mungiki did not start out as a criminal organization. Rather, the movement started as a Kikuyu ethnic group religious and cultural movement in the late 1980s, advocating a return to traditional customs and values (Wamue 2001, 456). Certainly the majority of the movement's rituals and organizational practices, such as initiation ceremonies, oaths, and the movement's cell structure, are inspired by old Kikuyu traditions and customs. Mungiki's stated aim was to free the Kenyan people from cultural, political, and economic oppression. When the movement was formed, Kenya was still a one-party state with little associational space, especially for oppositional politics (Nasong'o 2007; Ndeda 2009). After the 1992 multiparty elections, however, the hitherto oppressive Moi regime gradually allowed for more civic organizations, and grassroots associational life expanded. Dissatisfaction with President Moi's gerontocracy grew, and Mungiki became a focal point for calls for a new generational politics. Drawing on the old Kikuyu traditions of cyclical transference of ritualistic power from one generation to the next (the so-called *Itwika*), the movement claimed that it was time for the old leaders to step down and leave the scene for the young (Kagwanja 2005a, 2005b).

Mungiki quickly developed political ambitions, and after attempting to team up with existing parties, it registered as a political party under the name "Kenya National Youth Alliance" (KNYA) in 2004. The social ambition rooted in Kikuyu traditions appealed to many poor young Kikuyu, who joined the new party en masse, and as the movement grew, it spread from the central regions in the Kikuyu heartlands to the slums of Nairobi. As a result, the economic interests of the movement changed over time and became increasingly focused on the informal sector. Concomitantly, the movement was frequently accused of being engaged in criminal activities such as illegal taxation and extortion. Mungiki's consequent engagement in battles with other informal groups, including in particular ethnic gangs affiliated with non-Kikuyu tribes, led to it being widely labeled an ethnic street gang, compounded by the fact that the movement's political engagement saw it categorized as a vigilante group or political militia. Partly as a result of this violence, the KNYA was deregistered by the Kenyan government prior to the 2007 elections. The Mungiki leader Maina Njenga was also jailed in 2004 on what Mungiki claim were fabricated charges. On his release in late October 2009, he converted to a Pentecostal church and officially put an end to Mungiki. However, the movement clearly lives on with the same hierarchies, the same network, and the same organizational structure, the only difference being that it now officially has no name and is therefore supposedly nonexistent. However, the January 2010 burial of Maina Njenga's wife in a remote rural area south of Nairobi was attended by more than ten thousand young men and stands as proof that the organization is still very strong.

Before Mungiki turned to Pentecostalism, initiation into the movement took place through mass baptism rituals at riverbanks in the countryside. The baptisms were large gatherings where initiates would enter the river from one bank and reemerge from the other, before then passing through the thick smoke of fire—a "baptism through fire." Such baptisms came to be increasingly interrupted by the authorities during the 1990s, leading to running battles between the police and Mungiki, adding an extra, metaphorical dimension to the "baptism through fire" of initiation through hardship and battle. Certainly, as Dennis Rodgers (2006) has argued with regard to warfare between gangs in Nicaragua, conflict can often be socially constitutive.[3] After the movement was banned in 2002, Mungiki's rituals became smaller in scale and surrounded by greater secrecy. This led to numerous rumors and unsubstantiated tales about the movement emerging and circulating through Kenyan society. At the same time, this lent a certain aura to Mungiki, of which its members are very much aware.

During the course of a conversation I once had with a high-ranking member of Mungiki, he resorted to a vivid metaphor to describe the changes and shifts that the movement had undergone over the years since its foundation: "Mungiki is like a chameleon!" He, however, quickly added to this that "what keeps us together is the cause." The "cause" to which he referred was the fight against injustice and oppression. This meant—as he explained—the movement could logically both embrace Islam, as it did for a short period prior to the 2002 elections, and join a Pentecostal church, as it did upon the release of its jailed leader Maina Njenga in October 2009. Similarly, in politics, Mungiki have worked with government officials at some points in time, as well as with opposition politicians at others, depending on what the movement leadership felt was the best option in terms of moving toward fulfillment of the movement's overall goal.[4] In other words, much of Mungiki's transformation is highly instrumental. After the public conversion to Islam by the Mungiki leadership and large numbers of their adherents in 2000, they quickly returned to their initial beliefs, for example (Kagwanja 2003).[5] This instrumentalization is in fact often quite explicit. The Mungiki leader Maina Njenga has, for example, stated that his Pentecostal conversion signals that the movement is reformed and that the members should abandon their criminal activities, clearly an attempt to gain public legitimacy. The Mungiki leadership, in other words, claims that the movement is moving in the direction of further noncriminal and nonviolent interaction with society but, at the same time, admits that it is speculating in image control and self-presentation to position the movement in the best possible way in relation to its overall aims.[6]

At the same time, individual Mungiki members also drew on the chameleon metaphor to show that they, as Mungiki members, could change into whatever appearance is required. This was, for example, explicitly raised in conversation with Mungiki members as they explained to me how it was that they could look for jobs both as housekeepers and as security guards for international companies in Afghanistan, to suggest that they could adapt to whatever these different circumstances demanded. The same was also true of the Mungiki members from the city whom I met on a Mungiki farm, who used the chameleon metaphor to justify their having taken up farming. At the same time, individuals clearly used the metaphor to describe more than just an instrumental change but also a much deeper transformation. The transition from urban to rural life encompassed a transformation involving taking on wholesale a new livelihood, which required new skills and a new way of life. To this extent, the metaphor of the chameleon can be said to have worked both on individual and collective levels, as well as on instrumental and genuinely transformative levels.

The chameleon metaphor arguably captures the changing character of Mungiki very well, but it also touches on Mungiki members' presentation of themselves as a movement with a social cause rather than as a gang. That is, Mungiki might be changing its colors, but it sticks to its political and social cause—it is still a chameleon regardless of the color in which it presents itself. At the same time, however, another metaphor is also commonly invoked by Mungiki members to describe the movement—that of the *mugumo,* or fig tree. The *mugumo* tree grows like a parasite on other trees, with its branches establishing roots when they reach the ground, and then entangling and subsuming the host tree (Beech 1913, 4). Thus the *mugumo* tree metaphor also describes a process of transformation while staying the same, but with the added capacity of growing stronger while draining the host. Some *mugumo* trees are sacred in Kikuyu traditions, and many members of Mungiki refer to the tree when they explain the various transformations of the movement, stating that Mungiki can swallow the other religions or parties with which they have associated themselves.[7]

At the same time, it is important to stress that Mungiki is a heterogeneous movement where the local branches or factions might differ from each other in terms of what their primary activities are. Certain members or factions tend to be more interested in politics, others in religion, and still others join for economic reasons. Considering the size of Mungiki, internal variations come as little surprise. The actual size of Mungiki is difficult to establish, with some claiming that there are more than a million members, whereas others suggest that members only number one hundred thousand. Such disputes over the movement's size are part of a political game, where Mungiki claim a larger following than they might actually have to present themselves as both a political and a militant threat, while the authorities, of course, minimize them (Ruteere 2008, 16). At the same time, the movement's ability to mobilize thousands of people from different factions, very quickly, has been shown on multiple occasions over the years and indicates that, at one level, at least, Mungiki is a mass movement.

The burial of Maina Njenga's wife is a classic example highlighting the movement's ability to mobilize thousands of adherents, who, moreover, congregated in a remote field. This required substantial financial as well as good logistic and organizational capacity. The strength of the movement was further visible at the burial not only through the sheer number of people who attended but also through the members' submission to the movement: after driving for an hour across empty fields, the hearse's cortege entered a human alleyway of thousands of Mungiki members silently holding hands and bowing their heads in respect to their chairman's deceased wife. The organizational capacity and discipline of the Mungiki were evident on another occasion, when the venue of a planned peace meeting was changed from Nakuru to Nyahururu—two cities sixty-three kilometers apart—only two days before the event, yet several thousand Mungiki members nevertheless attended.

Transformations and the ability to adapt to changing situations are central elements of Mungiki's narrative. The many activities in which Mungiki is engaged and the different expressions of the movement show not only how Mungiki has been able to adapt to changing political contexts without losing its support but also how the movement has been able to reinvent and renew itself and expand its areas of operation. Conventional criminological studies see the volatility of gangs as a potential societal problem, because it makes them more difficult to control, but Hagedorn (2008, xxv) sees the potential of gangs to bridge several activities and take on different expressions as offering an opportunity to reduce violence and change gangs more permanently into socially positive forces. To determine to what extent this can be said of Mungiki, however, it is necessary to delve further into the underpinning dynamics of the movement and, more specifically, its relation to the Mau Mau movement, as the next section proceeds to do.

MAU MAU LEGACIES

Probably the most central theme invoked in Mungiki's narrative is the movement's Mau Mau legacy. Mau Mau fighters fought the British colonizers in the decade preceding Kenya's independence in 1963. Mungiki's cofounder, Ndura Waruinge, is the grandchild of former Mau Mau general Waruinge, and many Mungiki members in fact claim to be descendants of former Mau Mau fighters (Wamue 2001, 455). Certainly, during the interviews that I carried out with rank-and-file Mungiki members, they would often show me faded black-and-white photos of their grandfathers, more often than not typical images of Mau Mau warriors: young bearded and dreadlocked men, walking stick in hand, straightened back, with their chins lifted up in a self-assured pose. Indeed, it is very much a part of the Mungiki foundation narrative that the movement's two founders, the cousins Maina Njenga and Ndura Waruinge, consulted their Mau Mau grandfathers as teenagers in the late 1980s to obtain advice on how to best deal with their youthful grievances, and that they advised forming the Mungiki movement.[8] Thus, just as in the early 1950s, when the Mau Mau advocated a return to indigenous values and beliefs in opposition to the British colonial regime (Wachanga 1975; Anderson 2005), excluded youths in the 1980s began to express their increasing dissatisfaction with the Moi regime through calls to return to traditional values and beliefs, linking the religious aspect with the bloodline heritage from the Mau Mau.

The Mau Mau was a movement formed primarily by young Kikuyu members fighting for land and freedom from the British colonial rulers from the late 1940s until 1960 (Anderson 2005, 50–67). The Mau Mau fighters mainly operated from the forests around Mt. Kenya and the Aberdare mountains, although they did initially have close ties to allies in the cities, until the British managed to infiltrate and close these lines of supply (Anderson 2005, 212; Furedi 1973, 285).[9] Mau Mau were organized into cells, or *batunis* (platoons), that operated independently but under common leadership and coordination. Mau Mau were famous for their oaths of unity, which committed members to reject all European values and, to some extent, to use violence in pursuit of their goals (Anderson 2005, 56; see also Lonsdale 1992; Lonsdale 2003). Mau Mau primarily targeted Kenyan collaborators of the colonial regime, but from the early 1950s onward, they also began targeting whites, although few whites were actually killed, partly because the Mau Mau fighters were ill equipped and had few guns, mainly using *rungus* and *pangas,* wooden clubs and long knives used for work in the fields, respectively. As a result, they developed a reputation for slashing the throats of and decapitating their victims.

The British rulers declared a state of emergency in Kenya in 1952 and started to systematically persecute the Mau Mau by infiltrating and killing them, and by setting up camps where more than a hundred thousand innocent Kikuyu were detained (Anderson 2005; Elkins 2005). At the same time, Kikuyus opposed to the Mau Mau formed regiments of so-called Home Guards, who assisted the British (Anderson 2005, 140–41; Lonsdale 1992, 266). Kenya gained independence in 1963, and the Kikuyu Jomo Kenyatta became the first president. In postcolonial writing about Kenyan history, the internal strife within the Kikuyu tribe during the independence struggle has been suppressed, and the prevailing discourse is one that emphasizes a story of united Kikuyu support for the postindependence government, which, at the time, was very important for the construction of the new country's national project (Lonsdale 2003).

Mungiki frequently claim that they are "the true blood of the Mau Mau," both physically and metaphorically. A critical Mau Mau issue that has shaped Mungiki discourse is the fact that most Mau Mau fighters remained landless and poor after independence. Certainly this is an issue that has generated significant dissatisfaction within postindependence Kenyan society, where accusations of land grabbing by the Kenyan political elite are recurrent, including most recently public critique of Uhuru Kenyatta's enormous land holdings during the presidential campaign for the 2013 Kenyan elections. Mungiki often speak against this injustice, arguing that they have inherited a marginal position in Kenyan society from the original Mau Mau fighters, something that is further compounded by the fact that Mungiki argue that the Mau Mau were not given proper recognition for the brutality they suffered during the British persecution and in the detention camps and that Jomo Kenyatta alone was celebrated for achieving independence. The reference to Mau Mau is not only a way of legitimizing the Mungiki struggle against oppression, because the Mau Mau, in their view, never fully achieved their goals of egalitarianism and social integration, but it is arguably also a tool for the movement to position itself as marginalized in Kenyan society.

Part of the logic for the construction of this particular standpoint is clearly that Mungiki primarily recruits its members among the urban poor Kikuyu youths and among the victims of the large population displacements that took place in the 1990s, and it can use the socioeconomic parallel with the situation of the former Mau Mau fighters to promote recruitment. The illegalization of Mungiki in 2002 and the police persecution that followed only confirmed their position as marginal, forcing them underground and, indeed, strengthening the parallel with the Mau Mau, because it allows Mungiki to present themselves as an organization with a just cause that is being unfairly targeted. Some of the politicians in charge of banning Mungiki come from the Kikuyu ruling class, a fact Mungiki has turned into a story of rich and Westernized Kikuyus fighting poor and traditionally minded Kikuyus, just like the Home Guards were fighting the Mau Mau back in the 1950s.

The more recent recruits—many admitting to be school dropouts, small-time criminals, and alcohol abusers—often reiterate the story of how their parents have let them down by not teaching them about their traditions and the heritage of their grandfathers. In these stories, Mungiki has not only offered unity and brotherhood but has provided Kikuyu youth with a cultural power they say was almost lost to them. This reevocation of traditions is visible when the members exchange and share snuff tobacco, which will take place everywhere members meet, whether in a music shop in downtown Nairobi or in a shack in Kariobangi. On a less mundane scale, I also witnessed traditional practices at a reconciliation meeting in Dagoretti, where the slaughter and preparation of a roasted goat were followed by collective prayers, after which the goat was cut into nine pieces to symbolize the unity of the nine Kikuyu clans. The blood and the intestines of the goat were mixed and spread around the compound to keep away evil spirits. Thus Mungiki's references to Mau Mau and past cultural traditions are not only oral but also practiced.

The police actively accuse Mungiki initiation rituals involving the taking of oaths to be similar to the oaths of the Mau Mau, something widely seen in Kenyan society as inherently justifying the movement's persecution. Certainly the police have found goatskin and snuff tobacco at the sites of Mungiki ceremonies, both of which were important elements of Mau Mau rituals. Mungiki counter such rumors by telling stories of traditional sacrifices of goats to God, of the traditional use of snuff tobacco sniffed to communicate dissatisfaction with the political rule, and of oaths not like the Mau Mau oaths but rather similar to those repeated at the swearing in of a politician to parliament (Rasmussen 2010a). At the same time, however, as David Pratten (2008, 10) has shown in his studies of gangs and vigilantes in Nigeria, a group's narrative of precolonial secret practices, such as magic and witchcraft, can project particular images. Pratten argues that the relevance of the continued reference to such practices is not the suggestion of tradition itself but rather the ideas of power they evoke. What matters for Mungiki is not the reference to a particular type of oath; rather, it is the images of power the reference to oaths attributes to the movement. The mere association with the Mau Mau, irrespective of the actual content of the oaths, evokes images of a highly united, secretive, and courageous movement willing to use violence and willing to die for its cause, and it is this image, whether it is true or not, that invests power in the movement.

In his work on narratives, Bruner (1991, 20) argues that narrative is a means for creating a history and for constituting legitimacy. Through the repeated references to the Mau Mau in their stories and practices, Mungiki creates its own version of history while drawing on the legitimacy of the Mau Mau. But as David Denborough (2008, 41) argues, these historical narratives have the ability to transmit legacy from one generation to another. The Mungiki narrative's emphasis on the blood relation to the Mau Mau can be seen as an attempt to transmit the legacy from their grandfathers to themselves. At the same time, as Hannah Arendt (1958, 182–84) has argued, narratives are shared activities that transform events into something that is *collectively* meaningful. Mungiki projects its experiences of marginalization and misrecognition onto the marginalization and failed recognition of the Mau Mau, which helps the movement create unity and a sense of shared identity and allows for a metanarrative of a continuously just cause. At the same time, however, this narrative of injustices and marginalization arguably not only unites the movement but also reproduces the marginalization it wants to fight, because the narrative places Mungiki on the margins in relation to the rest of Kenyan society. This is similar to the reproduction of marginalization through gang narratives described by Steffen Jensen (2006, 291–92) in relation to Cape Town, South Africa, where the narratives include continued references to prison life and humiliation in prison. At the same time, however, the continuous reproduction of marginality has paradoxically helped the movement to institutionalize itself in Kenyan society by positioning it in direct opposition to the Kenyan state, as the next section explores.

MUNGIKI AGAINST THE STATE?

Mungiki was not criminal and violent in the first years of the movement's existence, but as the movement grew in numbers, especially in the urban areas, it developed a range of economic interests that led it to become involved in violence. At different times, Mungiki have been fighting with other criminal groups over rights and market shares, particularly in relation to the *matatu* (minibus) industry. The violent and criminal activities have been more prevalent in and around Nairobi, which has led some analysts to talk of a divide between the rural and the urban factions of Mungiki (Anderson 2002). Kenyan social scientist Peter Kagwanja goes so far as to label the urban faction of the movement as the "Mungiki Intifada" (Kagwanja 2003, 49).[10] At the same time, however, the Mungiki narrative concerning violence is very much at odds with such notions, not only with regard to its logic but also with regard to the actual enactment of violence.

From the middle of the 1990s, Nairobi developed a bad reputation for crime, which earned the city the nickname "Nai-robbery." As Mungiki recruited among the poorest and most marginalized urban dwellers, they started operating in areas of Nairobi where the police and the state had a poor presence. In the Mungiki narrative, the police had struggled to control crime for years and had difficulties operating in the most crime-infested estates around Nairobi. At a certain point, Mungiki decided to take action, and within a few days, the movement managed to make the most affected estates almost crime-free. Mungiki members from Nairobi's Kayole estate tell how the movement, through its local knowledge, ruthless fighting skills, and organizational strength and numbers, managed to take control of the estate and deal swiftly with any criminals in only five days. Mungiki forced out the Masai Morans (young warrior bands from the Masai tribe), who until then had controlled the area, and singled out known criminals and asked them to stop their criminal activities. Members stressed how the reputation of Mungiki meant that the movement did not even have to make a single arrest to establish order. Mungiki thus presents itself as both a security force working for the betterment of the local community and as a strong and powerful unit with the ability to create order where the state fails to do so.[11]

A similar presentation of the movement is contained in Mungiki's accounts of its role in water provision, electricity connections, garbage collection, rejuvenation of public toilets, and organization of *matatu* routes. In many of the poor and informal estates, service provision and sanitation are in bad condition, and according to Mungiki, the state has failed to improve conditions for its citizens. Mungiki has provided illegal power connections in some areas and organized distribution of water from the public taps, thus creating jobs for its members and providing services for the local communities for a small fee. As for the *matatu* industry, it was totally disorganized, and bus stops were crime ridden, when Mungiki decided to organize the vehicles into set routes and to provide security on board the vehicles and at bus stops—again, creating jobs for its members as drivers, conductors, and security guards, while providing services to the public for a small fee (Rasmussen 2012).[12] One can, for example, observe numerous young men writing down vehicle numbers in small notebooks at matatu ranks, keeping order and track of which vehicle can drive next and covertly collecting a daily fee for this service. Thus Mungiki's narrative projects an image of the movement managing to provide services and improve living conditions for the poor in areas where the state has failed or has not prioritized service provision for its citizens. Mungiki, in other words, presents itself as a state within the state, in a way that is analogous to Christian Lund's (2006) "twilight institutions," that is to say, organizations that operate as states without actually being states and without holding the legitimacy of the state. Such institutions capitalize on the state's failures and shortcomings but are not confined to the same rules of conduct as the state, which means they operate according to their own, sometimes arbitrary, rules.

In the case of Mungiki, the narrative of service provision presents the movement as powerful and as delivering where there is a need, and for the members and the communities where Mungiki operates, the narrative helps to build belief in the movement. As Hagedorn (2008, 9) has pointed out in relation to gangs, the institutionalization of such an organization depends on its ability to make its members and the surrounding community believe not only in individual members but, most importantly, in the organization itself. For Mungiki, the narrative of its ability to deliver basic services and its statelike powers are central in the institutionalization process of the movement.

Mungiki's narrative does not stand unchallenged, however, and what the movement presents as fair fees paid in return for services delivered by the movement are often presented in the Kenyan media as well-organized extortion rackets backed by threats and violence. In contrast, Mungiki claim that the government's introduction of new rules of conduct, taxes, and heavier traffic control and its prosecution of law breakers in the *matatu* industry are proof of a corrupt government that has no control over the industry but that "wants to harvest where it didn't sow." Mungiki claim that the state is trying to take away what Mungiki perceives as its rightful livelihood, invoking the image of the Mau Mau, who were barred from sowing and harvesting the land they claimed was rightfully theirs. To this extent, as Bruner (1991, 5) argues, Mungiki's narrative constitutes reality rather than simply representing it. Arendt (1965, 53) takes this argument a step further by stating that truth in narrative is relative to where we situate ourselves, and seen in this light, the narratives—Mungiki's narrative as well as the counternarrative—are best understood as means to an end in a struggle concerning the legitimization and institutionalization of Mungiki in Kenyan society.

There are, however, other aspects to the institutionalization of the movement than the narrative of service provision and control of the *matatu* industry. Mungiki became engaged in security operations on a larger scale at a time in the late 1990s when community-policing initiatives were widely introduced in the estates around Nairobi (Ruteere and Pommerolle 2003, 594; Brogden 2005, 75). For local vigilante groups and *jeshis*—a Swahili word meaning "army" or "militia"—the community-policing initiatives offered a legitimate way to become involved in local security (Ruteere and Pommerolle 2003, 63; see also Anderson 2002). The opening offered by the government through community policing was an opportunity for Mungiki to position its members strategically in the security business in many Nairobi estates, forming a visible and powerful force locally.[13] At the same time, Mungiki has been illegal since 2002, and the Kenyan police have actively persecuted the movement with varying intensity and brutality during the past decade. During the last years of Moi's regime, the police set up special units to target Mungiki through infiltration and supposedly formed pseudo-Mungiki gangs to commit crimes in the name of Mungiki to justify crackdowns (Kagwanja 2003, 41–42). In April 2008, and again in November 2009, a KNYA spokesman was shot dead, both times allegedly by the police. In 2009, the United Nations special rapporteur on extrajudicial killings released a report documenting more than five hundred killings and disappearances of Mungiki members at the hands of the Kenyan police (Alston 2009).

Having said this, Mungiki members are clearly also perpetrators of various kinds of violent acts. The best known such act is probably the Kariobangi massacre of March 2002, when Mungiki slaughtered members of the Luo-dominated vigilante group called "Taliban," in what Hervé Maupeu (2002a, 135–37; 2002b) suggests was an attack with the dual purpose of intimidating ethnic and political opponents and demonstrating that Mungiki was the most powerful vigilante group. Another massacre took place in April 2009, when Mungiki allegedly killed members of a local vigilante group in a retaliation attack in the rural area of Karatina. The massacres, which were conducted with machetes and crude weapons, earned Mungiki a reputation of having a trademark form of killing: decapitation. In the eyes of the public, the beheadings were seen as another reference to the Mau Mau, who were said to have taken a decapitation oath (see Alport 1955, 243).[14] When confronted with the possibility of a trademark killing, one member whom I interviewed dismissed the accusations as an attempt at demonizing Mungiki. On the contrary, he said, "the best way for a poor man, who can't afford a gun, to kill a man, is to cut his throat with a machete." Thus Mungiki's marginal position in society is reinforced and reproduced, even when they kill.

CONCLUSION

This chapter has presented key elements of the narrative Mungiki's members tell about their movement. I have argued that the transformative character of Mungiki is the critical aspect of this narrative. The other elements of Mungiki's narrative—whether they concern historical legitimacy through historical legacy or ritual practice, whether they refer to an inherited marginal position in society or formative battles with the police, or even prophetic powers and divine intervention—all refer to the movement's relation to broader Kenyan society, which is the catalyst for Mungiki's constant transformations. The fact that Mungiki has survived despite many transformations, multiple narratives, and opposition from the state as well as police persecution suggests that it is an institution that will endure. Certainly Mungiki's continued ability to mobilize large numbers would suggest it is by no means weakening.

At the same time, Mungiki's institutionalization has clearly occurred as a result of a range of factors, including the movement's social activities as local-level service providers; their capitalizing on openings in urban policies; the use of threats, violence, and extortion; and not least the projection and consequences of a particular narrative. In relation to this latter factor, Mungiki's narrative about itself is underpinned by a discourse of injustice and oppression by the Kenyan state, yet the narrative also clearly lacks a rational explanation for these injustices. It is quite contradictory, in the sense that it cannot answer why the Kenyan state is persecuting and killing Mungiki members if the movement is not a ganglike organization and is indeed working peacefully against oppression and for the improvement of the living conditions of poor youths, as the overall narrative suggests is the case.

Mungiki members simply answer this question by stating, "They are afraid of us, because we tell the truth!" Variations on this answer have come up during the course of my interviews, but they always revolve around the notion that Mungiki poses a threat to the state because it knows and is able to tell the truth. Certainly this is what I heard time and time again when I interviewed Mungiki members who were waiting to give testimony on extrajudicial killings to the United Nations rapporteur at the Kenya National Commission on Human Rights, and it is what I also often heard when I discussed the imprisonment of Maina Njenga with local members of the Pentagon, a formerly secret Mungiki meeting point in Nairobi. It was also the phrase used by Njuguna Githau, the now-deceased Mungiki spokesperson, to explain why the KNYA party was illegalized. In all these cases, the truth is presented as a truth with no specific content, thus emphasizing the will and the ability to speak the truth rather than its content. This is something that Michel Foucault (2001) discusses in a series of lectures dedicated to the Greek notion of *parrhesia*, which translates roughly as "free speech." The person who practices *parrhesia* is the one who speaks the truth, according to Foucault (2001, 11), who is less interested in the idea of telling the truth per se[15] but rather focuses on the figure of the truth-teller. In other words, Foucault turns his attention away from both the content and the purpose of a narrative to focus instead on the person who is narrating, arguing that the truth-teller is convinced that the truth he is telling is the actual truth because "there is always an exact coincidence between belief and truth" (15–16). He contends that this means that the truth-teller must have the moral conviction that he knows the truth and that he is obliged to tell the truth whatever dangers this might entail—even death. If the truth-teller is willing to take the risk of dying for what he believes is the truth, then it logically follows that there must be a relationship to another who can not only be hurt and harmed by the truth but also is more powerful than the truth-teller, so as to potentially cause his death (17).

In a pamphlet titled "The Unshakeable Foundation: Freedom, Justice, and Prosperity," Mungiki leader Maina Njenga writes about the relation to God and the truth and asks God to invest in him and in Mungiki the ability to speak the truth (Mungiki n.d., 2).[16] Mungiki's members perceive Maina Njenga as a prophet, and they believe that God speaks to the movement through him, either in the form of prophetic statements or else through reinterpretations of old Kikuyu prophets, especially Mugo wa Kibiro (see Anderson 2002, 5–6). The local members in Kayole spent a lot of time explaining Maina Njenga's reinterpretations of the Old Testament to me. They often quoted from a dog-eared copy of the Bible and especially emphasized a quote from the book of Zephania 3:10: "From beyond the rivers of Ethiopia, my worshippers, my scattered people, will bring me offerings." The Mungiki members would ask me, "Which country lies beyond Ethiopia?" and when I would say "Kenya," they would then triumphantly ask me whether the Kikuyu were not the scattered people of Kenya, being the victims of several forced removals since colonial times. Thus, they argued, in this quote was the proof of God's prediction of Mungiki.

The relation between God and truth is a critical factor in Mungiki's conviction of its ability to speak the truth, and it establishes a link between belief and truth. Because the prophecies are not given any credence or authority by outsiders, the fact that Mungiki holds them up as a source of knowledge and truth only emphasizes its perception that it occupies a marginal position in Kenyan society (Rasmussen 2010b; Lonsdale 1995). In other words, Mungiki's relation to Kenyan society is determined by a narrative move from *self-representation* to *self-perception,* where image and imagery are set aside to favor a focus on identity and belief instead.

This last idea would seem to very much go against Jerome Bruner's argument that narratives constitute reality rather than merely representing it. However, when looking at Mungiki's constituted reality, an underlying discourse concerning Mungiki's relation to the Kenyan state is revealed. This underlying discourse concerns Mungiki's self-perception—a self-perception that revolves around the ability to critically speak the truth against the people in power, even when risking death. This underlying discourse is central to Mungiki's narrative, as it presents and positions the movement as holding a moral high ground in relation to its opponents within Kenyan society. My intention here is not to say that Mungiki's narrative *is* the truth. The argument is rather that we gain an understanding of Mungiki's self-perception by first looking at its self-representation through its narrative and then applying the notion of the truth-teller to learn about its self-perception. Mungiki members claim to be willing to die for their cause, not for personal gain, but because they believe their cause to be right and true. The sense of a shared moral community that Mungiki has established within its ranks through the truth discourse helps justify the varied transformations of the movement and counters external constructions of the movement as a gang. It is not the activities per se that tie the movement together but rather the collective position and common relation to the rest of society, which perceived Mungiki as a violent gang.

NOTES

The financial support of the Danish Research Council for Communication and Culture (FKK) is gratefully acknowledged.

1. Bruner is generally interested in how people structure their sense of reality through cultural products, where narrative is an example of such cultural products. Bruner's analytical search for meaning and his focus on culture make his theories suitable for anthropological analyses of the collective influence and use of narratives. The journal *Ethos* has dedicated a special issue to Bruner's thinking and his influence on the relation between psychology and anthropology (Mattingly, Lutkehaus, and Throop 2008).

2. At the same time, Mungiki is clearly a multifaceted, amorphous, and ambiguous movement that is difficult to contain in a single descriptive or analytical concept. Indeed, Mungiki very much rejects the "gang" label and instead projects a narrative discourse that draws on historical accounts of the Mau Mau movement, a particular conception of Kenyan society, and opposition to the Kenyan state. But if we consider the label "gang" as a broad analytical category encompassing ambiguities and transformations, as suggested by Hagedorn, then it is arguably by no means unreasonable to ask whether Mungiki cannot be considered a gang.

3. Steffen Jensen (2008, 94–95) similarly refers to epic tales of battles between rival gangs in Cape Town, which end up constituting the gangsters and the gang as strong and proud of their collective identity.

4. For a detailed case study of how Mungiki change sides and how they have engaged in the game of political deception, see Rasmussen (2010b).

5. Certainly Mungiki members have been quite happy to show me photos of themselves in Islamic clothing despite having renounced the faith, while others have actually kept the registration papers attesting them to have officially converted to Islam, "just in case they need them again one day," as one person put it.

6. At the same time, these various transformations have clearly not changed the fundamental parameters of Mungiki. Despite initial anti-Christian proclamations, there have always been elements of Christian belief in Mungiki's blend of adapted traditions and beliefs, evident in their repeated references to the Bible, especially the Old Testament. Indeed, according to Kikuyu traditions, religion and state cannot be separated, and Mungiki in fact actively advocates for this connection (Kenyatta 1938, 177). The Pentecostal mission Njenga joined implicitly advocates the combination of politics and religion, as the bishop is a member of parliament and claims that her election was the will of God (Kavulla 2008). Ultimately, Mungiki members explain the religious shifts by arguing that God may have different names in different religions and that people may believe that God resides at different places, but ultimately it is the same God. It is interesting to note that Lonsdale (1992, 343) has described the Kikuyu theology as complex and heterodox, contending that the Kikuyus are monotheists but that their God—Ngai—is potentially multitribal.

7. Keeping the image of the Mugumo tree and its ability to swallow the host tree in mind, it is interesting to note that upon joining the Pentecostal mission, Mungiki leader Maina Njenga joked with the bishop that "this church is no longer yours. Now it is ours!" (*Daily Nation*, October 25, 2009).

8. There are two narratives concerning the decisive factor behind the cousins' approaching their grandfathers. One is a story where God approaches both young boys in their dreams. The other tells the story of how Maina Njenga died from a disease and resurrected, bound with a mission from God. The latter of the two versions was most prevalent during my fieldwork. As this was conducted at a time when Ndura Waruinge had abandoned the Mungiki movement to become a Catholic preacher, this might explain why the narrative leaving him out dominated. Following Njenga's release and Mungiki's public transformation, Waruinge has started interacting with the movement again, so it will be interesting to see how the narrative evolves.

9. The notorious Operation Anvil in 1954 forcefully removed half of Nairobi's Kikuyu population in an attempt to neutralise Mau Mau presence in the city (Anderson 2005, 200).

10. At the same time, there is a distinct rural bent to predominant Mungiki urban narratives. During a group interview with a Nairobi faction of Mungiki, they repeatedly stated to me that "the city is our forest!" This was clearly an implicit reference to the Mau Mau, who used to hide, regroup, and fight from the forests in the Central Province and Rift Valley. It is also interesting to note that Mungiki has recently started advocating for a return to farming and the rural areas. However, it is too soon to properly gauge the effects of this shift.

11. It was certainly clear while walking through the streets of Kayole with some Mungiki members that they had some local authority, as they constantly greeted people left and right, gave out orders to approaching youths, or rode the local *matatu* for free.

12. In this regard, Mungiki's discourse contains further implicit parallels with the Mau Mau, insofar as Mungiki seeks to empower youths economically and morally through various employment initiatives in the city, very similarly to the Mau Mau initiatives to empower the poor farmworkers by fighting against exploitation and for indigenous right to land.

13. Mungiki's venture into the Matatu industry has a similar trajectory, in the sense that the movement capitalised on a gap left by the government. In the 1980s, President Moi banned many worker's unions and associations, among them the Matatu associations (Nasong'o 2007). After years without a strong regulative body, powerful brokers who could provide security and order on the Matatu routes and stages could easily become influential on local routes. These opportunities for controlling and providing local security alongside establishing a solid economic base for the movement's members have, over the years, helped institutionalize Mungiki (Mutongi 2006). The movement's ordered approach to day-to-day problems, combined with the installment of belief in the movement through practice and narrative, has helped in the institutionalization process of Mungiki in Nairobi.

14. The oath described by Alport (1955) must be treated with some caution, as he noted it during the height of the British fight against Mau Mau, who were then largely represented as dangerous and vicious rebels, but it has nevertheless been part of the lasting picture of Mau Mau as brutal and secret.

15. Foucault traces the use of the word to Euripides's and Socrates's writings and argues that it constitutes the roots for what he calls "the critical tradition" in the West.

16. The pamphlet is undated, but on the basis of events mentioned in the pamphlet and the comments made to me by the member who gave it to me, it must have been published sometime between 2001 and 2004.

REFERENCES

Alport, C. J. M. 1955. "Kenya's Answer to the Mau Mau Challenge." *African Affairs* 53, no. 212: 241–48.

Alston, Phillip. 2009. *UN Special Rapporteur on Extrajudicial, Arbitrary, or Summary Executions Mission to Kenya.* New York: United Nations Office of the High Commissioner for Human Rights.

Anderson, David M. 2002. "Vigilantes, Violence, and the Politics of Public Order in Kenya." *African Affairs* 101:531–55.

———. 2005. *Histories of the Hanged: The Dirty War in Kenya and the End of Empire*. New York: W. W. Norton.

Arendt, Hannah. 1958. *The Human Condition*. Chicago: Chicago University Press.

———. 1965. *On Revolution*. Hammondsworth, U.K.: Penguin Books.

Beech, Mervyn W. H. 1913. "The Sacred Fig-Tree of the A-kikuyu of East Africa." *Man* 13:4–6.

Brogden, Mike. 2005. "'Horses for Courses' and 'Thin Blue Lines': Community Policing in Transitional Society." *Police Quarterly* 8, no. 1: 64–98.

Bruner, Jerome. 1991. "The Narrative Construction of Reality." *Critical Inquiry* 18, no. 1: 1–21.

Denborough, David. 2008. *Collective Narrative Practice*. Adelaide, Australia: Dulwick Centre.

Elkins, Caroline. 2005. *Britain's Gulag: The Brutal End of Empire in Kenya*. London: Jonathan Cape.

Foucault, Michel. 2001. *Fearless Speech*. Los Angeles: Semiotext(e).

Furedi, Frank. 1973. "The African Crowd in Nairobi." *Journal of African History* 14, no. 2: 275–90.

Gecaga, Margaret Gathoni. 2007. "Religious Movements and Democratisation in Kenya: Between the Sacred and the Profane." In *Kenya: The Struggle for Democracy,* edited by Godwin Murunga and Shadrack Nasong'o, 58–89. Dakar: Codesria Books.

Hagedorn, John. 2008. *A World of Gangs: Armed Young Men and Gangsta Culture*. Minneapolis: University of Minnesota Press.

Jensen, Steffen. 2006. "Capetonian Back Streets: Territorialising Young Men." *Ethnography* 7, no. 3: 275–301.

———. 2008. *Gangs, Politics, and Dignity in Cape Town*. Oxford: James Currey.

Kagwanja, Peter Mwangi. 2003. "Facing Mount Kenya or Facing Mecca? The Mungiki, Ethnic Violence, and the Politics of the Moi Succession in Kenya, 1987–2002." *African Affairs* 102:25–49.

———. 2005a. "Clash of Generations? Youth Identity, Violence, and the Politics of Transition in Kenya, 1997—2002." In *Vanguards and Vandals: Youth, Politics, and Conflict in Africa,* edited by Jon Abbink and Ineke van Kessel, 81–109. Boston: Brill.

———. 2005b. "Power to Uhuru: Youth Identity and Generational Politics in Kenya's 2002 Elections." *African Affairs* 105, no. 418: 51–75.

Kavulla, Travis. 2008. "Our Enemies are God's Enemies: The Religion and Politics of Bishop Margaret Wanjiru, MP." *Journal of Eastern African Studies* 2, no. 2: 254–63.

Kemp, Ross. 2008. *Gangs II: More Encounters with the World's Most Dangerous Gangsters*. London: Penguin Books.

Kenyatta, Jomo. 1938. *Facing Mt. Kenya*. New York: Vintage Books.

Lonsdale, John. 1992. "The Moral Economy of Mau Mau: Wealth, Poverty, and Civic Virtue in Kikuyu Political Thought." In *Unhappy Valley. Book 2:*

Violence and Ethnicity, ed. John Lonsdale and Bruce Berman, 315–467. Oxford: James Currey.

———. 1995. "The Prayers of Waiyaki: Political Uses of the Kikuyu Past." In *Revealing Prophets: Prophecy in Eastern African History,* edited by D. Anderson and D. H. Johnson, 240–91. London: James Currey.

———. 2003. "Authority, Gender, and Violence: The War within Mau Mau's Fight for Land and Freedom." In *Mau Mau and Nationhood: Arms, Authority, and Narration,* edited by John Lonsdale and Atieno Odhiambo, 46–75. Oxford: James Currey.

Lund, Christian. 2006. "Twilight Institutions: An Introduction." *Development and Change* 37, no. 4: 673–84.

Mattingly, Cheryl, Nancy C. Lutkehaus, and C. Jason Throop, eds. 2008. "Special Issue: Troubling the Boundary between Psychology and Anthropology: Jerome Bruner and His Inspiration." *Ethos* 36, no. 1: 1–169.

Maupeu, Hervé. 2002a. "Mungiki et les elections. Les mutations d'un prophétisme kikuyu (Kenya)." *Politique africaine* 87:117–37.

———. 2002b. "Physiologie d'un massacre: la tuerie du 3 mars 2002, Kariobangi North (Nairobi, Kenya)." In *Annuaire de l'Afrique Orientale 2002,* 339–67. Paris: L'Harmattan.

Mungiki. n.d. "The Unshakeable Foundation: Freedom, Justice, and Prosperity." Pamphlet produced and circulated by the Mungiki movement in Kenya.

Mutongi, Kenda. 2006. "Thugs or Entrepreneurs? Perceptions of Matatu Operators in Nairobi, 1970 to the Present." *Africa* 76, no. 4: 549–68.

Nasong'o, Shadrack. 2007. "Negotiating New Rules of the Game: Social Movements, Civil Society, and the Kenyan Transition." In *Kenya: The Struggle for Democracy,* edited by Godwin Murunga and Shadrack Nasong'o, 19–57. Dakar: Codesria.

Ndeda, Mildred. 2009. "The Struggle for Space: Minority Religious Identities in Post-independence Kenya." *Les Cahiers d'Afrique de l'Est* 41:107–81.

Pratten, David. 2008. "Introduction: The Politics of Protection: Perspectives on Vigilantism in Nigeria." *Africa* 78, no. 1: 1–15.

Rasmussen, Jacob. 2010a. "Mungiki as Youth Movement: Revolution, Gender, and Generational Politics in Nairobi, Kenya." *Nordic Journal of Youth Research* 18, no. 3: 301–19.

———. 2010b. "Outwitting the Professor of Politics? Mungiki Narratives of Political Deception and Their Role in Kenyan Politics." *Journal of Eastern African Studies* 5, no. 1: 435–49.

———. 2012. "Outside the Law—inside the System: Operating the Matutu Sector in Nairobi." *Urban Forum* 23, no. 4: 415–32.

Rodgers, Dennis. 2006. "The State as a Gang: Conceptualising the Governmentality of Violence in Contemporary Nicaragua." *Critique of Anthropology* 26, no. 3: 315–30.

Ruteere, Mutuma. 2008. *Dilemmas of Crime, Human Rights, and the Politics of*

Mungiki Violence in Kenya. Occasional Paper 01/08. Nairobi: Kenya Human Rights Institute.

Ruteere, Mutuma, and Marie-emanuelle Pommerolle. 2003. "Democratizing Security or Decentralizing Repression? The Ambiguities of Community Policing in Kenya." *African Affairs* 102:587–604.

Wachanga, H. K. 1975. *The Swords of Kirinyaga.* Nairobi: Kenya Literature Bureau.

Waki Report. 2008. *Report of the Commission of Inquiry into Post-election Violence.* Commission of Inquiry into Post-election Violence.

Wamue, Grace Nyatugah. 2001. "Revisiting Our Indigenous Shrines through Mungiki." *African Affairs* 100:453–67.

11

Gang Politics in Rio de Janeiro, Brazil

ENRIQUE DESMOND ARIAS

In May 2002, Tim Lopes, a reporter for the Globo media conglomerate, Brazil's largest television network and the publisher of Rio's most important newspaper, went to the *favela* (shantytown) of Vila Cruzeiro on Rio's working-class north side to report on rumors that drug dealers paid adolescent girls to perform sexual acts at the *favela*'s gang-sponsored *baile funk* (funk dance ball). The reporter had a history of daring undercover investigations, including one a few months earlier, where he had secretly filmed a major open-air drug market in the same neighborhood, leading to heavy police repression in the area. Local gang members recognized the reporter and murdered him.

Lopes's murder became a major story in Rio and around Brazil. In one of a series of periodic flare-ups, the city's press took notice of the gang problem. Newspapers and magazines published stories highlighting the problem of criminal dominance of shantytowns, even suggesting that parallel states existed with drug traffickers acting as the feudal lords of their own microscopic political systems (Alves Filho and Pernambuco 2002).

While drug trafficking, violence, and crime are all serious problems in Rio, the press and most of the political establishment have long misapprehended the nature of their power and the role they play in the city. Gang members in Rio de Janeiro come predominantly from the city's poorest neighborhoods, and even within these communities, they often hail from some of the most disadvantaged households. They almost universally have poor educations and few job skills. Drug traffickers come from one of the most disempowered segments of Brazilian social life, but they are blamed for many of the problems facing Rio and other Brazilian cities.

Building on more than a decade of research, I argue that to understand Rio's gangs, we need to look at these organizations not as systems somehow apart from the wider political system operating as parallel political entities, as is often suggested in media narratives; rather, understanding Rio de Janeiro's gangs necessitates understanding how they are part of the country's wider political and social system (Arias 2006). In particular, I argue that there is a political interest in maintaining a systematic misperception of gang activities to obscure the role of the current social, political, and economic system in perpetuating gangs and gang violence that is abetted by both politicians and the media. This allows contradiction to continue within a political system that claims to guarantee basic equal citizenship rights to all citizens but where many of the country's poor have substantial difficulty realizing those rights (Holston and Caldeira 1999).

GANGS IN THE MARVELOUS CITY

Brazil is by far the largest country in Latin America, with two hundred million inhabitants spread across a land area the size of the continental United States. It is also the seventh richest country in the world, with a gross domestic product of US$2.25 trillion. At the same time, however, with a GINI coefficient of 54.7 (World Bank 2013a, 2013b), Brazil is one of the world's most unequal places. Brazil's immense but poorly distributed wealth has played a substantial role in the country's history. High levels of natural resources, a robust agricultural system, and, later, substantial industrial capacity have enabled Brazil to build a robust and active government that has, for the past eighty years, played a critical role in national development.[1]

Heavy government investment in industry led to a rapid urbanization of the major metropolitan areas in the southeast of the country during the middle twentieth century. Without an effective national housing policy, migrants often clustered in shantytowns, where social and political life usually focused around local service and leisure organizations. Most famously, these took the shape of the *samba* schools, especially in the North Zone *favelas*. In the 1950s, however, the Roman Catholic Church and the state government began to organize *favela* residents into local representative organizations known as Associações de Moradores (Resident's Associations, or AMs), which would work to meet local need through cooperative labor and by negotiating with the state for resources (Leeds and Leeds 1978). These organizations have long maintained clientelist exchanges with wealthy and powerful political patrons but have also operated under a state umbrella group to advocate on behalf of *favela* dwellers around the city and, after the fusion of the former federal district into the surrounding region, the state of Rio. These groups reached their political apogee during the 1960s, when they fought *favela* removal efforts sponsored by the military dictatorship that ruled the country from 1964 to 1985. However, state repression weakened their umbrella group, and the remaining community leaders sought clientelist exchanges with the political machine that dominated state-level politics in the 1970s (Baumann Burgos 1998, 35; Leeds and Leeds 1978, 235–38; Perlman 1976, 258–60). The AMs expanded their activities during the transition to democracy in the early 1980s and were a critical component in the election of Leonel Brizola, a leftist former exile who ran on a populist platform, to governor in 1982 (Gay 1994, 31, 40–41). The newly revitalized community movements, however, found themselves on hard times as the government, in delivering basic services with some effectiveness, undermined these organizations' position in poor areas by partially diminishing local needs for their activities and coopting their leaders into partisan activities.

The 1980s were a period of growing social violence in Rio and São Paulo. Andean cocaine traffickers were looking for new routes to send their drugs to developed markets and began shipping narcotics through Brazil with the tacit or active support of some elements of the state's security forces. Drugs began flowing through Rio and São Paulo, and both cities experienced a substantial uptick in rates of violence during this period. In Rio, the drug trade was consolidated in *favelas,* which served as hubs for receiving the drugs and transshipping them out of the country and into the local retail drug trade. With their irregular and often unmapped street patterns, known best by those who had grown up in these areas, they provided a perfect place for gang security and sanctuary for contraband.

The cocaine trade put a lot of money in play, and the small-time drug dealers operating in the city's *favelas* rapidly grew in importance in the 1980s. Initially these gangs had an informal and decentralized structure, but they rapidly developed a degree of coherence. The drug gangs that dominate many Rio *favelas* organized under the umbrella of one of several *facções*, or "prison gangs," that control cell blocks dominating internal illegal markets. *Facções* have limited control of gangs on the outside but do have a say in actions taken against high-ranking *facção* members. The oldest is the Comando Vermelho (Red Command, or CV), which was organized in the now-defunct prison on Ilha Grande, an island several hours from Rio. The CV emerged out of the efforts of political prisoners to inculcate common prisoners with revolutionary ideals and tactics during the dictatorship.[2] Over time, a number of other *facções* emerged, such as the dissident Comando Vermelho Jovem (Young Red Command), the Terceiro Comando (Third Command), and the Amigos dos Amigos (Friends of Friends).[3]

The *facções* function primarily as prison gangs and have little say over the day-to-day operations of their street-based affiliates. Member gangs are able to switch affiliations and develop temporary alliances against other gangs that are part of their *facção*. Although gang leaders frequently develop alliances with politicians during elections, there is no evidence of systematic political activism, though the CV does use some left-wing rhetoric. Over the last fifteen years, as some state officials have sought to curtail criminal power in prisons, the CV has pushed back by ordering businesses in Rio to shut down on pain of violent retaliation and, in the process, has published declarations using strongly left-wing rhetoric (Penglase 2005).

Within particular shantytowns, gangs are more hierarchically organized. Gang leaders are referred to as *donos* (owners). In a large community, a *gerente geral* (general manager) will work under them and oversee a number of other *gerentes* (managers) in charge of a range of operations such as cocaine sales, marijuana sales, and security. Below them sit *vapores* (literally, "vapors," but in this context, dealers) and *soldados* (soldiers), who may have had some formal military training. At the bottom of the drug-trafficking hierarchy are *olheiros* (lookouts) and *fogueteiros* (firecracker lighters), who watch and warn of incursions by the police or other gangs (Dowdney 2003).

In general, members of these gangs are mainly in their adolescent years and twenties. The vast majority are male. Commonly there will be some members as young as ten or eleven who work as *olheiros*. Among younger traffickers, there is permeability between hanging out in the *favela* streets and becoming a member of the gang. A young boy who spends his time around other gang members will eventually come to be seen as a gang member by members of the gang and the community and will often be given some low-level work. Over time, he will move up to positions of greater responsibility. Some low-level members may drift in and out of these activities, although once they have advanced to a certain point, leaving a gang is quite difficult. Older *donos* may be in their thirties. Over time, traffickers are either killed, sent to prison, or seek another way out of the gang, which might include advancing into new criminal activities, joining an evangelical church, or moving to another city.

Although gangs as a whole operate under the loose umbrella of the *facções*, wholesale trafficking is not directly linked to any particular *facção*. Wholesalers, known as *matutos* (literally, "men from the forest"), are not affiliated with particular gangs or *facções*, though they may have emerged from a specific gang (Dowdney 2003, 39–42). Once working on the wholesale side, these large-scale dealers separate themselves from the conflicts associated with individual gangs. Major drug trafficking in Brazil is not characterized by public rivalries or violence. Those involved in this trade are occasionally *donos* who have done well for themselves, but this group also includes members of the armed forces and others from better-off backgrounds (Torres Maia 1999, 10; Gay 2005, 31).

GANGS AND *FAVELA* POLITICS

Drug gangs in Rio have a complex, contentious, collaborative, and ambiguous relationship to the state. Trafficker power exists, in many ways, as a systematically obscured subaltern adjunct to state power, maintaining order in regions of the city that the government has little interest in directly policing or governing. The presence of drug gangs in these areas creates conditions that make most political organizing difficult and in some ways constrains the ability of residents to act collectively and through civic organizations to make demands of the political system.

In general, the gangs operating in *favelas* have little political power.

They are vilified in the media and the subject of many police operations. They are made up of some of the most discriminated against and disempowered residents of the city: young, poorly educated, impoverished, nonwhite men. To make matters worse, they are in constant competition with other drug gangs and with the *milícias,* mafialike organizations operating in some parts of Rio that bring police together with other criminals to support protection rackets (Arias 2009, 90–93). To overcome these challenges, and build legitimacy in the communities in which they operate, many drug gangs maintain contacts with politicians. To this end, drug gangs work through the leadership of local AMs to negotiate deals with politicians in which a political candidate may be guaranteed a monopoly on access to the neighborhood in exchange for providing assistance to the community. In recent years, powerful gangs in the large *favelas* of Rocinha and Complexo do Alemão have helped to elect *favela* residents closely connected to them to the city council in the complex open-list proportional representation system used for most legislative elections in Brazil. Finally, drug traffickers maintain corrupt relations with different policing organizations. Traffickers bribe police on a case-by-case basis or are part of a long-term arrangement, which is often renegotiated at the point of a gun or when an important criminal is jailed.

As I have noted in my book *Drugs and Democracy in Rio* (Arias 2006), traffickers usually build their political activities through local AMs or other civic organizations. Thus the city councilor from Rocinha was the president of the *favelas* AM, and the politician elected from the Complexo do Alemão runs a charitable organization in that area. In general, however, gangs do not use elections to bring a *favela* resident to office. Most Rio *favelas* are too small to concentrate enough votes to elect even one city councilor. While the open-list proportional representation system leads to some anomalies in which the member of a successful party or multiparty coalition may win office with very few individual votes, most officeholders for this basic elected office received at least ten thousand votes in the 2008 election. With the secret ballot, traffickers have a very hard time ensuring that residents actually vote for the candidate the traffickers support. Thus, in Rocinha, a community with more than one hundred thousand residents, a politician with extensive trafficker support and protection still only generated around ten thousand votes. To further complicate matters, the electoral efforts of the traffickers in Rocinha led to substantial negative press and focused unwanted public attention on the gang.

Rather than support candidates from the *favela,* traffickers in most areas seek to benefit financially from a political campaign by controlling access to a community. Thus, if a politician wants to campaign in a particular neighborhood, she needs to negotiate access to the community with traffickers or their representatives. In general, as a result of the potential for political embarrassment, politicians conduct these negotiations through intermediaries, though on at least one occasion, I observed a politician directly negotiating with one gang leader. These negotiations often involve the politician hiring a certain number of local residents named by the traffickers or their intermediaries and providing some limited investment in the community, such as improving basic infrastructure. This can involve building a sports court, improving a stairway, or paving a road (Arias 2006). In general, the idea is that traffickers and the individuals most closely connected to them will benefit the most from these exchanges but that some benefits will be delivered to the rest of the community to shore up support for the traffickers who secured the deal with the politicians.

Historically, none of this is unusual. Prior to the rise of drug trafficking in Rio, AM leaders and other respected neighborhood residents would work to bring politicians to their communities to negotiate block voting in exchange for the delivery by politicians of some benefits to the community (Gay 1994). In this earlier form of clientelism, local civic leaders had the ability to negotiate on behalf of area residents with different politicians for the best benefits for the neighborhood. An unsuccessful local leader could, through open elections or other mechanisms, be replaced, thereby creating a system of accountability to ensure that residents could work to achieve higher benefits from clientelist agreements between local leaders and politicians.

This structure creates what has been referred to in the Colombian context as a form of "armed clientelism," in which criminals take control of the political resources that they then redistribute to themselves and the voting population (Easton 2007). The result is that the gangs take an increasingly larger cut of patronage payments to the detriment of what the population might have expected to receive. Clientelistic support still trickles down to the general population, but at a significantly lower level than previously. Trafficker-connected community leaders have expressed frustration that their efforts to secure votes by their constituents in Brazil's reliable, secret ballot–based elections have failed, suggesting that the intervention of drug traffickers may be hindering the ability of patrimonial politicians to build a strong popular base of support among the population in some *favelas*.

The dominance of powerful criminals in local clientelist relations is related to other similar patrimonial processes in Brazil. In the Brazilian Northeast, powerful landlords, referred to historically as *coroneis* (colonels), have substantial power over the lives of the poor who live in their areas. These *coroneis* had local police and political powers that reinforced local economic dominance. Despite the fact that the more formal roles of these actors in the political system ended in the 1930s with the consolidation of central state power during the so-called Estado Novo, or "New State," *coroneis* and their descendants have continued to maintain a degree of localized power in some parts of the country. The central role of the *coronel* was to aggregate local support for political leverage and to use police power, local favors, and efforts to improve local conditions as means of maintaining local support (Nunes Leal 1977, 14–20). This was an unequal reciprocal exchange relationship in which bosses received considerable resources and commanded large amounts of local power and violence and in which individual tenants, landless workers, and smallholders received limited support in exchange for voting with the *coronel*. Of course, this is only one side of the political narrative of gangs in Rio today. Although many politicians are willing to build ties to traffickers to gain access to votes, once elected, they may very well adopt hard-line anticrime rhetoric supporting repressive hard-line policies against residents of *favelas*.

Another important component of the complex relationship between the state and gangs is the police. The police adopt multiple and contradictory modes of operation with regard to gangs. On one hand, police occasionally engage in brutal efforts to repress gangs. Rather than maintaining a regular presence in the communities, police often intervene at different moments to attack traffickers, make arrests, and seize drugs. These interventions result in large amounts of abuse and large numbers of killings. Though these actions do result in some contraband seizures and arrests, they also allow for corruption. For example, arrested traffickers are often released after the payment of bribes, and Rio's police occasionally sell seized contraband to other gangs. Police also engage in more ongoing exchanges with traffickers. In some cases, police take regular payments from dealers in exchange for not acting against them. Alternatively, sometimes transactions are nonmonetary, with policemen occasionally servicing gang members' weapons for them, for example. All of this said, there are many well-intentioned police who seek to better protect citizens.

These interactions with government officials show that traffickers, far from operating in opposition to the political system, actually operate in conjunction with elements of the state. Traffickers themselves have no interest in bringing down the government but rather seek to engage with the government to guarantee security for their activities. At the same time, elements of the state seek to engage with traffickers to gain access to resources from illegal markets to supplement meager salaries and to gain easy and perhaps exclusive access to a group of voters at a relatively inexpensive rate. Furthermore, allowing traffickers to maintain order and resolve local disputes has the effect of demobilizing *favela* residents politically and limiting the effectiveness of civic leaders making demands for improvements. This enables the government to avoid expanding and developing the police to effectively provide security to these communities, and instead allows the state to rely on criminals to resolve disputes and maintain some sort of order in these neighborhoods. It further provides a buffer that keeps poor neighborhoods controlled by rival gangs divided from one another and compromises the leaders of those areas, thereby preventing the organization of a powerful popular movement that could make demands to address the substantial problems facing the working class in Rio.

CONCEPTUALIZING GANGS

Despite these multilayered connections between state actors and drug gangs, the Brazilian and international media promote a stark and threatening vision of Rio de Janeiro's gangs not just as a menace to the underlying public order but as the leaders of alternative parallel powers or polities. In other words, gang members are not just threats to the individual and broader civic safety but pose, on some levels, profound localized threats to the power of the Brazilian state. In using the term *parallel power* or *polity*, the media narrative of *favelas* further suggests that Rio's drug gangs have something in common with the parallel state formations that have existed in revolutionary movements in China, Peru, and Vietnam. Underlying this idea of the parallel state is the concept that traffickers dominate areas that somehow become separate from or independent of the city and that, within *favelas,* traffickers maintain a brutal and unquestioned order in some ways similar to state power.

In the wake of the murder of Tim Lopes in 2002, *Istoé,* a major Brazilian newsweekly akin to *Time,* published a cover titled "Por Dentro do Estado Paralelo" (Inside the parallel state) that starkly illustrates this conception of trafficker power. The cover contains a caption that sensationally reads, "*Istoé* reveals the barbarous world that came to light with the murder of the Globo reporter. Traffickers impose terror, move billions of dollars, oppress society, and challenge duly constituted powers."[4] The actual cover image goes further, placing a gilded frame in the center in which a nonwhite young man holds a rifle and masks most of his face with a T-shirt, while wearing a presidential sash in yellow and green, Brazil's national colors. The gilt frame sits on the rough wood wall of a shantytown home. Arrayed below the frame on a table, the viewer sees guns, drugs, cigarettes, bullets, drug paraphernalia, a half-empty glass of beer, a cellular telephone, a compact disk player, and sunglasses. This image, which in many ways is not unique in the history of how Brazilian news magazines have graphically treated the trafficking in Rio,[5] offers profound insights into the media narrative about gangs in Rio. The first element here is the notion of these actors, generally poorly educated, impoverished, nonwhite adolescents, as representative of a parallel state that directly challenges formal political power. It suggests that their activities are also barbarous and uncivilized. This depiction suggests gangs exist in opposition to society as well as the state, rather than being products of or acting in conjunction with other elements of state and society. The nonwhite, armed, and faceless antipresident who sits at the center of the cover clearly embodies this confrontation. The details of the threat are then arrayed at the bottom of the picture in terms of the sale of drugs; the profligate use of dangerous substances such as guns, liquor, and cigarettes; and a relationship between popular, working-class consumer aspirations, such as owning sunglasses, a cellular telephone, or a compact disk player, and the dangers of the drug trade.

The juxtaposition of civilization and barbarity in urban violence in

Rio plays an important role in understanding both gangs and shanty-towns in the city. The historic vision of Rio's shantytowns (*favelas*) is as rural areas divided, or marginalized, from the rest of the city. At the same time, for Rio intellectuals and others, the *favelas* in the context of the city represent the duality of Brazil as a country where a shantytown reflects "a traditional system of patrimonial organization, retrograde and poor, based on personal relations of dominations, loyalty, and mutual obligations," as opposed to "a capitalist industrial system in expansion, progressive and rich, founded on the concept of profit, that rationalization of productive processes, and the bureaucratization of institutions, the impersonality of interpersonal relations" (Eunice Durham, as quoted in Zaluar and Alvito 1998, 12).[6] In this frame, the *favela* is a space of rural and traditional otherness to the modern metropolis. Rural Brazil, in this wider context, is the traditional site of the violence and patrimonial inequity that led to interclass conflict and uprisings of social bandits known as *cangaceiros* in what the intelligentsia saw as a wider pacific and industrious country (Messeder Pereira 2000). The notion of barbarity reflected on the cover not only engages the level of violence in the *favela* but puts that violence in opposition to the city, to the state, and to modern Brazilian civilization. The gang is the other on which the media narrative constructs the more peaceful reality of the modern metropolis of Rio. This otherness is framed in a historic context of violence by the poor and working class. The specific nature of the threat to the state in the engagement in conspicuous consumption, however, sets the modern trafficker apart from the traditional *cangaceiro* not as a social bandit but, in the image presented earlier, as a brutal contemporary entrepreneur operating in a traditional space of otherness. To be sure, other media narratives do acknowledge some of the social contributions of gangs to the communities they dominate, but they do so in a way that is not incorrect, but that ultimately emphasizes their violence and the role of social investment in promoting dominance. At the center of the media narrative is the idea of the gang and of the *favela* as separate from other actors and institutions in the city.

The cover discussed previously is, of course, only one among many other media portrayals of gangs in Brazil. However, the cover is in some ways representative of the sensationalism of media representations of gangs and their focus almost exclusively on the violent activities of gangs and gang involvement in the drug trade. Although the media is right to draw attention to these components of gang activities, a deeper understanding of gangs necessitates going beyond these activities to understand how gangs are produced by society and politics in Rio.

THE SOCIAL ROLE OF GANGS IN *FAVELAS*

Facing public vilification in society at large, drug gangs seek to augment their own safety and protect their operations by developing tight political, military, and social control over the neighborhoods where they concentrate their operations. Within the *favela*, as discussed earlier, the head of the gang is referred to as the *dono*, a term that we can translate as "owner" or "landlord." As many of the cities' older shantytowns are built on hills, a gang leader may be referred to as the *dono do morro* (owner of the hill). This terminology comes out of the history of *favelas* sitting apart from the city as a whole, despite their deep social and economic integration, and it reflects the view held by some within a community that the community has a landlord to whom residents owe a certain allegiance, including responsibilities such as maintaining their silence or offering shelter in times of need. This allegiance comes in exchange for those same gang leaders providing some limited protection and assistance to residents in their times of need. This unequal and often exploitative relationship can be compared in some ways to the complex reciprocal expectations that James Scott (1976, 44–52) saw as underlying landlord–tenant relations in some parts of Southeast Asia. This notion of ownership and of having seigniorial right over the territory of *favelas* dovetails with media interpretations of traffickers' power, which, as discussed earlier, depicts drug dealers as local feudal political leaders who dominate areas and create systems of parallel power and politics.

Rio gangs, however, have a much more dynamic relationship with the communities they control. Historically, gangs have made significant efforts to maintain positive relations with the residents of their communities to gain protection against the police and other gangs that may try to take over their areas of activity. These efforts have usually involved providing some extremely limited social support, such as paying for the funerals of the very poor, throwing parties for children on saint's days, and hosting *baile funks* and other parties for adults. Drug traffickers also take control of and redistribute some state political resources to the community. Finally, traffickers resolve disputes and prevent certain forms of crime against residents, though there is evidence that they enforce these rules unequally and in ways that are biased toward individuals connected to traffickers (Arias and Davis Rodrigues 2006).

Drug gangs are deeply embedded in their communities and are dependent on their relations to individuals in those communities for their success. These relationships involve formal and pseudo-familial ties.[7] Drug gangs often consist of the young men from a community and, as a result, often have a number of familial relations within the community. Powerful gang leaders also maintain sexual relationships with a number of women who may bear them children, who they support economically, and who provide them with protection in difficult times (Gay 2005). In one case that I observed, a powerful trafficker made an important community leader in the *favela* he dominated the godfather of one of his children to solidify their relationship. In other cases, leaders of community organizations are direct relations of powerful gang leaders (Arias 2006). Gang members who are from a particular community will also maintain multiple friendships with non–gang members in the community. Finally, traffickers also establish a series of other relationships in their communities, including semilegitimate business relationships in which they might become partners with local entrepreneurs in taverns, entertainment venues, and gymnasiums.

These activities were particularly important as survival mechanisms among poor *favela* dwellers in the 1980s and 1990s as a result of the economic dislocations associated with the deregulation of the economy that forced many into the informal sector (Leeds 1996). Individuals who did not have access to regular work or government aid in many cases depended to some extent on traffickers, trafficking, and other elements of the illegal economy to survive. In addition, *favelas* remained outside of the law in ways that went beyond drug dealing. The neighborhoods all depend on informal economic and legal arrangements. In squatter settlements, most residents have no legal title to their land and pay no property taxes. Ownership of homes has always depended on informal mechanisms and has been regulated by AMs (de Sousa Santos 1995). As traffickers have taken larger roles in these communities, they have played a role in resolving local disputes and, at times, enforcing payment of membership fees to the AMs. These fees and some support from traffickers contribute to the ability of local civic leaders to provide services to the residents of some *favelas*.

Over the last decade, drug gangs have expanded, and traffickers have come to dominate different communities. Some have suggested that gangs have decreased their services to residents and have become involved in wider illegal and semilegal businesses. Though I have not found evidence that traffickers have eliminated the very limited social services they offer, there is some evidence that traffickers have become more commercially oriented, to the detriment of resident welfare. For example, traffickers are at times accused of regulating what businesses can operate in communities. Some have suggested that traffickers involve themselves in regulating the sale of cooking gas canisters by imposing monopolies or oligopolies that drive up prices. This shift into commercial activity can chafe relations between gang leaders and residents as residents increasingly perceive gang members as not only bringing danger to the community but also profiting economically from local economic activities beyond drug trafficking. At the same time, however, the growing economic dominance of traffickers in some communities reflects their own market power; their ability to capitalize on informal economic activities, providing new services to residents; and, most importantly, their right, as landlords in the traditional Brazilian context, to exercise some dominance over economic activities in the area they control.[8]

The activities of drug traffickers within the *favelas* have evolved over time. The underlying narrative of drug gangs, and in particular of gang leaders, is one of ownership and reciprocal obligations. Traffickers engage in unequal, reciprocal patron–client relations with the residents of the communities they dominate. In return for silence, protection, and an acceptance of dominance in a variety of realms, traffickers provide very limited social support to residents, support some chosen local civic groups, such as AMs and *samba* schools, and resolve disputes and provide protection to residents. Their management of these relationships, despite a wider narrative of obligation, reflects different types of connections gang members maintain to different residents of communities. These activities are part of local survival strategies in which poor citizens who cannot survive in the formal economy or must resolve disputes and have their property protected through informal mechanisms turn to gangs to deal with quotidian problems that the formal economic, political, and social systems do not address. Gangs, thus, emerge out of historical, social, political, and economic relationships that are spread across the working-class neighborhoods of Rio and, in contrast to the dominant media narrative, are intimately linked to processes of exclusion and inequality that operate in the wider historical, political, and economic context of late-industrial Brazil.

CONCLUSION: THE FAILURE TO COMPREHEND RIO DE JANEIRO'S DRUG GANGS

Armed groups are deeply embedded in Rio de Janeiro political and social life. The media narrative of gangs, however, suggests that criminals are an almost external threat to society and, indeed, the state. Drug traffickers, these stories say, operate parallel states in the midst of the second largest city and undermine the very idea that Rio operates under the modern state system. The only response to this is brutal police operation and repression. This narrative exists in contrast to the localized reality of traffickers within *favelas* providing minimal support to some elements of the population in difficult times and serving as important, though quite dangerous, interlocutors with the state. Both police and politicians use their relationships with gangs to fulfill their economic and political projects. In practice, rather than in the narratives of journalists and many politicians, *favelas* and the gangs that control them are not separate from and opposed to the rest of the political system. Drug gangs are an integral part of these economic, social, and political systems and are in many ways important to the operation of existing political and social networks.

This gap between the terms of public debate and the reality in the shantytowns has created significant difficulties for efforts on the part of government and civil society to build successful policies and programs to address the challenges that gangs pose to both the city as a whole and to the populations that live in the *favelas*. The rhetoric of separateness, of an alternate state, supports a set of policies focused on reconquering the rebel space held by drug traffickers. Indeed, Rio de Janeiro's current marquee program to control *favela* violence is a policing program called the Unidade de Policia Pacificadora (Police Pacification Unit), which focuses on sending elite police units into *favelas* to pacify the areas by suppressing gang activity and then seeks to develop a type of community policing program to help residents collaborate with police to maintain limits on gang activities. Although there is much to be lauded in this program, and initial government reports on program efforts are positive, the underlying logic of the policy continues to see *favelas* as areas of rebellion, as parallel states, where the population needs to be pacified, language which was used to describe the efforts of the U.S. government to control guerillas during the war in Vietnam (Pinard 2002). The program, in all likelihood, will have relatively little impact on the underlying conditions of political corruption and mass poverty that give rise to these types of criminal organizations. Over time, the success of state efforts will depend on the ability of the political and police officials implementing the programs to fully understand the deep interrelationships between gangs and political and social life in the city and to develop effective ways of transforming those relationships to minimize their embeddedness.

The narrative of the parallel state obscures connections between the political and social order in the power of gangs in shantytowns. This narrative, however, plays an important function in providing legitimacy to state and social institutions that claim Brazil to be a racial democracy with reasonable levels of opportunity for its population, despite the widespread context of pervasive, racially tinged inequality and the existence of ineffective political institutions that often operate to benefit the well-off and well-connected at the expense of everyone else. Such a narrative excises the gang from the body politic and constitutes it as a threat to state and society. This enables the intellectual reconciliation of what James Holston and Teresa Caldeira (1999) have called a "disjunctive" political system, in which formal rights and guarantees are extended to a citizenry in which the less well-off almost never have the resources to fully realize their rights and participation in the democratic political economy.

NOTES

1. On the development of the Brazilian state, see Collier and Collier (1991, 169–95, 360–402).

2. On the history of the Comando Vermelho, see Amorim (1993). Also see Leeds (1996, 62–56) and Dowdney (2003, 29–32).

3. On the factions, see Dowdney (2003, 42–46).

4. Original text: "Istoé revela o mundo bárbaro que veio à tona com a morte do reporter da Globo. Traficantes impõem o terror, movimentam milhões de dolares, oprimem a sociedade, e desafiam os poderes constituidos."

5. Presentation by Urbiratan Ângelo, former Comandante Geral of the Polícia Militar do Estado do Rio de Janeiro, at the conference on Community Policing in Latin America, October 2006.

6. Original texts: "A organizção patrimonial do sistema tradicional, retrograde e pobre, baseado nas relações pessoais de dominação, lealdade, e obrigações mútuas" and "um sistema capitalista industrial em expansão, progressista e rico, fundado na concepção do lubro, na racionalização do processo produtivo, na burocratização das instituições, na impessoalidade das relações interpessoais."

7. On pseudo-familial relations, see Liebow (2003).

8. More recently, as gangs have become more professionalized, there is some evidence that in a handful of *favelas,* there are laboratories that process cocaine base into powdered cocaine. This potentially positions Rio's gangs to expand their projection into other regions of the country and increase their profits, though at the same time, it is something that will likely create greater stress on the community in which these factories operate.

REFERENCES

Alves Filho, Francisco, and Marcos Pernambuco. 2002. "No Front Inimigo." *Istoé* (São Paulo), June 19, 24–37.

Amorim, Celso. 1993. *Comando Vermelho: A História Secreta do Crime Organizado.* Rio de Janeiro: Editora Record.

Arias, Enrique Desmond. 2006. *Drugs and Democracy in Rio de Janeiro: Trafficker, Social Networks, and Public Security.* Chapel Hill: University of North Carolina Press.

Arias, Enrique Desmond. 2009. "Dispatches from the Field: Rio de Janeiro." *America's Quarterly* 3, no. 2: 90–93.

Arias, Enrique Desmond, and Corinne Davis Rodrigues. 2006. "The Myth of Personal Security: A Discursive Model of Local Level Legitimation in Rio's *Favelas.*" *Latin American Politics and Society* 48, no. 4: 53–81.

Baumann Burgos, Marcelo. 1998. "Dos Parques Proletários ao *Favela*-Bairro: As políticas públicas nas *favelas* do Rio de Janeiro." In *Um Século de Favela,* edited by Alba Zaluar and Marcos Alvito, 25–60. Rio de Janeiro: Fundação Gétulio Vargas.

Collier, Ruth Beirns, and David Collier. 1991. *Shaping the Political Arena: Critical Junctures, the Labor Movement, and Regime Dynamics in Latin America.* Princeton, N.J.: Princeton University Press.

de Sousa Santos, Boaventura. 1995. *Towards a New Common Sense: Law, Science, and Politics in the Paradigmatic Transition.* London: Routledge.

Dowdney, Luke. 2003. *Children of the Drug Trade: A Case Study of Children in Organised Armed Violence in Rio de Janeiro.* Rio de Janeiro: 7 Letras.

Easton, Kent. 2007. "The Downside of Decentralization: Armed Clientelism in Colombia." *Security Studies* 15, no. 4: 533–62.

Gay, Robert. 1994. *Popular Organization and Democracy in Rio de Janeiro: A Tale of Two Favelas.* Philadelphia: Temple University Press.

———. 2005. *Lucia: Testimonies of a Drug Dealer's Woman.* Philadelphia: Temple University Press.

Holston, James, and Teresa Caldeira. 1999. "Democracy and Violence in Brazil." *Comparative Studies in Society and History* 41, no. 4: 691–720.

Leeds, Anthony, and Elizabeth Leeds. 1978. *A Sociologia do Brasil Urbano.* Rio de Janeiro: Zahar.

Leeds, Elizabeth. 1996. "Cocaine and Parallel Polities on the Brazilian Urban Periphery: Constraints on Local Level Democratization." *Latin American Research Review* 31, no. 3: 47–84.

Liebow, Elliot. 2003. *Tally's Corner: A Study of Negro Streetcorner Men.* Lanham, Md.: Rowman and Littlefield.

Messeder Pereira, Carlos Alberto. 2000. "O Brasil do Sertão e a Mídia Televisiva." In *Linguagens da Violência,* edited by Carlos Alberto Messeder Pereira, Elizabeth Rondelli, Karl Erick Scholhammer, and Micael Herschmann. Rio de Janeiro: Rocco.

Nunes Leal, Vitor. 1977. *Coronelismo: The Municipality and Representative Government in Brazil.* Cambridge: Cambridge University Press.

Penglase, Ben. 2005. "The Shutdown of Rio de Janeiro: The Poetics of Drug Trafficker Violence." *Anthropology Today* 21, no. 5: 3–6.

Perlman, Janice. 1976. *The Myth of Marginality: Urban Poverty and Politics in Rio de Janeiro.* Berkeley: University of California Press.

Pinard, Matthew D. 2002. "The American and South Vietnamese Pacification Efforts during the Vietnam War." Master's thesis, Louisiana State University.

Scott, James C. 1976. *The Moral Economy of the Peasant: Rebellion and Subsistence in Southeast Asia.* New Haven, Conn.: Yale University Press.

Torres Maia, Monica. 1999. "White admite conhecer acusados de tráfico na FAB." *O Globo,* May 19, 10.

World Bank. 2013a. "GDP Ranking." http://data.worldbank.org/data-catalog/GDP-ranking-table.

———. 2013b. "GINI Index." http://data.worldbank.org/indicator/SI.PV.GINI.

Zaluar, Alba, and Marcos Alvito. 1998. "Introdução." In *Um Século de Favela,* edited by Alba Zaluar and Marcos Alvito, 7–24. Rio de Janeiro: Fundação Getúlio Vargas.

12

"Hecho en México": Gangs, Identities, and the Politics of Public Security

GARETH A. JONES

As I sit on the pavement with a group of young people passing the time near a bustling market in the city of Puebla, central Mexico, I listen to Ramón as he describes his worries over recent events. He is uncharacteristically nervous, unable to sit still, and his eyes are scanning the street. During our previous meetings, Ramón would take little notice as passers-by shot disapproving glances at his often bare-chested, muscular, although sometimes disheveled appearance—a look that communicated drug use and little consideration for conventional employment. Nor, unlike others in the group, would Ramón approach the police to pay for their "cooperation" for a hassle-free life, preferring to remain near the back of a shaded area of trees and stalls out of sight, or he would invent a reason to cross the road to the market and return once the coast was clear. But today he was alert. In recent weeks, the area of Hidalgo market, one of the city's major locations for the sale of smuggled, stolen, and prohibited goods, had become a quasi-militarized zone. Apparently in search of contraband, the Agencia Federal de Investigación (AFI), a police agency staffed with many ex-military personnel and with all the paraphernalia and finesse of a paramilitary unit, had been conducting operations in the market. Moreover, a new state-level police force known as the Metropolitana had also been in the area, repeatedly driving by in large pickup trucks, the men dressed in black fatigues, wearing balaclavas and touting assault rifles. Both the AFI and the Metropolitana are less reliable than the local police, and they exude menace.

As a unit of the Metropolitana passed our seated position, Ramón muttered under his breath. But once the pickup had gone a safe distance, he got up and, without intending for his voice to carry, shouted a string of obscenities in their direction. He sat back down, still worried, and commented that "everything had gone to shit around here." As a contributor to what most people would consider to be the "shit" of the Hidalgo area, Ramón's reflection was that the norms that guided antisocial behavior, including crime, had shifted, and the change had been away from the conditions to which he was accustomed. In short, policing had become military-style "public security"; indeed, through the unfolding war on drugs, it had become legitimated as "national security."[1] This was not a welcome shift for somebody like Ramón or, indeed, for most young people caught up in the *razzias,* the police and military sweeps of streets and clubs, which often involve meting out violence (Castillo Berthier and Jones 2009). Ramón's agitation was heightened, however, by what he referred to as some "awkward business," possibly linked to his roles in armed robbery or low-level drug deals. Although details were hazy, it appeared that some people were looking for him, and he was contemplating acquiring a handgun for protection. As we talked, he revealed that there were people at the back of the market who "rented" guns and that he was deciding between three models.[2] The new policing situation, however, was a cause for concern, as possessing a weapon—he motioned to placing a gun in the belt of his jeans behind his back—would be dangerous if he were detained. And despite his streetwise demeanor, Ramón was often detained.

In these circumstances, Ramón raised the seemingly sensible option of leaving Puebla. Like many of his peers, his life history revealed considerable mobility as well as dreams of travel (Jones and Thomas de Benítez 2009). But our discussion of the flight option took an unexpected turn when Ramón mentioned that he might be better off in Tepito, a central *barrio* in Mexico City associated with crime, and where he had previously lived. He dismissed the alternative of going to Los Angeles, which he declared he knew quite well (despite having previously denied ever having been in the United States). Moreover, it transpired that in both Tepito and California, he had been involved with gangs. Would the solution to the "awkward business" in Puebla be found by reacquainting himself with his old gang, and if so, why opt for Tepito and not the United States? This chapter explores how Ramón and young men like him are caught between the threat posed by more draconian forms of public security, on one hand, and by a group of potential assailants, on the other, and how involvement with gangs is understood as a possible solution. I argue that, for Ramón, the gang exists as a social space in which connections are made and opportunities are opened up, sometimes allowing him to cement ties with other young men and to extract some fun from a "hard life."

Drawing on Charles Tilly (2005), my claim is that young people go to considerable lengths to form social relations within the gang that compound into collective identities that, in turn, provide a sense of physical protection, belonging, and reputation. However, unlike the term *gang* in English, which has a relatively generic application, and, indeed, can be applied to describe a range of different social relations and settings, in Mexico, it is important to understand specific usages of *gang* terms. As I discuss in the next section, different terms for *gang* in everyday life imply nuances of social relations, albeit distinctions missed or misinterpreted by lawmakers and police. I note how Ramón constructs discursive boundaries around his gang identities that differentiate between social relations formed by "hanging out" and occasional criminal activity and involvement in more organized social groups, including those with transnational dimensions.

MEXICAN GANGS IN HISTORICAL PERSPECTIVE

As anybody familiar with Luis Buñuel's 1950 film *Los Olvidados* or the work of Oscar Lewis will be aware, the idea of youth gangs is not new to Mexico. In his classic text *The Children of Sánchez*, Lewis (1983, 36–38, 73–74, 145–47) makes numerous references to the presence of gangs in the Tepito district of Mexico City during the late 1950s. The gangs described in the "autobiographies" of Manuel, Roberto, and Marta marked out important "turf"; engaged in petty crime; and created opportunities for bonding with peers, access to marijuana, and sexual conquests. Some gangs, seemingly those joined earlier in life and tied to the *vecindad* (tenement) of Casa Grande, the Sánchez family's principal residence during the time period covered by the book, were limited to a few members but still had "beating in" rituals and a leadership hierarchy.[3] Although not all the violence described every few pages by Lewis was on account of gangs, the book's temporal structure indicates that early confrontations with fists were replaced later in life with sticks, knives, and, in the case of Roberto, the use of a handgun. Importantly, the gangs in *The Children of Sánchez* seem to be ever present in the social landscape of central Mexico City, without being dominant organizations. Family members' lives are interleaved with the gangs, serving to shape gender relations, the use of space, and interactions with more powerful agents, both in terms of the police and criminal organizations in the barrio and in prison.[4] Lewis sees gangs as part of communities and place rather than as outside and delinquent, describing their activities in the same paragraphs as other goings-on rather than pulling them out as special. Hence they are just one indication of the poor's ability to organize socially and construct identities. But people's economic and social lives do not seem to have been determined by gangs, which ultimately appear epiphenomenal and, with the exception of Roberto, have limited impact on how eventual life paths developed and might be explained.

Lewis's work on what he termed the "culture of poverty" would be the subject of vociferous critiques, notably from academics influenced by neo-Marxism (see Leacock 1971).[5] Nevertheless, Eric Wolf (1962, 619) considered *The Children of Sánchez* to be "burningly relevant to the world in which we live" and placed it with "only a few books by anthropologists that have so affected our public view of the world." Despite Wolf's apparent encouragement, studies of gangs in Mexico since *The Children of Sánchez* have been piecemeal and rarely supported by ethnographic enquiry. Rather, attention focused on understanding the "Mexican" gang as a cipher for cultural change and the nation, particularly through the influence of Octavio Paz's short essay on "The Pachuco and Other Extremes," published as part of *The Labyrinth of Solitude* (Paz [1961] 1990). Paz shifted the optic from the uncomfortable social implications of Buñuel and Lewis's work to how the gang represented a possible consciousness of being "Mexican." Paz's essay was based on a visit to Los Angeles, where he witnessed youths of Mexican origin—*pachucos*—organized into gangs who had developed new forms of speech, deportment, and clothing, notably the zoot suit. According to Paz, these gangs demonstrate a desire neither to "vindicate their race" nor to assimilate into U.S. society but rather a "fanatical will-to-be" (14).

The focus on the *pachuco* is a timely reminder that the present-day attention to the "transnational gang" is not new and that Paz had effectively already raised concern with the process of cultural hybridity. A host of more recent studies have taken up the theme, shifting the emphasis to explore how the gang experience in Mexico reflects the long-standing cultural contact of young people with the United States, including through involvement with gangs or knowing people who have gone north (Hernandez León 1999; Nateras Domínguez 2007). This is not always a case of youths in Mexico borrowing and adapting gang styles from the United States. As Rogelio Marcial (1997) and Robert Smith (2005) have outlined, the return of gang-involved youths from the United States can provoke contests over identity with those left behind (known as "regulars"), which can occasionally turn aggressive. Paz's observation, however, also helpfully raises the role of the gang as a social space. In exerting their "fanatical will-to-be," these "extreme Mexicans" flaunt their difference from society around them. This process follows what Tilly (2005, 131–52) calls "boundary change," whereby groups work through their social relations attempting to reconcile how others, notably the state and media, construct boundaries of meaning, in terms of gangs, for example, as delinquent, criminal, and dangerous, with their self-perception and own sense of agency.[6]

The description of gangs provided by Lewis gives a sense that boundary formation was largely under the control of youths themselves. *The Children of Sánchez* reveals an incipient subculture in which being young in Tepito and being in a gang were relatively indistinct, social behavior was largely benign—captured by the term *palomilla* to refer to gangs in the 1950s[7]—and ties within the group were relatively short-lived. More established associations of the period, such as Los Tarzanes, Los Nazis, Los Roquets, Los Feos, and Los Panchitos, which emerged in the 1960s, display a stronger sense of a group identity constructed around dress codes, drawing from the influence, in some cases, of the *pachuco,* the consumption of alcohol and cigarettes, and their presence in pool and dance halls (Valenzuela Arce 2007). These gangs exerted a territorial control over important working-class neighborhoods in Mexico City, such as Portales, La Industrial, and Anahuac, through involvement in petty street crime, running numbers rackets, enforcing debt repayments, and fending off rivals. Reflecting the heightened contestation of youth identity norms, the innocuous term *palomilla* is dropped from colloquial and academic usage, to be replaced by the terms *banda* and *pandilla.*

The state's attitude toward gangs until this point was to decry their immorality and lack of "loyalty" to the "system," meaning a concern with the undermining of social institutions, such as the family and church, and the threat to the one-party state and the way of doing politics.[8] But, as Héctor Castillo Berthier (2004) notes, the state became increasingly active from the late 1960s in attempts to define the meanings of *banda* and *pandilla* and, crucially, the difference between the two. Following Tilly, we might view this involvement as preemptive of social reality—an attempt by the state to influence the boundaries of group identity through recognition of certain norms and outlaying the means for treating transgressions. In 1968, the Penal Code established that anyone identified as a *pandillero* would, upon conviction, have their sentence increased by one-half (Article 164, *Diario Oficial,* March 8, 1968). The code considered *pandilla* to be akin to a criminal organization, motivated, strategic, and undertaking hard-core gang behaviors, whereas *banda* was shorthand for social relations that might be ascribed as ganglike or "gang-lite." That is, *bandas* were affective relations perceived to be antisocial from the outside but not likely to be permanent and dominant organizations.

Research tended to confirm that the social identities and quotidian practices of *banda* were little different from previous iterations of youth association. Most *banda* consist of young men, mostly from around age twelve to their late twenties, with the primary intent to "hang out" and have fun (Castillo Berthier 2002; Gigengack 2006). Although often perceived as countercultural, in some cases, *bandas* were involved with civil society organizations such as sports teams and social clubs. The dominant treatment of the *banda,* however, has been to focus on the appropriation of styles, ranging at different moments from punks to *metaleros* and *raztecas,* and later to *goticos, darquetos, eskatos,* and hip-hop, as well as to identifications with and practices of tattooing, body piercing, graffiti, and tagging (Castillo Berthier and Jones 2009; Cruz Salazar 2004; Nateras Domínguez 2002, 2006). Noting how these practices contest social and cultural norms, and, in the case of graffiti and tagging, may possess an overtly political content, José Manuel Valenzuela Arce (2007) has gone so far as to suggest that *bandas* might be thought of as social movements (see also Reguillo Cruz 1991). Such an argument is probably not widely shared on the ground, as it were, in the neighborhoods, markets, and colleges where groups of young people hang out smoking, drinking, taking drugs, listening to music, getting into fights, taunting passers-by, and getting involved in petty crime.

In people's daily lives, the distinction between *banda* and *pandilla* may seem rather abstract.[9] In his excellent study of neighborhood gangs in Zamora, Marcial (1997) employs the term *banda* in accordance with the identification used by his informants. The *banda* appears to be widely identifiable to residents by name and seems to have an inter-generational dimension. As Marcial describes, the *banda* is intimately embedded within the neighborhood, although it has an antagonistic relationship with it, vandalizing property, fighting, and mugging residents. Yet it retains the nomenclature of *banda*. Sonnevelt (2009), conversely, notes how residents in her study settlement in Guadalajara would interchange between referring to young people as being part of a *pandilla* or else as *los muchachos* (the boys), a proximate of *banda*. The distinction does not appear to follow a simple fear–tolerance divide. Residents talk of gangs in reference to misguided or delinquent behavior and express frustration at noise, vandalism, and general signs of declining standards in the area or society in general (see also Castillo Berthier 2004). But they would also consider the gang a source of authority and call on it for conflict resolution (Sonnevelt 2009). These relations in the neighborhoods of Zamora and Guadalajara are possible because the gang's influence is restricted to its *facha,* or local area. This presence is maintained on a semipermanent basis against competition from other groups, including other *banda* and local police, with only occasional resource to violence beyond fistfights, throwing rocks, and using knives. In conceptual terms, then, the boundaries of young people's social identities are established with other actors, who are also relatively local and whose actions are not too dissimilar from the motives of the *banda* and *pandilla* themselves.

Ramón's anxiety over contemporary events in Puebla, however, indicates that we cannot understand gangs, as either *banda* or *pandilla,* without reference to the changing landscape of public security. The rise of certain forms of criminal activity, including kidnap, gun trafficking and drugs, in particular, as well as the state's response by declaring a war on drugs, has recast the boundaries between all youths, those identified with delinquency and the state.[10] The boundary between youth, gangs, and society is being reconfigured around young people's relationship with "security" and the gang as an actual or potential link to drug-trafficking organizations (DTOs), and as an actual or potential transnational actor. Commentary has also shifted from a more or less exclusive focus on the neighborhood or city to a wider panorama of geopolitics. Without radically altering their behavior, young people such as Ramón find their identities being described and interpreted using new vocabularies, with assumptions of new social ties and behaviors, and with very different potential consequences. The hitherto blurred distinction between *pandilla* and *banda* in practice becomes more important.

PUBLIC SECURITY AND THE NEW GANG

The presence of military-style public security measures in large parts of Mexico is legitimated by a series of discourses that trace, on one hand, rising levels of organized crime and, on the other hand, the sense that the state, and especially the police, are untrustworthy and incapable of maintaining control.[11] At the furthest extremes of this discourse is the idea that Mexico teeters on the brink of becoming a "failed state," a contention hotly refuted by (then) President Felipe Calderón, who nevertheless readily invoked the language of "war" backed up with large-scale troop deployment (Jones 2012). As an indication of what is apparently at stake, a report by the U.S. Joint Operating Environment (U.S. Joint Forces Command 2008, 34, 36) declared that the "growing assault by the drug cartels and their thugs on the Mexican government over the past several years reminds one that an unstable Mexico could represent a homeland security problem of immense proportions to the United States" before identifying Mexico with Pakistan as the two countries most prone to "rapid and sudden collapse." It is a position endorsed by a range of think tanks and commentators, a number of whom elide gangs together with DTOs (see Killebrew and Bernal 2010; Manwaring 2005, 2008; Strickland 2009; Wilson and Sullivan 2007).[12]

Gangs have become situated in a policy frame, political discourse, and daily reality that perceive their actions, and even their simple presence, as evidence of and contributing to a regional and national security threat. By these accounts, the street corners of Mexico and the United States are linked by youths that are actually or potentially part of "networked criminal insurgencies" (Killebrew and Bernal 2010; Manwaring 2005). To emphasize the point, Robert Killebrew and Jennifer Bernal

(2010, 40) suggest that "to average Americans, the most immediately threatening 'tactical' manifestations of the cartel networks are the gangs they read about in the local press or that leave graffiti on the side of the local convenience store."[13] Their argument is that, by the time a gang presence is noticed, it is too late; "homegrown" gangs will be already contributing to the transnational gang network by selling drugs, identifying recruits, and contributing to an atmosphere of lawlessness. Other observers warn that the conventional territorially based gangs can transform rapidly into extraterritorial organizations—so-called third-generation gangs—with the capacity to establish relations with groups as varied as Al-Qaeda, Hezbollah, or FARC, as well as pirates, anarchists, and DTOs, to form "plug-and-go" networks engaged in "fourth-generation"—that is, nonstate—warfare (Sullivan and Elkus 2008; Teicher 2009; Wilson and Sullivan 2007). The sense is that gangs, in Mexico and elsewhere, represent an imminent form of "insurgency."

As applied to Mexico, the credibility of "transnational gang" arguments rests on the integrity and fragility of the state; its ability to secure its southern border; its ability to conduct domestic security; and its ability, therefore, to protect its northern border with the United States. The cipher for state fragility and transnationalization was for a long time the presence of the notorious *maras*—both the Mara Salvatrucha (MS-13) and Calle 18—in Mexico (see Franco 2008; Seelke 2009; Strickland 2009). The presence of *maras* would certainly mark a dramatic departure from the gangs depicted in *The Children of Sánchez*. Unlike the 1950s *palomillas*, the *maras* undertake a range of criminal activities from kidnapping to extortion, are accredited with a command structure, and use violence to dominate social institutions and carve out space within which they may exert hegemonic control over the local state (Armijo, Benítez Manaut, and Hristroulas 2009; Lara Klahr 2006; Valenzuela Arce 2007; see also *La Jornada,* December 6, 2004).[14] Lending credence to the transnationalization case, *mara clicas* (chapters) were identified in the areas of Tapachula, Suchiate and Huixtla in Chiapas, and parts of Oaxaca and Tabasco in the late 1990s and early 2000s, with numbers climbing to perhaps three thousand in 2001 (Comisión Nacional de Derechos Hermanos [CNDH] 2008; Santamaría Balmaceda 2007). The headline of the major national daily, *El Universal,* on December 7, 2003—"Chiapas invadido por 'maras'" (Chiapas invaded by *maras*)—is fairly typical of the alarm.[15]

Claims of a significant *mara* presence outside of a few municipalities in southern Mexico and of links with Mexican DTOs are controversial (*El Universal,* February 19, 2009). In 2008, the Comisión Nacional de Derechos Humanos (National Commission for Human Rights, or CNDH) identified *maras* in twenty-three states and the Federal District but suggested numbers in most areas were small (CNDH 2008). By contrast, the Centro de Investigación y Seguridad Nacional, the Mexican intelligence agency, USAID, and some journalist accounts claim that there are between five thousand and twenty thousand *mara* members in Mexico, with growing numbers along the border with the United States and in Mexico City, in particular (Fernández Menéndez and Ronquillo 2006; USAID 2006).[16] One newspaper article in 2004 reported claims by city politicians that MS-13 alone may have had a thousand members in the capital (*El Universal,* February 25, 2004). Yet, when journalists report in more detail, the case for a *mara* "invasion" seems weaker. An article prompted by the concerns of a *mara* presence in the Pensil Norte neighborhood relied on a claim by the neighborhood Mothers' Committee of a possible link between a Honduran man arrested elsewhere in the city and Pensil Norte, the presence of "*mara*-type" graffiti in the area, and the assertion of a city congressman for the Partido Acción Nacional political party that the *maras* are recruiting members from people on the streets (*Crónica de Hoy,* May 18, 2004).[17] Nevertheless, a short time later, director of public security for Mexico City and future mayor Marcelo Ebrard announced that an anti-*maras* unit had been established within the city's police force.[18]

The presence of more than one thousand MS-13 members in organized *clicas* beyond the purview of the state is unlikely, even in a city as large as Mexico City, not least given the aggression displayed by *maras* to rival gangs and more subtle differences such as accents and local street slang versus gang idiom *(caló).* Rather than an "invasion" of Mexico by transnational gangs marching on to the United States, what appears a better explanation is a process of *mara*-ization. Despite seemingly limited "incentives," to follow Tilly (2005), this process reflects an antagonistic "boundary readjustment" of a minority of young people to their ongoing exclusion in Mexico. Young Mexicans are involved in a process mimicking *mara* styles, building on already existing forms of gang identity (Armijo, Benítez Manaut, and Hristroulas 2009; Santamaría Balmaceda 2007). This is not an entirely benign process, with some observers arguing for a more deliberate "cloning" whereby adoption of *mara* lifestyles lends itself to incorporation into criminal networks (Lara

Klahr 2006).[19] Yet it is consistent with the observation of the CNDH (2008) that upward of 70 percent of apprehended *mareros* are Mexican and with colloquialisms in, for example, Chiapas, where Mexican *mareros* have acquired the name *Chiapatruchas*. In circumstances in which gang narratives are elastic, mimicking a *mara* "look" provides an added countercultural dimension to identity construction. As Alfredo Nateras Domínguez (2006) has perceptively discussed, *maras* and what he terms *cholos* share certain motivations and representations in styles of dress, tattoos, and deportment, but also some marked differences.[20] Unlike the *maras*, whose intent is to have "power over" others, these *mara*-type arrangements do not appear to break ties with the neighborhood and its social institutions, despite their enthusiasm for transgressing their norms; in short, they act in ways long recognized for *bandas* and *pandillas*.

Concerns with *maras* appear to have abated, in Mexico at least, since the late 2000s, but the state's scrutiny of gangs has become more intense and pervasive. The establishment of police anti-*maras* units and the more general militarization of security forces is part of a process whereby the state has toughened its stance to all gangs, whether *bandas* or *pandillas*. In 1996, a new Law against Organized Delinquency brought both *bandas* and *pandillas* under the rubric of "organized crime," initially justified through links with assault, robbery, and vehicle theft, but reforms to the Penal Code in 2007 and 2009 associated gangs with kidnapping, drugs, and terrorism.[21] Public and national security agencies also became more prominently involved in attempts to measure gang presence.[22] The Subprocuraduría de Investigación Especializada en Delincuencia Organizada (Attorney General's Special Investigative Office for Organized Crime) estimated in 2008 that there may be as many as fifteen hundred gangs and twenty thousand young people linked with drug-related violence, and a 2010 submission by the Procuraduría General de la República (Attorney General) to a Special Session of the Organization of American States on "Pandillas Delictivas" (Delinquent Gangs) estimated that there were 214 gangs in Mexico with links to DTOs.[23]

In a few cases, these *narco-pandilla* have grown from existing *bandas* and *pandillas*. Recent reports for Tepito, for example, suggest that a leading gang, the Ojos (Rojos), which has been involved with protection, contraband, and drug sales for many years, has been challenged by the La Mano de Osos gang to take over drug distribution. Unlike previous turf wars that would be resolved with fights and a body count kept to a minimum, La Mano de Osos is openly engaged in the killing of rival distributors and gang members. Intergang rivalry for control of the drug trade—Tepito is an important center for both small-scale drug sales *(narcomenudeo)* and wholesale distribution—has been the explanation for the killing of six young people in Tepito in October 2010. The killings were attributed to another long-established gang, Los Perros, that took the uncharacteristic step of using a drive-by shooting (*Proceso,* October 28, 2010). These *pandilla* to *narco-pandilla* conversions remain rare, however, and crucially, most *pandillas* lack the skills and tactics employed by the paramilitary-style "new gangs" directly under the command of the DTOs.[24]

For the past decade, the most organized, sophisticated, and violent of the new gangs have been the "Mexican" gangs originating in the United States. There is fairly credible evidence that gangs of Mexican origin but U.S. citizenship are key actors in the present drug violence in Mexico (U.S. Department of Justice 2010, 13–17, 64–65).[25] The best-known example of this new type of gang is La Eme (aka the Mexican Mafia). Reportedly established in Maravilla in East Los Angeles by second-generation Mexicans during the 1950s, La Eme split from the Maravilla gangs; consolidated a powerbase in the California prison system; and gradually extended its influence through control of drugs and protection rackets, setting up *clicas* across the southern United States and developing links with other Latino gangs, possibly even controlling Calle 18 (Morales 2006). Involvement in Mexico can be dated at least to 1997, when La Eme was linked with the attack on Jesus Blancornelas, owner of the *Zeta* newspaper, as well as to the killing of Cardinal Juan Jesús Posadas Ocampo in Guadalajara (*La Jornada,* December 1, 1997). More recently, a report informed by the head of the Anti-gang Division of the Los Angeles Police Department claims that the DTOs are deliberately hiring individuals of Mexican origin with U.S. citizenship residing in California—a suggestion of La Eme—to conduct killings in Tijuana, Mexicali, and Rosarito (*Milenio,* May 29, 2008). It is even claimed that La Eme may be involved directly in the drug trade in Baja California, either in partnership with the Arellano Felix DTO or, given its weaker position since the mid-2000s, as its replacement (*La Jornada,* January 27, 2006).

The upsurge of drug-related killings in Ciudad Júarez has also been linked with "Mexican" gangs, specifically the Aztecas (aka Barrio Azteca), acting on behalf of the Júarez DTO, and the Mexicles (from Mexica), acting for the Sinaloa Pacific DTO, as well as the smaller Artistas Asesinos (aka Doble A).[26] All three gangs were established in Texas, the Aztecas and Mexicales in the mid-1980s by "Mexicans" Longo Fernández and José Marquez, respectively.[27] As with La Eme, the core membership of these gangs remains quite small—the Aztecas and Los Mexicles claim a combined membership of about three thousand people. Moreover, only some of these members have the necessary skills to operate as a quasi-paramilitary organization. Rather, the narco-pandillas have adopted a different process to extend their influence in Mexico. The Aztecas, the Mexicles, and Doble A appear to recruit existing pandillas or pandilleros in Mexico to their ranks, including from within the prison system, or in the case of the Aztecas paramilitary arm, called La Linea, from corrupt elements of the police (Proceso, December 14, 2008). Importantly, membership in this "new gang" arrangement involves the deliberate construction of identity boundaries, to confer a sense of belonging and respect. Narco-pandillas have invented roles and rituals to cement loyalty, including a rite-of-passage killing, the heavy use of tattooing—members of the Aztecas have tattoos of Aztec warriors—and the incorporation of oaths and ceremonies during meetings or before conflicts.[28] Once recruited, pandillas become involved in activities that are an extension of previous practices, including drug distribution, trafficking, and extortion, as well as the possibility of graduation to roles as malandrines or gatilleros (gunmen) or sicarios (hit men)—all terms in ever greater usage in the media.

The most likely victims of the narco-pandilla hit men are the members of other gangs or one's own. Evidence, for example, for the violence in Ciudad Juárez during 2007 and 2008 suggests that DTOs were engaged in "cleaning up" gangs affiliated with their organizations to remove addicts or potential informants (Padilla 2008). The available statistics confirm that being identified with a pandilla brings risks but being associated with a narco-pandilla brings all the more. Murder is the eighth ranked cause of death across all age groups in Mexico, but it is the fifth for males aged fifteen to sixty-four and the second for males aged fifteen to nineteen (Alvarado 2009). Males aged eighteen to thirty-five record the highest prevalence of drug-related killing nationally. These data point to a situation in which the war on drugs has not only adjusted the boundaries of how gangs are represented and reduced the scope for young people to redetermine those boundaries but has affected the material outcomes of these identity adjustments. As we sat on the sidewalk, the dilemma for a young man such as Ramón became apparent. His identity construction marked him out to most casual observers as *banda,* whereas his reference to "awkward business" away from the street corner suggested activities that the authorities would identify with his being a *pandillero.* The changed identity boundary would shift Ramón's relationship with the state, drawing him away from the municipal police demanding "cooperation" to the security agencies scouring the area.

YOUTH, GANGS, AND IDENTITY MATTERS

From our discussion, it was clear that Ramón saw no advantage to re-solving his present difficulties by leaving Mexico for the United States. His description of being in California appeared to have been both an unhappy one and, if repeated, likely not to aid resolution of his dilemma. During his brief time in Los Angeles, Ramón had been a member of what he specifically underscored was a "Mexican" gang. The name of the gang was not offered, Ramón pointing out simply that his *clica* was involved in battles with the cholos.[29] It was through the *clica* that Ramón claimed to have learned about guns, although he also showed a wound in his leg which he claimed to be the result of having accidentally shot himself. He also described how, having been in Los Angeles for only a short while, he was arrested and put in prison, and that while in de-tention, he had begun to use heroin and other drugs. It was not clear whether Ramón was released and returned to Mexico voluntarily or whether he was deported, but he expressed little pride or boast of his California gang experience, and he did not seem to have maintained a "transnational" gang affiliation.[30]

By contrast, Ramón appears to have remained in contact with other gang arrangements in Tepito, specifically the Osos Leyes.[31] He describes the gang as a tough outfit involved in territorial disputes and recalls briefly how they would catch enemies if they crossed their street and deal with them by whatever means necessary, using blows (*garrotazos*), belts, bottles, and knives. Ramón would later show the scars on his body from some of these fights and his "VL" tattoo, standing for "Vato Loco" (Crazy Guy). He would also explain that while in Tepito, he would carry a .38 revolver in his belt just in case matters required it. Ramón discussed the Osos in very different terms to the LA gang and claimed that he would return to Mexico City if he were ever needed. Nevertheless, he had left Tepito for what appeared to be a fresh start in Puebla: he had sold the gun and worked for a time at the city's Wholesale Centre (Central de Abastos).

Over the course of a few years, however, Ramón would join a gang in Puebla—indeed, he described himself as having formed the gang—and spend time in prison for armed robbery. His prison life also led him to acquire a range of tattoos—including one of a Santa Muerte (a death saint) across his chest that is often associated with a *pandillero* "look" (see Jones, Herrera, and Thomas de Benítez 2007). The gang, which at the time of our principal interview still had no name, consisted of people from the Abastos area and people who had met up in prison. He claimed that the gang had more than twenty members but that its principal purpose was to hang out, take drugs, go to parties, beat up other kids, and fight rivals such as Los Ricolinos to gain their respect. From conversations with Ramón and others, it appeared that he had become involved in robberies, including break-ins and the use of weapons. The *banda*-type activities that Ramón associated with hanging around the Hidalgo market were clearly taking a more serious turn with his mates at the Abasto.

His friendship with Rodrigo, who also occasionally hung out at the Hidalgo market and had multiple gang involvements in his background, had become more serious.[32] Rodrigo was a member of a well-known gang called Hecho en México (Made in Mexico; HEM), and the area around the Hidalgo market had much graffiti featuring the HEM symbol. Members of HEM, according to Rodrigo, had to "apply themselves," meaning a commitment to paint graffiti of the gang's emblem throughout the city as a sign of its influence; to hold parties featuring hip-hop music, copious quantities of alcohol, and drug consumption; and to provide support for other members during fights with lead pipes, stones, or, occasionally, firearms. HEM membership required a twenty-nine-second beating-in administered by several other members and was indicated by the use of tattoos and cigarette burns, in Rodrigo's case, three burned dots on the back of his hand, supposedly to represent "money, drugs, and women" and to indicate both a belonging and a tolerance for pain.[33]

In our last meetings, just some weeks after he had been released from prison, it was clear that Ramón was becoming involved with minor drug dealing. He was often distracted by friends passing on mopeds with whom he would engage in secretive conversations and sometimes jump on and speed off. Others in the area now seemed wary of Ramón and warned openly that I needed to be careful being around his new acquaintances. On our last meeting, as I glanced over to where Ramón was talking with someone I did not recognize, one of the kids hanging around on the corner physically caught me by the arm and pulled me into a conversation, turning me away from what was going on and whispering that the situation was dangerous. Ramón's wariness of the Metropolitana and the AFI was more than a young person's antagonism to authority but reflected a very real threat to how his new gang involvement had shifted into more sustained criminal activity.

Ramón's personal narrative shows a complicated relationship with gang life. He had begun with a fairly hard-core gang in Tepito, before going to the United States, where he joined a *clica* but seemed to regret the experience and returned to Mexico. In Puebla, he hung out for a number of years on the street corner running errands, taking drugs, and having fun, but he combined this existence with forming a new gang, one that seemed to be becoming increasingly involved with drugs or other criminal activity. Faced with the consequences of this last move, Ramón contemplated flight to Mexico City rather than leaving behind gang involvement, a move that was unlikely to put him at lesser risk in the medium term. This, however, is to offer a general and outsider's perspective on Ramón and the gang. In his own words, he is careful in the terms he deploys to distinguish between different registers of *gang* and to suggest that his social identity relates differently to each. Ramón seemed to take care with how the term *banda* was applied.

In conversations and interviews about his gang involvement in the United States, Ramón used the term *clicas* and did not refer to either *banda* or *pandilla*. But when describing his involvement with gangs in Tepito and Puebla, he used the term *banda*, a term that he retained even as the Puebla gang transitioned to more hard-core activities. To the best of my recollection, Ramón never used the term *pandilla*. The inference we may draw is that Ramón considered this gang activity as involving primarily a set of social relations, drug taking, violence, and crime conducted among friends. He would also avoid referring to his hanging out on the streets around the Hidalgo market as *banda,* despite this group's intense bonding, including use of drugs and resort to and being victims of violence. Indeed, attempts to identify this group with *banda* or *pandilla* by nongovernmental organization street educators—who would self-consciously back up this boundary marking by interspersing conversation with swearing—would be ridiculed or met with an angry put-down.[34] To Ramón and others of the group, this hanging about was an arrangement that implied "work"—as windscreen washers and running errands—an opposition to involvement with crime and long periods of "having fun" (Herrera, Jones, and Thomas de Benítez 2009).

Shortly after leaving Puebla, I received a short newspaper article. It showed a picture of Ramón wearing a sleeveless Puma T-shirt and a Santa Muerte pendant draped down his front. He was looking, somewhat bewildered, off to his left. From the right side protruded a gloved hand, presumably of a police officer, holding up a large knife. The accompanying report described the knife, with a twenty-three-centimeter blade, as being found on Ramón when he was apprehended by a police tactical group called La Guardian. According to the article, Ramón had been spotted walking down a street near the Hidalgo market holding a bottle of PVC (glue)—an action very much out of character as neither he nor the others took their bottles or other inhalant devices into public view (Herrera, Jones, and Thomas de Benítez 2009). On stopping him, the officers found the knife, and on registering positive for alcohol, Ramón was sent to the Ministerio Publico office (Attorney General) for charging. For the third time in as many years, Ramón would now spend time in prison, this time for a federal charge. His previous time in prison had appeared to draw him closer to harder gang behaviors. Now he was facing more jail time.

CONCLUSION

At a time when "gangs" are being folded into a national and regional security discourse, this chapter has argued that it is vital to attend to the boundaries and ignore the different modi operandi of *maras,* "Mexican" transnational gangs, *pandillas,* and *bandas.* It is especially important not to draw young people who join *bandas* and who admittedly may be engaged in organized criminal activity into the same frame as *narco-pandillas*. Yet a great deal of the literature, media, and policy-oriented discourse seem to do just that. This chapter has attempted to elucidate how gang membership is most often an ascribed identity provided by others, notably the media, lawmakers, and the police, who tend to use the term *pandilla* in preference to *banda*, or Anglophonic "security" think tank commentators, who rarely make any distinction except between national and transnational gangs and offer ahistorical analyses that miss any nuance between *pandillas* and *bandas*. From either quarter there seems to be little concern to understand why young people, mostly male, join gangs—*bandas* or otherwise—and why they continue to do so in the context of apparently strong disincentives (viewed from a rational perspective). Being associated with a gang will increase young people's stigmatization, their chances of being picked up by a growing array of security agencies, and of being beaten up and possibly killed.

Almost a half a century on, Lewis's account of the *palomilla* in Teipto gangs seems *superficially* out of step with the contemporary "public view of the world." While the *banda* is an extension of the *palomilla*, the difference is that young people at the present juncture seem to possess less control over gang identity formations. Lewis portrayed the *palomilla* as relatively autonomous groups, neither dominating nor dominated by social institutions. In the present context of a war on drugs and its geopolitical framing, the boundary of the "gang" is determined beyond social institutions but by geopolitical forces, both of the national state and of DTOs. In practice, gangs with different modi operandi have emerged, aiming to secure spaces for drug sales through the removal of competitors. These new gangs—*narco-pandillas*—are similar to *pandillas*, through which they sometimes recruit members, but they are more likely to use violence as a principal activity and with a view to controlling local social institutions. Unlike the *palomilla* or *banda*, these arrangements determine life paths.

However unfortunate one might perceive Ramón's life as he navigated between errands, drug use, petty crime, and prison, his power was not so limited as to deny him an attempt to construct an identity in constrained circumstances. The accounts of young people such as Ramón indicate the plasticity of social identities linked with the gang. Sitting on the pavement, he was working out whether to stay in Puebla or rejoin his *banda* in Tepito, having seemingly rejected the possibility of going to the United States. He took some care in positioning boundaries around competing gang identities, as indicated, for example, in the deployment of the term *clica* to describe his experience in California and *banda* for his gang life in both Puebla and Mexico City. In both locations, the *banda* existed as one possible social space for mucking about, drug taking, and sharing interests in music, parties, girls, and crime. Importantly, Ramón avoided *pandilla* as shorthand to describe gang arrangements. In representing his gang life as being that of the *banda*, at least to himself, Ramón nevertheless undertook with some excitement and awareness greater involvement in crime. Ultimately, this step seems to have been a mistake. A gang life that had hitherto displayed the characteristics of an epiphenomenal social process, and in which the locus afforded Ramón a degree of control, had brought him closer to activities that the security and criminal justice systems, and media, consider as *pandilla* life. Indeed, in 2012, on release from prison, Ramón was arrested once more and sentenced to a twenty-year jail term for what his friends claim was probably murder.

NOTES

Research for this chapter was supported by ESRC grant RES 148-25-0050. I acknowledge the financial support of the ESRC and am extremely grateful to Sarah Thomas de Benítez and Elsa Herrera. The field research employed street ethnography, through which I met regularly with two groups of street-based youth between 2005 and 2009, and less frequently since.

1. I draw the same distinction in the text as my informants, between low-level policing and "public security" by a range of new or reformed agencies and units. Policing is usually described as an irritant and is responded to with feigned humor, when describing officers as *pitufos* (smurfs), for example. By contrast, *la seguridad* is referred to with caution and apprehension.

2. Ramón used the term "rent," although the prices suggest purchase, possibly on a sale-use-return basis. The going rate for a .22 was MX$1,500, and a .38 automatic was MX$3,000, or US$120 and US$240, respectively.

3. Lewis's observations were consistent with Buñuel's challenge to ideas of progress, the moral strength of the family, and the role of the state, portraying a group of boys from poor *vecindad* and *ciudades perdida* (shack settlements) engaging in crime and violence and apparently immune to "reform."

4. Lewis (1983, 145–47) makes a brief mention of an all-girl gang joined by Marta in her early teens, which was mostly engaged in group exploration of sexuality and smoking marijuana. Although the perceived norm of gang violence is that it does not often involve women as protagonists or victims, few studies back this up (for a study of female-on-female violence, see Cummings 1994).

5. Whatever the merits of these critiques, Lewis raised important points about gangs. First, he seems not to have regarded the modi operandi of gangs in Mexico City to be any different from those in Chicago that, courtesy of Frederick Thrasher, dominated most debates in sociology. Second, and unlike those of many of his critics, Lewis's methodology was sensitive to and not condescending of the accounts of his respondents. He avoided enveloping gangs with broader conceptual labels that regarded young people's lives as subnormative or lumpen.

6. It is important to distinguish these social boundaries from the terms used in everyday exchange. Young people in a variety of circumstances, gang related and not, will refer to friends and acquaintances as *carnal* (brother), *chamaco* (lad), *cabrón* (git), and a host of other colloquialisms.

7. There is no simple translation of *palomilla,* which, in this context, covers equivalents of "kids," "ragamuffins," "layabouts," "vagabonds," and "hooligans." However, and as with *banda,* to which I refer later in the chapter, *palomilla* is occasionally used in general speech, among men and across class, to refer to a group of "mates."

8. The state, or at least the ruling Partido Revolucionario Institucional political party, was not averse to using gangs as agents of political control, using some members as enforcers *(matones)* or to infiltrate student organisations *(porras)*.

9. A reform to the code in the 1980s revealed the state's uncertainty about how categorical boundaries might be drawn between *pandilla* and *banda.* The revised code defined a *pandilla* as a group of young people who meet for noncriminal purposes, whereas a banda referred to three or more people who meet for the purpose of delinquency. The harsher penalty, including the possibility of a five- to ten-year prison term and a fine equivalent to between one hundred and three hundred times the official minimum daily wage, could be applied to members of a *banda.* Castillo (2004) suggests that the confusion of lawmakers gave police leverage to extort money from many more young people who could be readily identified as *banda.*

10. After a decline in the murder rate over fifteen years to 2006, data show a dramatic increase year on year to early 2011, more or less doubling in four years and quadrupling the total number of dead from 2006 to 2011 compared with from 2000 to 2006 (Ríos and Shirk 2011). Within the general data for homicide, new categories of drug-related "executions" and "confrontations" have been created.

11. For data on kidnap, see IKV Pax Christi (2008); for data on money laundering, smuggled goods, and people trafficking, see United Nations Office on

Drugs and Crime (2007). Impunity and corruption of the justice system are discussed by Zepeda Lecuona (2004); for details on police reform and the prison system, see Davis (2006) and López Portillo (2004).

12. For a more complicated and less excitable reading of the rise of the DTOs in Mexico and the effects of attempts to confront them, see Jones (2012).

13. Transnational gangs are defined by Killebrew and Bernal (2010, 41) as much by ethnic identity as by geographical presence, noting that they are "primarily Latino gangs." These are distinct from the so-called homegrown variety, which appears to be either Caucasian or African American.

14. The numerous media reports of *maras* often appear prompted by an interview with a government official or human rights organization or to coincide with a regional summit or binational cooperation announcement, rather than by discussion with young people, gang members or not (*La Jornada*, September 12, 2005).

15. Despite the *maras*, Chiapas has one of the lowest homicide rates of any Mexican state (Ríos and Shirk 2011).

16. When arrested, *mareros* appear to be poorly armed, often possessing no more than machetes and rudimentary pistols, and show little sign of a command structure or of links outside the immediate area.

17. Pensil was known for its gangs at least as far back as the 1950s, when it was the base to *Los Gatos* and *Los Charros Negros*.

18. The national government responded to concerns for transnational gangs with a range of plans and strategies, mostly notably the Operación Acero (Operation Steel) from 2003 to 2007 and the 2005 Plan International de Operaciones Simultáneous contra Pandillas, which involved security forces from Mexico, El Salvador, Guatemala, Honduras, and the United States. A number of states formed "anti-*mara*" police units during the 2000s, and state governors held high-profile meetings to discuss the *mara* problem and the appropriate response.

19. In Culiacán, for example, so-called *narco-juniors* have conducted unprovoked attacks, seemingly with no financial reward or instructions from *narcos*, with the intention of spreading a sense of insecurity (*La Jornada*, November 23, 2006).

20. Cholo is often referred to as a hybrid transnational youth style, often ascribed as a border identity derived from the Pachuco style of the 1940s and combining today a wide range of dress styles, verbal codes, and music, all of which can be incorporated into gang identities.

21. To this point, gangs are responsible for a relatively small proportion of reported crime—less than 0.5 percent in the Federal District, with the highest percentage claimed by Chiapas at 24.3 percent (*La Jornada*, February 11, 2007).

22. The media and state agencies have produced a battery of unreliable estimates, focusing on a number of gangs rather than members, and not contextualizing to total population size as the need for a headline dictated (see Castillo Berthier 2004). For the federal District of Mexico City alone, the Secretaria de

Desarrollo Social has estimated at least 351 major gangs and possibly as many as 1,000.

23. See http://www.mision.sre.gob.mx/index/php.

24. The Michoacán-based DTO La Familia Mexicana has used Los Historicos and Los Cobradores de Deudas to carry out intimidation and hits, and both it and the Gulf and Juárez DTOs used Las Zetas. These groups are paramilitary in organization and operation and draw from police and military units, with little evidence that they have acquired members directly from gangs.

25. Much of the geopolitical "security" literature represents the "Latino" gangs, such as the Calle 18, as of Central American origin, when, according to the Los Angeles Police Department, 80 percent of the forty thousand gang members in Los Angeles are Mexican or Mexican American.

26. *La Jornada* (December 9, 2004) noted that some of the three hundred *pandillas* in Ciudad Juárez were working as distributors, and occasionally as enforcers, for the Juárez DTO as far back as 2004.

27. Until the late 1990s, the Aztecas and Mexicles were allied, along with other border and prison-based gangs of Mexican origin. But involvement with the drug war has fragmented this bond, resulting in intergang violence. In 2009, the Aztecas killed twenty members of the Mexicles and Artistas Asesinos within a Juárez prison.

28. The Aztecas consider the Bible a sacred document for swearing of oaths and incorporate the use of feathered headdresses *(penaches)* and drums in pre-conflict ceremonies.

29. In the sense used by Ramón, *cholo* is most likely a derogative against Mexicans appropriating U.S. styles, closer to the term *naco*.

30. Working out the possible time frame, Ramón was almost certainly a minor while in the United States. Although he used the term *prison* to describe incarceration, it is possible that he was in a juvenile correctional facility, but without ID, he may have been confused for an adult.

31. Extensive searches of newspaper accounts of gangs in Tepito and La Merced have been unable to confirm the presence of the Osos Leyes from among the eighty or so gangs in these districts. *Oso* (bear) is a common ascription to both gangs and gang-member nicknames and is frequently referred to in Tepito, including for a famous drug-sales point and as the nickname of a notorious gang leader. I confirmed with Ramón that *leyes* (laws) was not a mistake for *reyes* (kings), another common name, including of another gang leader in Tepito.

32. Rodrigo had spent time in prison and had appeared to gravitate away from the Hidalgo area, in part trying to spend more time with a partner and young family but also with HEM.

33. The standard interpretation of three dots is "mi vida loca" (my crazy life), indicating the plasticity of gang tattoo iconography, though not in this instance contradictory to "money, drugs, and women."

34. From his study of young people on the streets of downtown Mexico City,

Gigengack (2006) prefers the term *bandas* to *street children,* noting some (self) identify as *bandas,* whereas others are closer to the *chavos bandas* engaged in street crime. Usefully, Gigengack draws out the identification of community without losing the highly fluid associations within and without such groups.

REFERENCES

Alvarado, Arturo. 2009. "The Crisis of Public Security and Challenges to Judicial Reform in Mexico." Paper presented at the Institute for the Study of the Americas, University of London, April 30.

Armijo, Natalia, Raúl Benítez Manaut, and Athanasios Hristroulas. 2009. "Las 'Maras' y la seguridad del triángulo México-Estados Unidos-Centroamérica." In *Gobernabilidad, Seguridad y Defensa,* edited by Carlos Barrachina, 339–69. Mexico City: Plaza y Valdes.

Castillo Berthier, Héctor. 2002. "De las bandas a las Tribus Urbanas." *Desacatos* 9:57–71.

———. 2004. "Pandillas, jóvenes y violencia." *Desacatos* 14:105–26.

Castillo Berthier, Héctor, and Gareth A. Jones. 2009. "Mean Streets: Gangs, Violence, and Daily Life in Mexico." In *Youth Violence in Latin America: Gangs and Juvenile Justice in Perspective,* edited by Gareth A. Jones and Dennis Rodgers, 289–315. New York: Palgrave.

Comisión Nacional de Derechos Humanos. 2008. "Informe Especial de la Comisión Nacional de Derechos Humano sobre Las Pandillas Delectivas Transnacionales Conocidas como 'Maras.'" Mexico City: Comisión Nacional de Derechos Humanos.

Cruz Salazar, Tania. 2004. "Yo me aventé como tres anos haciendo tags, sí, la verdad, si fui ilegal! Grafiteros: arte callejero en la ciudad de México." *Desacatos* 14:197–226.

Cummings, Laura L. 1994. "Fighting by the Rules: Women Street-Fighting in Chihuahua, Chihuahua, Mexico." *Sex Roles* 30, nos. 3–4: 189–98.

Davis, Diane E. 2006. "Undermining the Rule of Law: Democratization and the Dark Side of Police Reform in México." *Latin American Politics and Society* 48, no. 1: 55–86.

Fernández Menéndez, Jorge, and Victor Ronquillo. 2006. *De Los Maras a Los Zetas: los secretos del narcotráfico, de Colombia a Chicago.* Mexico City: Grijalbo.

Franco, Celinda. 2008. "The MS-13 and 18th Street Gangs: Emerging Transnational Gang Threats?" Washington, D.C.: Congressional Research Service.

Gigengack, Roy. 2006. "Young, Damned, and Banda: The World of Young Street People in Mexico City, 1990–1997." Ph.D. diss., University of Amsterdam.

Hernández León, Ruben. 1999. "A la Aventura! Jovenes, Pandillas y Migración en la Conexión Monterrey-Houston." In *Fronteras Fragmentadas,* edited by Gail Mummert, 115–43. Zamora, Spain: El Colegio de Michoacán.

Herrera, Elsa, Gareth A. Jones, and Sarah Thomas de Benítez. 2009. "Bodies on the Line: Identity Markers among Mexican Street Youth." *Children's Geographies* 17, no. 1: 67–81.

IKV Pax Christi. 2008. *Kidnapping Is Booming Business: A Lucrative Political Instrument for Armed Groups Operating in Conflict Zones.* Utrecht, Netherlands: IKV Pax Christi.

Jones, Gareth A. 2012. *Drugs, Violence, and Insecurity in Mexico, an Europa Regional Survey of the World: South America, Central American, and Caribbean.* London: Routledge.

Jones, Gareth A., Elsa Herrera, and Sarah Thomas de Benítez. 2007. "Tears, Trauma, and Suicide: Everyday Violence among Street Youth in Puebla, Mexico." *Bulletin of Latin American Research* 26, no. 4: 462–79.

Jones, Gareth A., and Sarah Thomas de Benítez. 2009. "Tales of Two or Many Worlds? When 'Street' Kids Go Global." In *Theorizing Identities and Social Action,* edited by Margaret Wetherell, 75–94. Basingstoke: Palgrave Macmillan.

Killebrew, Robert, and Jennifer Bernal. 2010. "Crime Wars: Gangs, Cartels, and U.S. National Security." Washington, D.C.: Center for a New American Century.

Lara Klahr, Marco. 2006. *Hoy Te Toca La Muerte: el imperio de las Maras visto desde adentro.* Mexico City: Planeta.

Leacock, Eleanor Burke, ed. 1971. *The Culture of Poverty: A Critique.* New York: Simon and Schuster.

Lewis, Oscar. 1983. *The Children of Sánchez: Autobiography of a Mexican Family.* New York: Penguin Books.

López Portillo, Ernesto. 2004. "La reforma a la seguridad pública." *Nexos* 323:17–24.

Manwaring, Max G. 2005. *Street Gangs: The New Urban Insurgency.* Carlisle, Pa.: Strategic Studies Institute, U.S. Army War College.

———. 2008. *A Contemporary Challenge to State Sovereignty: Gangs and Other Illicit Transnational Criminal Organizations (TCOs) in Central America, El Salvador, Mexico, Jamaica, and Brazil.* Carlisle, Pa.: Strategic Studies Institute, U.S. Army War College.

Marcial, Rogelio. 1997. *La banda rifa: Vida cotidiana de grupos juveniles de esquina en Zamora, Michoacán.* Zamora, Spain: El Colegio de Michoacán.

Morales, Gabriel. 2006. *Varrio Warfare: Violence in the Latino Community.* San Antonio, Tex.: Munguia Press.

Nateras Domínguez, Alfredo. 2002. "La identificaciones en los agrupamientos juveniles urbanos: 'graffiteros y góticos.'" In *Sociologia de la Identidad,* edited by Aquiles Chihuamparán, 185–221. Mexico DF: Miguel Angel Porrua.

———. 2006. "Violencia Simbolica y Significacion de los cuerpos: tatuajes en jóvenes." *Revista Temas Sociologicos* 11:71–101.

———. 2007. "Adscripciones Juveniles y Violencias Transnacionales: Cholos y Maras." In *Las Maras: identidades juveniles al limite,* edited by José Manuel Valenzuela Arce, Alfredo Nateras Domínguez, and Rossana Reguillo Cruz,

127–55. Mexico City: Universidad Autónoma Metropolitana Iztapalapa.

Padilla, Héctor. 2008. "Las fronteras de la gobernabilidad: el caso de la Ciudad Juárez." Paper presented at the Coloquio Internacional Gobernabilidad, Gobernanza y Buen Gobierno, UAM-Iztapalapa, September 17–19.

Paz, Octavio. (1961) 1990. *The Labyrinth of Solitude*. London: Penguin.

Reguillo Cruz, Rossana. 1991. *En la Calle Otra Vez: Las Bandas—Identidad Urbana y Usos de la Comunicación*. Guadalajara: ITESO.

Ríos, Viridiana, and David A. Shirk. 2011. *Drug Violence in Mexico: Data and Analysis through 2010*. San Diego, Calif.: University of San Diego Transborder Institute.

Santamaría Balmaceda, Gema. 2007. "Maras y pandillas: límites de su transnacionalidad." *Revista Mexicana de Política Exterior* 81:101–23.

Seelke, Clare Ribando. 2009. *Gangs in Central America*. Washington, D.C.: Congressional Research Service.

Smith, Robert Courtney. 2005. *Mexican New York: Transnational Lives of New Immigrants*. Berkeley: University of California Press.

Sonnevelt, Monique. 2009. "Security at Stake: Dealing with Violence and Public (In)security in a Popular Neighborhood in Guadalajara, Mexico." In *Youth Violence in Latin America: Gangs and Juvenile Justice in Perspective*, edited by Gareth A. Jones and Dennis Rodgers, 45–62. New York: Palgrave.

Strickland, Tina S. 2009. "Mara Salvatrucha: A Threat to U.S. and Central American Security." In *The World's Most Threatening Terrorist Networks and Criminal Gangs*, edited by Michael T. Kindt, Jerrold M. Post, and Barry R. Schneider, 247–74. New York: Palgrave.

Sullivan, John P., and Adam Elkus. 2008. "State of Siege: Mexico's Criminal Insurgency." *Small Wars Journal*, August, http://smallwars.org/jml/art/state-of-siege-mexicos-criminal-insurgency.

Teicher, Dario E. 2009. "The Mexican Drug Cartels: At War for Control of the US–Mexico Border." In *The World's Most Threatening Terrorist Networks and Criminal Gangs*, edited by Michael T. Kindt, Jerrold M. Post, and Barry R. Schneider, 209–34. New York: Palgrave.

Tilly, Charles. 2005. *Identities, Boundaries, and Social Ties*. Boulder, Colo.: Paradigm Books.

United Nations Office on Drugs and Crime. 2007. *Crime and Development in Central America: Caught in the Crossfire*. Vienna, Austria: United Nations Office on Drugs and Crime.

USAID. 2006. *Central America and México Gang Assessment*. Washington, D.C.: USAID.

U.S. Department of Justice. 2010. *National Drug Threat Assessment 2010*. Johnstown, Pa.: National Drug Intelligence Center.

U.S. Joint Forces Command. 2008. *The Joint Operating Environment: Challenges and Implications for the Future Joint Force*. Suffolk, Va.: U.S. Joint Forces Command.

Valenzuela Arce, José Manuel. 2007. "La Mara es mi Familia." In *Las Maras: identidades juveniles al limite,* edited by José Manuel Arce Valenzuela, Alfredo Nateras Domínguez, and Rossana Reguillo Cruz, 33–61. Mexico City: Universidad Autónoma Metropolitana Iztapalapa.

Wilson, Gary I., and John P. Sullivan. 2007. "On Gangs, Crime, and Terrorism: Defense and the National Interest." February 28. http://www.d-n-i.net/fes/pdf/wilson_sullivan_gangs_terrorism.pdf.

Wolf, Eric. 1962. "Review of *The Children of Sánchez*: Autobiography of a Mexican Family." *American Anthropologist* 64:619–21.

Zepeda Lecuona, Guillermo. 2004. *Crimen sin Castigo: Procuración de Justicia penal y ministerio público en México.* Mexico City: Centro de Investigación para el Desarrollo A.C.

Afterword

The Inevitable Gang

SUDHIR VENKATESH

Rodgers and Hazen sum up the motivating spirit behind *Global Gangs* succinctly when they write that this volume highlights the "socially embedded nature of all gangs, regardless of their location, and how different environments can affect their origins and their transformation." In the area of gang studies, this is no small accomplishment. Gangs perplex us. All manner of explanation—biological, genetic, psychological, environmental—continues to proliferate in our attempts to answer the question, Why do gangs exist? Collections of research findings often have difficulty sorting through the muck to deliver a tight, polished thesis. This volume breaks that mold.

So successful is this global tour of gang life that *Global Gangs* motivates this reader to ask an entirely separate question: Why *shouldn't* gangs exist? From the Siliwangi Boys of Indonesia to the West Side Boys of Sierra Leone to Russia's Khadi-Taktash, the richly detailed studies of youth in this volume show repeatedly that gangs are a logical and inevitable expression of local social structure. Rather than focusing on the gang as an exception, perhaps we should be accounting for the diversity of factors that bring them about—with the assumption that it is our job to investigate those social conditions leading to such diversity. In fact, in many of the contributions to *Global Gangs,* the through line illuminates this very point: the gang is as much lens as social problem; it is both an object to be explained by societal factors and a means by which to see those dynamics unfold.

After leaving this volume, one is hard-pressed to see the gang as a marginal social group. This status seems more an artifact of the intellectual historical habitus that assigns gang studies to the branch of criminology, which has always been viewed as a tier below its sisters in the social sciences. This should not be the case, because so many of the foundational works in social science have stemmed from a study of deviance. And yet, that is precisely where we sit.

The marginalization of gang studies is partly an outgrowth of its founder Frederick Thrasher, in whose shadow gang scholars still labor. Thrasher (1927) repeatedly juxtaposed the wildness of the gang to the civilizing project of managing the industrial American metropolis. To Thrasher's contemporaries, the gang was a weed. It disturbed the natural ecological equilibrium of *urbs en hortus*. It required attention as a misfit in the family requires care and, at times, quarantine for the household to remain functional.

The gang fascinated, but the fascination was short-lived. Legitimating the study of gangs via the odd and sometimes disturbing qualities of their members was not without consequence. Those in Thrasher's wake, operating primarily within a "social disorganization" perspective in criminology, would fix the gang in time and space as a black sheep. The analytic value that the gang held for the sociologist was as violation of macrosocietal values. The gang became the place to study societal difference—not social relation. Cohen's (1955) use of *subculture* and Cloward and Ohlin's (1960) focus on *illegitimate opportunity structure* are two examples.

If one configures an object of study as being marginal within society, one cannot then rightfully enforce the claim that the knowledge produced holds general applicability. Criminology began losing the battle for relevance. Robert Merton's writings notwithstanding, the field became deeply atheoretical and anti-intellectual in the decades following the Second World War. It was quickly overwhelmed by a programmatic, social-work focus on recovering lost youth. At least, this was the American story. In the United Kingdom, as the cultural studies movement took hold, social scientists would eventually pick up a study of gangs, as they might a study of revolution, to understand society broadly. That work has been nearly completely ignored by the mainstream of U.S. criminology and gang research.

At long last, this momentum has changed. The essays in *Global Gangs* bring a sharpness of theory and a commitment to transcending the social problems framework. Across the world, the youth gang is a means to grapple with the tensions at the core of a social body. The essays make clear that youth gangs must be considered very much at the center of the transformations taking place in society. These are not insignificant achievements. This volume must be appreciated not simply for the breadth of cases that it features but also for the collective work of its authors in refashioning a century of theory that relegated the gang to oddball status.

Rodgers and Hazen write that this volume consequently "seeks to encourage a more relational and interdisciplinary approach to study-ing gangs by focusing on comparisons across gangs, their practices, and their contexts." It is legitimate to ask what the results would be if gang research were to groove intellectually on this dance floor. And, turning this volume's pages, one finds that the contributing authors answer this question.

As Rodgers and Hazen point out, "properly exploring gang dynamics demands a comparative perspective across both time and space." Many of the essays take care to situate the gang in wider urban and national contexts. In the very first essay, Steffen Jensen argues that gangs "became a way that government made sense of life in the urban fringes." What better way to begin reframing gang studies than by using the social deviants to reconceptualize the role of the state? Other essays also move in unexpected directions, taking a standard national history or urban social dynamic and rearticulating it with the gang at the center.

The methodological breadth of the historical essays is particularly attractive. Most of the authors move with ease across multiple levels of abstraction. They are as comfortable discussing the biographical foreplay of leaders engaged in turf battles as they are re-presenting a vision of macrosocial change. Consider Salagaev and Safin's provoca-tive analysis of the genesis of gangs in the Soviet Union. In just this statement, the authors move deftly across several terrains, including an analysis of (1) overall demographic shifts in the Soviet Union, (2) cultural transformations of the nation's long-standing traditions, and (3) interorganizational disputes among various youth constituencies:

The rural population moving to the growing cities and newly built towns of the Soviet Union in the 1960s and 1970s often preserved their norms, values, and traditions when they came into their new urban environments. Among these traditions were traditional forms of intervillage ritualized feuding in which the majority of the male population of these villages generally took part. This became transformed in the cities into intrayouth fighting over turf between different neighborhoods and streets of the cities affiliated with rival villages. This helped cement territory-based unity as the basis for gang identity.

In the main, studies of gangs tend not to emphasize a temporal perspective. At times, the reader may find allusions to historical abstractions—*gangs emerged because of gentrification, gangs are the product of deindustrialization, segregation created ethnic divisions among youth that led to gangs forming,* and so on. However, these accounts appear most often in the beginning of an article or book, where they feel obligatory, as if the scholar were displaying membership in a political party. They are rarely picked up as threads in the remainder of the work. Contrast that to the essays in *Global Gangs,* in which there is a rich institutional analysis of governments, police agencies, corporations, and nongovernmental organizations. One might teach any of these essays in a class on social movements, political conflict, or state formation and reproduction.[1]

This volume is deeply attentive to the discursive frames through which gangs become meaningful in everyday life.[2] Jensen's observation of South Africa would easily apply to other national contexts: "Gangs and gang culture have occupied central positions in the imaginaries and anxieties of mainstream society in South Africa for more than a century." However, in most scholarly treatments, there is usually little analysis of media accounts, citizen voices, law enforcement explanations, and so on, that could situate the youth organizations in their respective societies (those who embrace the cultural studies perspective or who labor in anthropology departments are the obvious exceptions). And yet, as Arias shows, it is *the construction of the gang as a social problem* that must first be explained before the gang can be analyzed *as* a social problem. We might extrapolate from Zhang's phrasing, made in the context of his analysis of China's gang "problem":

In sum, although youth gangs are widely seen as having emerged as a significant social problem in China as a result of the nation's rapid social and economic changes, the extent to which this is a real or perceived issue is unclear.

This line of argumentation appears also in Arias's inquiry into gang politics in Rio de Janeiro:

> Armed groups are deeply embedded in Rio de Janeiro political and social life. The media narrative of gangs, however, suggests that criminals are an almost external threat to society and, indeed, the state. Drug traffickers, these stories say, operate parallel states in the midst of the second largest city and undermine the very idea that Rio operates under the modern state system. The only response to this is brutal police operation and repression. This narrative exists in contrast to the localized reality of traffickers within *favelas* providing minimal support to some elements of the population in difficult times and serving as important, though quite dangerous, interlocutors with the state. Both police and politicians use their relationships with gangs to fulfill their economic and political projects. In practice, rather than in the narratives of journalists and many politicians, *favelas* and the gangs that control them are not separate from and opposed to the rest of the political system.

One wonders why it is that more scholars do not argue for the importance of gangs for general understandings of social reproduction. As Rodgers and Hazen observe,

> On one hand, gang studies exists almost as an autonomous sub-discipline and rarely relates with other fields of study, including, for example, those considering the nature of potentially analogous phenomena such as other armed groups and those exploring the broader structural contexts within which gangs emerge, both of which would arguably have much to offer when considering the evolutionary nature of gangs.

It is simply not common practice for scholars to "relate to other fields of study," however.[3] It cannot be because gangs in other cities are not "embedded in political and social life." Nearly every newspaper report offers some potential means of tying a gang to wider social processes.

Perhaps it is because of the methodological difficulties of studying gangs up close such that details on the organization's social, political, and financial activities can be gleaned. Or, as stated earlier, it may arise because researchers see the gang as a problem to be eviscerated, not as one for general social scientific questions.

As a faculty member supervising independent research, I can share this volume with students who wonder whether the study of gangs can be brought outside the camp of criminology. The studies offer direct examples to young investigators who are interested in studying the gang of how to address a wide range of sociological questions. Those students already committed to comparative historical research will, it is hoped, be drawn to gang studies as a site to pursue those interests. As someone who studies gangs, I am less certain how to make use of the assembled work. On one hand, the essays offer numerous examples of methodological and narrative strategies that might enable us to weave data in more compelling ways. Rodgers and Hazen are right to suggest that their global perspective is a necessary antidote to both the parochial nature of U.S. gang research and the more limited potential of a transnational focus. But innovation requires that a community of scholars find the perspectives and frameworks useful for their own work. I think most authors in this volume would probably agree that much more needs to be done to make the study of gangs accessible to a wider range of scholars.

Each of these essays succeeds, however, because it raises compelling questions about the role that gangs play in their respective national contexts. Such is the mark of achievement of a paradigm shift—it disrupts while clarifying. But it will require the energies of researchers working in various capacities, with diverse methods and tools, to make this disruption a lasting, productive one. There is certainly the need for such transformation. The global gang phenomenon does not appear to be diminishing.

NOTES

1. The authors also situate the gang in wider developmental pathways of nation-state making, community formation, city building, and so on. At the same time, because the national record offers few possibilities for re-creating an

accurate, empathetic account of youths who are recruited into armed combat, authors such as Sen turn to the voices of the youths themselves to provide an historical view of child soldiering.

2. As an aside, it is rare that scholars might juxtapose the discursive frames of multiple societies, as Utas does in his engaging reading of the gangs of Sierra Leone through the epistemic frameworks of U.S. gang scholarship.

3. After reading these essays, one is struck by one particular construction of the gang. Namely, many street gangs around the world appear to have intricate relations with militaristic organizations in their respective nation-states. For example, in Ryter's account, the gang phenomenon makes sense only when one understands how youths are mobilized as political objects by the powerful in Indonesia: "Why the need for this quasi-gang at all? The reformation of 234 SC can be seen in this context as a way for Japto to build support for his political party, and hence as yet another example of the tendency to mobilize gangs in politics. From another perspective, however, this reawakening indexes a profound dissatisfaction with the politicization of gangs and heralds a desire for a return of the days when gangs were gangs, or at least seemed to be." This kind of connection certainly exists in the United States, but it is rarely developed as a theme in studies of American gangs. And yet, when such interconnections are discovered, there is tremendous potential for analysis to open up unforeseen avenues.

REFERENCES

Cloward, R. A., and L. E. Ohlin. 1960. *Delinquency and Opportunity: A Theory of Delinquent Gangs.* New York: Free Press.

Cohen, A. K. 1955. *Delinquent Boys: The Culture of the Gang.* Glencoe, Ill.: Free Press.

Thrasher, F. 1927. *The Gang: A Study of 1,313 Gangs in Chicago.* Chicago: University of Chicago Press.

Contributors

Enrique Desmond Arias is an associate professor in the School of Public Policy at George Mason University. He is the author of *Drugs and Democracy in Rio de Janeiro: Trafficking, Social Networks, and Public Security* and coeditor of *Violent Democracies in Latin America.*

José Miguel Cruz is the director of research at the Latin American and Caribbean Center and visiting assistant professor in the Department of Politics and International Relations at Florida International University. He was previously director of the University Institute for Public Opinion at Universidad Centroamericana in El Salvador and is the author of several books on Central American gangs.

Jennifer M. Hazen has worked with International Crisis Group/Freetown, the United Nations Peacekeeping Mission in Sierra Leone, the Small Arms Survey in Geneva, Switzerland, and BAE Systems, working in support of U.S. Africa Command. She is the author of *What Rebels Want: Resources and Supply Networks in Wartime.*

Steffen Jensen is a senior researcher at DIGNITY–Danish Institute against Torture in Copenhagen and is also associated with the University of the Philippines. He is the author of *Gangs, Politics, and Dignity in Cape Town* and coeditor of *Human Rights and State Violence: State Officials in the South, The Security–Development Nexus: Expressions of Sovereignty and Securitization in South Africa,* and *Histories of Victimhood.*

Gareth A. Jones is a professor of urban geography at the London School of Economics and Political Science. He is the coeditor of *Housing and*

Finance in Developing Countries, Youth Violence in Latin America: Gangs and Juvenile Justice in Perspective, and *Bringing Youth into Development.*

Marwan Mohammed is a research fellow in the Centre Maurice Halbwachs, École Normale Supérieure, Paris, where he is a member of the research team on social inequalities. His research focuses on youth gangs and urban riots in France. He is the author of *La formation des bandes de jeunes: Entre la famille, l'école et la rue* and coeditor of *Les bandes de jeunes, des "Blousons noirs" à nos jours.*

Jacob Rasmussen is an assistant professor in the Department of International Development Studies, Roskilde University. He has published on urban politics, violence, youth, and grassroots politics in South Africa and Kenya.

Dennis Rodgers is a professor of urban social and political research in the School of Social and Political Sciences at the University of Glasgow. He is the coeditor of *Youth Violence in Latin America: Gangs and Juvenile Justice in Perspective* and *Latin American Urban Development into the Twenty-first Century: Towards a Renewed Perspective on the City.*

Loren Ryter is a faculty affiliate at the Center for Southeast Asian Studies at the University of Michigan and has taught comparative politics and Southeast Asian history at Cornell University and the University of Michigan. He has researched and published extensively on youth, criminality, and the state in Indonesia.

Rustem R. Safin is a senior research fellow in the Center for Analytic Studies and Development, National Research Technological University, in Kazan, Russian Federation. He has published on ethnic discrimination, racism, youth delinquency, and religious extremism.

Alexander L. Salagaev is a professor, head of the Social and Political Conflict Studies Department, and director of the Center for Analytic Studies and Development, National Research Technological University, Kazan, Russian Federation. He is the author or coauthor of several books on Russian youth gangs and delinquent subcultures.

Atreyee Sen is a lecturer in contemporary religion and conflict in the Department of Religions and Theology at the University of Manchester. She is the author of *Shiv Sena Women: Violence and Communalism in a Bombay Slum* and coeditor of *Global Vigilantes: Contemporary Perspectives on Violence and Justice.*

Mats Utas is an associate professor in cultural anthropology and leader of the Conflict, Security, and Democratic Transformation cluster at the Nordic Africa Institute, Sweden. He has written extensively on child and youth combatants; the politics and economy of informality; the media, refugees, and gender in Liberia, Sierra Leone, Ghana, Côte d'Ivoire, and Somalia.

Sudhir Venkatesh is the Williams B. Ransford Professor of Sociology at Columbia University. His work has appeared in numerous national publications, including the *New York Times,* the *Chicago Tribune,* and the *Washington Post.* His books include *American Project: The Rise and Fall of a Modern Ghetto, Floating City: A Rogue Sociologist Lost and Found in New York's Underground Economy,* and *Gang Leader for a Day.*

James Diego Vigil is a professor in the School of Social Ecology at the University of California at Irvine. He is the author of *Barrio Gangs: Street Life and Identity in Southern California, A Rainbow of Gangs: Street Cultures in the Mega-City,* and *The Projects: Gang and Non-gang Families in East Los Angeles.*

Lening Zhang is a professor in the Department of Sociology and Criminal Justice and director of the Rural Center for Applied Social, Health, and Behavioral Research at Saint Francis University, Loretto, Pennsylvania. He has published numerous articles on crime and social control in China.

Index